"For the last 25 years, I have worked with [illegible] administrative roles responding to their questions and concerns regarding the future of family members who have disabilities. Always I wished I would have had this type of information available. This book is very well written and I really can't think of a piece of information that is missing."

—Sister Elaine Weber, O.S.F., Executive Director,
St. John's Villa, Carrollton, Ohio

"Planning is this book's overriding feature—no matter what the disability or how small or large the income, if there is a well-considered and thoughtful plan ... children with disabilities will have a greater chance of enjoying the best possible health and security. This book is a must purchase for all parents who have children with emotional, physical, or mental disabilities."

—*Legal Information Alert*

"Expert information on this very important often complicated topic. Very valuable for parents and professionals."

—Stanley D. Klein, Ph.D., Editor in Chief, *Exceptional Parent Magazine*

"Using this book may be the single most important step that one takes in planning for a family member with a disability."

—The National Alliance For The Mentally Ill

"I congratulate the authors for their approach, their comprehensiveness, and their obvious commitment to people with disabilities. This book should be read numerous times before and during estate planning with one's own advisors."

—Marilyn Price Spivak, Founder, National Head Injury Foundation

"A comprehensive publication which presents an easy to follow approach to addressing vital questions and burning issues that caregivers and consumers encounter. A must for every professional in the field of mental retardation."

—B.R. Walker, Ph. D., Past President, AAMR

"*Planning For The Future* is a book we distribute at all Arc events. We have found it to be a great deal of value and very easy to understand for all parents concerned about planning."

—TONY PAULAUSKI, EXECUTIVE DIRECTOR, ARC OF ILLINOIS

"*Planning For The Future* is the most complete compilation which I have seen of useful information for planning the future of a mentally disabled family member. The authors layout the issues and options in great detail, including sample letters. They also skillfully take the mystery out of legal jargon. Highly recommended."

—E. FULLER TORREY, M.D., AUTHOR OF *SURVIVING SCHIZOPHRENIA*

"When educators assemble libraries, they tend to select two categories of books: those for themselves as instructor and those to be shared with persons with disabilities, their families, and their caregivers. Educators concerned with transition will find that this indispensable book can fit into either category."

—GERALD GIORDANO, PH.D., BOOK REVIEW EDITOR,
CAREER DEVELOPMENT FOR EXCEPTIONAL INDIVIDUALS

"Estate planning for families with children who have a disability is quite different from other types of estate planning....*Planning For The Future* draws on the authors' extensive personal experiences, providing a number of case histories and specific examples to enable readers to understand the planning process. Numerous worksheets, sample documents, and useful charts are included. This book is easily understood and very helpful in addressing the many issues that face parents with disabled children."

—NANCY SHURTZ, PROFESSOR OF LAW, UNIVERSITY OF OREGON LAW SCHOOL, IN A REVIEW BY *ESTATE PLANNING MAGAZINE*

"Now, as the time arrives to look to the future of a child with a disability, a future in which families will be absent due to aging, illness or death, the need to plan becomes urgent. This book is the place to begin the process of future care planning. It is comprehensive and thorough, taking the reader through each step and available option. The authors are generous and accurate in the information they provide."

—CAROL OBLOY, CHAIRMAN, GUARDIANSHIP AND TRUSTS NETWORK, NATIONAL ALLIANCE FOR THE MENTALLY ILL, FROM A REVIEW IN THE *NAMI ADVOCATE*

PLANNING FOR THE FUTURE

PROVIDING A MEANINGFUL LIFE FOR A CHILD WITH A DISABILITY AFTER YOUR DEATH

L. MARK RUSSELL ATTORNEY

ARNOLD E. GRANT ATTORNEY

SUZANNE M. JOSEPH C.F.P.

RICHARD W. FEE M.ED., M.A.

AMERICAN PUBLISHING COMPANY,
P.O. BOX 988, EVANSTON, IL 60204-0988

Disclaimer

This book is intended to provide accurate information. It is not intended, however, to render any legal, tax, accounting or other professional advice or services. You should therefore use this book as a general guide only. In addition, this book contains information that was available only up to the time of printing. Laws do change with some frequency.

That's why you must discuss your estate planning with a qualified attorney before relying on the information you may find here or anywhere else.

Library of Congress Number: 93-070321
Printed in the United States of America
ISBN 0-9635780-0-6
Fourth Edition

Editor: Doug Utigard
Design: Rivera Design & Communications

American Publishing Company
P.O. Box 988
Evanston, IL 60204-0988

Acknowledgments

The practice of estate planning, particularly in the area of planning for children with disabilities, has grown in sophistication over the past decade. The authors want to thank all the professionals involved for contributing to the growing excellence in this very specialized field.

Many people have helped us with this book. We extend our very sincere gratitude to Margaret Grant. She worked beside us throughout the entire process of developing, writing, and designing this book. She always made herself available to help us. We also want to extend our sincere gratitude to a number of our professional colleagues who graciously took time from their busy schedules to comment on prior drafts of our book. Special thanks to Grace Allison, tax counsel at The Northern Trust Company of Chicago, and adjunct professor at IIT Chicago-Kent College of Law; Robert Borden, former chairman of the mathematics department at Knox College, and member of the Board of Directors of The Community Workshop and Training Center in Peoria, Illinois; Richard Kazarian, professor of finance at the graduate school of business at the University of Michigan; Maurice P. Wolk, of counsel to the law firm of Ross & Hardies, and a practicing attorney with more than 30 years experience in the estate planning field; and Brian Ziv, principal of Ziv Asset Management, Chicago, Illinois.

A special thanks should also go to our clients. The love that you so obviously feel for your children has energized us throughout the entire process, providing needed incentive when this book was no more than an idea in a hopeful mind.

Table of Contents

INTRODUCTION

WHEN WE FIRST SAT DOWN TO WRITE THIS BOOK, WE thought about the many elements that we consider essential to a *comprehensive* estate plan where a person with a disability is involved. We thought about the importance of developing a life plan for your child and the importance of communicating that plan to future caregivers in order to provide continuity of care after you are gone. We thought about the importance of a financial plan and the difficulties inherent in providing for the lifetime needs of a person with a disability. We thought about the various legal documents involved—trusts, wills, and powers of attorney—that will enable you to leave property to your child in a form that will permit proper management, while at the same time not imperiling your child's eligibility under government benefit programs that can be so vital. We thought about estate-tax planning, probate avoidance, and the protection of assets from the devastating costs of old age.

All of these items are important, and the major goal of a comprehensive estate plan is to deal with each of them. Omission of any one of these crucial elements from your estate plan could jeopardize your child's security.

Two real life situations demonstrate the unfortunate results of inadequate planning.

The first involved a client who came to us in near-panic to get her estate plan prepared. Apparently the woman's neighbor had died, leaving two children, a nine-year-old son with autism and a twenty-year-old college student who was away at school. The neighbor had done no estate planning, all her relatives lived out of town, and the younger child was left alone, with no where to go and no one to take care of him. All the details future caregivers needed to know—the child's medical history, his favorite foods, favorite activities—died with the parent. No financial planning had been done, and no one had any idea who was to look out for the child or provide for the child's future. Eventually the child was placed in an institution, but there had been no investigation of alternatives, no search for a proper placement.

The second situation involved one of our very first clients, a man whose mother had died without a will, owning more than $200,000 in property. Our client's sister, a forty-five-year-old woman with mental retardation, was residing in a state-funded residential facility. Under the probate laws in the state where the man's mother resided, his sister was entitled to one-half of her mother's estate. The state's Medicaid authorities seized the property for past cost-of-care liabilities. This left the woman with nothing.

There is much that both of these families could have done if only they had engaged in timely estate planning. The goal of this book is to discuss all the elements of a comprehensive estate plan and to convince you to begin the process of having such a plan prepared for you and your family.

Estate planning for families with a member who has a disability is different from other types of estate planning, because there is so much more that has to be done. Our goal is to convince you that estate planning is *essential* for every family and not an activity *only* for the wealthy. Parents must plan their estates, regardless of size, to secure the continued care and well-being of their child. Future caregivers must be selected, living arrangements investigated, and alternatives discussed. Families with limited financial resources must learn to maximize government benefits so that their child's financial needs will be satisfied.

As we discuss later in this book, many of these government benefits are unavailable to people who have more than an insignificant amount of property. In Chapter Six we will show how you can leave property to your child in trusts that will provide for effective management and supplement government benefits, without affecting your child's eligibility for such benefits or subjecting the inheritance to government seizure under a cost-of-care claim. In fact, in many cases avoidance of government cost-of-care claims and maintenance of eligibility for government benefits are among the most important goals of an estate plan. Many of our clients are shocked to learn that the cost of purely private lifetime care can exceed one million dollars.

Although there are many alternatives that all parents with children who have disabilities should consider, there is no single magic formula for creating the appropriate estate plan. Every estate plan should be custom-fit to the family's circumstances and the needs of its members. The size of a family's estate affects the need for estate-tax planning and the importance of government benefits. The nature and degree of your child's disability will help determine the type of living arrangement that will be appropriate. The ages of your children—both those with disabilities and those without—affect your need for insurance. The size of your family might influence the distribution of property. The age and maturity of children without disabilities will determine whether you will need trusts for them, as well as for the child with the disability. In other words, estate planning is a process of weighing numerous alternatives and making decisions that you hope will improve and secure your child's life now and in the future.

The task is daunting, but it is achievable. We have helped many clients who have children with disabilities develop effective estate plans. Our book is intended to be a guide to effective decision making for parents who have children with disabilities. It explains the estate-planning process in an understandable, comprehensive way and provides methods of integrating the planning for children who have disabilities within the estate-planning process in general.

A final warning. Our book is not intended to be a substitute for the services of attorneys and other advisors. Rather, it is intended to be a guide for parents in dealing with their advisors and a guide for advisors through the comprehensive estate-planning process. We prefer a team approach in which the family works closely with a skilled attorney, financial planner, and with those who are knowledgeable about living and care facilities for people with disabilities to develop and implement effective life and estate plans.

It is important to find professionals who are expert in estate planning and appreciate the special problems involved for families with members who have disabilities. Most lawyers and financial planners have *not* been exposed to the special problems affecting families with children who have disabilities and may be unaware of much of the specialized information contained in this book. For this reason, parents should consider sharing this book with their attorneys and other advisors. This may provide the professional with helpful direction and consequently may save both time and money.

For example, if an attorney is not familiar with planning for people with disabilities, he or she may make some critical, though unintentional, errors in preparing the plan. For instance, if a typical trust format is used for an individual with a disability, the state government might collect the trust property in repayment for benefits received by the individual. Such a trust might also make the person with a disability ineligible for current government benefits. Similarly, financial planners may direct funds from insurance policies or investments directly to the person with a disability, again disqualifying the person from much needed entitlements.

Many states have attorneys who specialize in estate planning for families with children who have disabilities. In fact, in many areas of the country, teams of specialists are available—financial planners, attorneys, and mental health professionals—who work together to help families develop comprehensive estate plans, all at a very reasonable cost.

Parents may find professionals who have the necessary specialized background by asking other parents who have children with disabilities for references. People who have already been through the estate-planning process may be willing to share recommendations about attorneys, as well as information about costs and special planning problems they encountered and solved. You should also consider contacting local advocacy organizations or service providers that you may have worked with in the past. Many of the organizations listed in the Directory of Organizations in the back of this book can also be of help.

It is important to discuss your advisors' fees at the initial consultation, before hiring. However, while it is natural to want to pay the lowest possible fees, parents should place the greater emphasis on the professional's special knowledge and experience in estate planning for families with children who have disabilities.

Remember that this book is not intended to be the only resource in estate planning for families that have children with disabilities. Laws and requirements about estate-planning methods are changing constantly. It is therefore necessary to check all your plans closely with a knowledgeable attorney before they become final. Once a plan is prepared, it should be periodically evaluated and revised to guarantee the maximum possible care for your child in light of changes in his or her life and changes in your financial situation.

Although there can be no guarantee that an estate plan will provide lifelong care and protection for your child, a plan is essential for parents who are concerned about what will happen to their children after they are gone. With a proper estate plan, parents can avoid a drastic interruption in care and do everything that is possible to ensure that their child will have a comfortable and fulfilling life.

Chapter 1

The Life Plan

Estate planning for families with children who have disabilities begins at the most basic level. How can you, as a parent, be assured that your son or daughter will lead as full and complete a life as possible after your death? What can you do to make sure your hopes and aspirations are realized?

In this chapter we take the first step toward answering those questions. We discuss the process of developing a *life plan*, which is simply a way of encouraging you, as a parent, to sit down and think about what you want for your son or daughter and, equally important, what your son or daughter wants for his or her self. This important information must be communicated to those who will have primary responsibility for your child's care after your death.

To aid you in the process, we discuss a number of options available to people who have disabilities, such as group living arrangements and supervised employment opportunities. Many of the items discussed in this chapter will be of immediate interest to you. You may have a child living with you now who you believe is ready to "leave home" for another supervised environment, perhaps living with peers but having trained staff members available to help with everyday needs, and one or more of the alternatives discussed in this chapter may be what you are looking for.

Not all of the alternatives discussed in this chapter will be appropriate for everyone. Like everyone else, your child has likes and dislikes, abilities and disabilities, and it will be up to you, as a parent, in consultation with your child and other family members and advisors, to cull through the alternatives and develop a life plan for your child that is most appropriate given his or her abilities, desires, and aspirations.

What Is a Life Plan and How Do I Develop One for My Child?

Most parents never find time to really sit down and discuss what their future intentions are for their child. At best, Mom and Dad may talk about the matter while driving home from some family gathering and, in most cases, nothing will ever be resolved. The discussion will typically end with something like, "I'm sure Aunt Bessie will look out for Fred; she's responsible and she's certainly family oriented," or "Brother Bob loves him, and I'm sure he'll take care of him." No effort is ever made to inform Brother Bob or Aunt Bessie that they are expected to perform as future caregivers, or to tell them of Fred's needs and desires, or to investigate whether living with Bob or Bessie is the best alternative. The assumption is simply made that these relatives will gladly step into the parent's role and that they will know what to do as well as Mom and Dad do.

A comprehensive life plan leaves nothing to chance. Issues are addressed openly and in depth, with active participation by family members and others who will be expected to carry on when you, the parents, are deceased. Often the person with the disability will be the most important participant, and we think it is right that this should be so. After all, it is your child's future that is under discussion. Depending on the type of disability involved, your child may have definite ideas that deserve respect and consideration.

This is not to say that you should frighten or intimidate your child by talking about your death in an open and direct way, or that you should base the life plan entirely on what your child says. It is often possible to get vital information from your child in nonthreatening ways. For example, Fred's parents could ask him where he would want to live if he couldn't live with them. Perhaps he would indicate that he wanted to live with his brother Bob, or maybe he has a friend who lives in a group home that he would like to try. Or they may ask him about the types of social activity that he prefers, or the type of job he might like to try.

Even if Fred's answers do not initially appear realistic, it is often possible to cull useful information from them. For example, Fred may express a desire to become a doctor. While this may be unrealistic given Fred's disability, it may be possible for him to get a job as an orderly, or to work in a hospital in some other capacity.

Now that we know who we should talk with in developing our life plan, what is it that we should talk about? In a phrase, *everything that is important in your child's life*. Only you, as a parent, are the real expert on your child, and you must ask yourself what information you want to pass on to future caregivers. While professionals have come and gone, you have seen what has worked for your child, and what has not.

If you were to die today, what are the three priorities you would want for your child in terms of residential care? Would you want your child to live with Aunt Bessie, or with Brother Bob? Should your child live in a group home? If so, what size? Should your child have a private room or share a room with another? Where should the home be located?

William, the son of one of our clients, enjoys going to church on Sundays. It is something he looks forward to every week, and it is also the place where he is most integrated into the community. So it was important to find a place for William within walking distance of a church. His family didn't even know such a place existed. But William's father had indicated in his Letter of Intent (see Chapter Two) that he was looking for a six-bed group home within walking distance of a church where William could have his own room. The advance planning gave guidance to the entire family, and when William's father became aware of the existence of such a facility, the family was ready to act. William was put on the waiting list and when one of the residents moved out, William was ready to move into his new home.

Because the home was funded by private charities and the state in which William resided, the cost was negligible. As we discuss later in this chapter, many states and private corporations provide residential facilities for people who have disabilities and charge according to the residents' ability to pay. Because William has no assets in his name, the cost of the facility is borne entirely by private charities and the government. The federal government pays a percentage based on William's father's work history under the Social Security Disability Income Maintenance Program (SSDI). The remainder of the cost is paid by private charities and the state government under Medicaid and other programs. SSDI, Medicaid, and other government programs are discussed in detail in Chapter Four. As we discuss in Chapter Six, it is possible to use trusts to supplement the income available to your child from government programs without reducing the benefits paid by those programs.

Thinking about your child's future social life is also important. Social activities are often the difference between a meaningful lifestyle and a neglected one. For example, William's father has made it clear that he wants William to visit his relatives in New York once a year, to go to rock concerts, to go to religion camp every summer, and to have money to buy radios (William goes through about two a year).

Debbie, one of our clients, loves to bowl and also enjoys attending church. She was living with her mother and was showing signs that she wanted independence. Fortunately, Debbie's mother heard of a state-funded group home being constructed close by and was able to secure a place for Debbie. The home is near enough that she can drive Debbie to church and bowling. The facility even has a regular bowling league for its residents on Thursday nights.

Debbie's mother was also concerned about Debbie's diet. She was worried that Debbie might gain too much weight. Her Letter of Intent instructs future caregivers to give Debbie low-calorie foods such as fruit for dessert. She also listed a number of foods that Debbie relishes and recommended that Debbie's clothes be bought through an L.L. Bean catalogue. Debbie is quite hard on clothes, and her mother has found L.L. Bean clothing to be the most durable. She wanted money available to pay for Debbie to wear nice, age-appropriate, clothing.

Employment and education are other important categories. We are still not far removed from the days when those with disabilities were simply warehoused in institutions with little in the way of programming or activity. As described in detail later in this chapter, there is an increasing array of job opportunities for people with disabilities.

For example, one of our clients who owns his own business has employed his daughter, who has schizophrenia, in a clerical position for many years. Our client was able to persuade the man who is to take over the business when our client retires to keep a job for his daughter. Another client has a son with mental retardation who works in a laboratory at a major university.

The following is a chart of priorities that we typically ask our clients to complete as a first step in the life planning process. You may wish to use the chart yourself. Keep one thing in mind, however. The life planning process is an ongoing job. As your child changes, and as you and other family members become aware of new and different opportunities, the plan will need to be revised.

In the next chapter we will describe how you can organize the life plan that you develop in the form of an instruction sheet called a *Letter of Intent.* This letter communicates your wishes to future caregivers. It is a good idea to review this letter on a periodic basis so that the letter remains accurate through all the changes in your child's life. One possibility may be to review the letter each year on your child's birthday, as well as whenever a life change dictates a change in planning.

RESIDENCE:

(If you don't wake up tomorrow or if you go into a nursing home, where do you want your child to live?)

1.
2.
3.
4.

EDUCATION:

(You have a long perspective of your child's capabilities, share it!)

1.
2.
3.
4.

EMPLOYMENT:

(What has your child enjoyed? List his or her goals, aspirations, limitations, etc.)

1.
2.
3.
4.

SOCIAL:

(What activities make life meaningful for your child? List sports, hobbies, etc.)

1.
2.
3.
4.

RELIGIOUS:
(Is there a special church or synagogue for fellowship?)

1.
2.
3.
4.

MEDICAL CARE:
(What has and has not worked?)

1.
2.
3.
4.

BEHAVIOR MANAGEMENT:
(Does your child have special behavior problems? What behavior management techniques have been effective in the past?)

1.
2.
3.
4.

FINAL ARRANGEMENTS:
(Remember, you will not be there. What dignified final arrangements do you want to provide for your child?)

1.
2.
3.
4.

ADVOCATE/GUARDIAN:
(Who will look after your child, fight for your child, and be a friend?)

1.
2.
3.
4.

TRUSTEES:
(Who do you trust to manage your child's funds?)

1.
2.
3.
4.

OTHER AREAS OF CONCERN:

1.
2.
3.
4.

Obviously, developing an effective life plan requires a great deal of thought and consideration. In the remainder of this chapter we discuss a number of options relating to residence, education, employment, and social activities. Advocacy and guardianship are discussed in Chapter Three, and considerations relevant to the selection of a trustee are discussed in Chapter Six.

What Options Are Available to My Child in the Way of Residential Care?

There are several ways to obtain information about the types of residential alternatives available for persons who have disabilities. Obviously, finances are a major factor. One of our clients, who owns a large farm in the state of Wisconsin, indicated in her Letter of Intent that she wants her daughter to live on the farm and authorized the trustee of the trust she established for her daughter to hire full-time attendants to help her daughter with daily living needs. Her daughter has Down syndrome and very much enjoys riding horses that are boarded at the farm. Other clients have left homes in trust for their children, with the understanding that friends or relatives would also reside in the homes on a rent-free basis to help with living needs.

These options are not for everyone, both because of the cost involved and because they may not meet the particular needs of your son or daughter. First-rate living accommodations are available for persons who have disabilities, without regard to financial cost. However, these facilities are scarce, and parents should begin the search well in advance of the time they expect their child to move out of the house. We have already discussed group homes, many of which are paid for entirely by the government. Other options are discussed in this section.

After completing this chapter, you will need to investigate the alternatives available in your area. Several sources of information are available to you. One of the best is word of mouth. Perhaps you know others who have family members with disabilities, and they may have ideas about living options. You should also consider contacting local advocacy organizations or service providers that you may have worked with in the past.

It is also possible to obtain information from state and federal agencies. Most state and local governments have public agencies responsible for meeting the needs of persons with disabilities. You can obtain the names of the responsible agencies in your state through your local advocacy organization, at your local library, or by calling the general information number at your state capital.

On the federal level, information can be obtained from the National Information Center for Children and Youth with Disabilities, a federally sponsored clearinghouse for information on planning for persons who have disabilities. The Center provides referrals to local agencies as well as information packets that answer many questions relating to planning issues. You can contact the National Information Center by calling 1-800-999-5599. Another helpful information source, the National Information System and Clearinghouse, can be reached at 1-800-922-9234. Information can also be obtained from many of the organizations listed in the Directory of Organizations at the end of this book.

Family-Type Living Arrangements

Approximately one-half of our clients live with their children for their entire lives, and many of them prefer to keep their children in family-type situations after their deaths. Such clients generally feel that it will be less disruptive to continue family-type living, by having the child live with friends or other family members after they die.

Where this situation is possible, it can work quite well. Friends and relatives can be expected to know your child better than anyone else, and therefore may be in the best position to help your child in his or her daily life, particularly with the aid of information provided in the Letter of Intent. The critical factor is the choice of caregiver. Caregivers should not be selected without complete and open discussion with the person who is to be selected because, depending on the type of disability involved, the caregiver's responsibility can be quite extensive. As a parent, you know the level of responsibility required better than anyone, and it is important that the person you select as caregiver have as complete an understanding as possible.

Family-type living arrangements can be established in your home or in the home of the caregiver. If your son or daughter is to live in the caregiver's home, you can arrange for your son or daughter to pay rent, either with his or her own funds (perhaps through a trust which you may have established) or with funds provided by the government, such as Social Security Disability Income or Supplemental Security Income. These programs are discussed in detail in Chapter Four.

If the caregiver is to live with your child in your home, it is possible to permit the caregiver to live in your home on a rent-free basis. One of our clients selected a sister to act as caregiver, with the provision that the sister was to receive the home at the death of the person with the disability.

If the family-type living arrangement is selected, special attention should be paid to the employment, educational, and social categories. These activities may not be as readily achieved as they might if your child stays in a professionally managed residential setting and special attention will need to be paid to them. Some states have in-home support programs to help pay for items such as supervision.

If the caregiver is to live with your child in your home, you should make sure your child's resources are sufficient to pay real estate taxes, make required mortgage payments, and pay for general upkeep. As discussed in Chapter Six, payments would typically be made through a trust that you would establish for your son or daughter either while you are alive or at your death.

Adult Foster Care

Adult foster-care homes are similar to the family-type living arrangements discussed above. A person who has a disability lives with a caregiver in a small family-type environment. Unlike the family-type arrangement discussed above, however, the caregiver is typically not a friend or relative but is instead a concerned community member who has opened his or her home to others out of a desire to help. The caregiver usually receives expense reimbursements from the government.

Adult foster care has many of the strengths of the family-type living arrangements discussed above. The homes are generally small, and the living situation is generally family-like. In addition, adult foster care homes are regulated by governmental agencies.

However, there are risks involved in such living arrangements as well. A great deal depends upon the skill and character of the foster caregiver. It is the caregiver who will determine how well the home will meet your child's needs in terms of social, developmental, and educational programs; state supervision may not be adequate to ensure the quality of the home. In other words, you will be relying a great deal on the caregiver, and you will need to investigate the setting to assure yourself that the caregiver will do a quality job. This should include interviewing potential foster caregivers, requiring references, and interviewing those who give references.

Moreover, there is always a risk that a foster caregiver will decide to stop providing care for your child. In such circumstances your child would be forced to find a new residence, which could be upsetting.

Thus, while many foster homes are very good, and while many adults with disabilities are undoubtedly very happy in them, great care should be taken in the investigatory process before such an approach is adopted.

The Group Home

"Group home" is a generic term that covers a wide variety of living arrangements. The distinguishing characteristic is that group homes tend to house several unrelated individuals who have disabilities.

Group homes can be owned by the state or by private corporations that may be operated on a for-profit or a not-for-profit basis. Some homes are even purchased by parents or groups of parents, sometimes with the aid of outside investors or charitable organizations. Parents then supply rooms for caregivers and other persons who have disabilities. Some parents may even leave their home to a child with a disability (typically in a trust) after their deaths and instruct the trustee to hire a qualified caregiver to live in the home and rent rooms to other persons with disabilities. Other parents will leave their home to a charity, with the understanding that the charity will run it as a group home.

As a consumer, you will probably be indifferent to the form of ownership of any group home that you may be considering unless, of course, you decide to purchase a group home yourself. For you, the critical issue will be the quality of the services provided and the cost of those services. So far as we are aware, there is no reason to believe that a home owned by the state will be any better or any worse than a home that is owned and operated by a private company, whether that company is operated for-profit or on a not- for- profit basis.

As for cost, residents of publicly owned facilities typically pay on an "ability to pay" basis. Assuming the resident has little in the way of income or assets, payment is usually limited to the residents' entitlements under the Social Security Disability Income or Supplemental Security Income programs. This is true of many privately run homes as well, whether run by for-profit or not-for-profit companies. Such homes tend to charge residents under the same financial needs formulas employed by public facilities, with the company operating the home receiving additional payments from the state under the Medicaid or other programs.

Some privately run group homes are quite expensive, however, and before deciding on a particular group home, you should make sure you have a clear understanding of the cost to you and your child and whether that cost will be met by government programs.

Many of our clients who do not choose a family-type living situation for their children select some type of group home alternative, and frequently the living arrangement is set in place long before our clients' deaths. In fact, in many cases the person with the disability has entered into a group living arrangement before the client contacts us.

For people who select the group home alternative, it is generally advisable that the person with the disability enter the group home before the parents die. This is recommended for two reasons. First, obtaining a place in a particular group home can be very difficult, and parents will want to make sure the most appropriate home is selected. Second, having the living arrangement in place before the parents die will ease the transition when the parents actually do die. The death of a parent is traumatic enough, and the situation is only compounded if the person who has the disability also has to move to an unfamiliar environment.

Community Residential Settings. Within the group home continuum, a wide variety of choices is available. Many communities have homes located in residential neighborhoods that house people who have disabilities. These homes are generally referred to as "community care homes" or "community residences" and may be indistinguishable from other homes in the neighborhood.

Residents may have their own bedrooms, or they may share a room with someone else. The homes may have been converted from single family use, or they might be slightly larger, specifically constructed for group home living. It is possible that such homes already exist in or around your neighborhood and that you have no knowledge of them.

The level of care provided at such community residences generally depends upon the needs of the residents. Many such homes have live-in managers who are responsible for seeing to the needs of the house and the residents. Duties often include preparation of meals (frequently with the aid of the residents) and the development and implementation of training and social programs. Other homes employ rotating staff rather than house managers. Still others provide a combination of the two approaches, with house managers available for daily living needs and other staff members available for emergency situations and to provide the house managers with time off according to a regular schedule or on an "as needed" basis.

Where the disabilities of the residents are less severe, the level of supervision is reduced. In such circumstances there may be no staff member who lives in the home on a full-time basis or works a regularly scheduled shift. Instead, assistance may be provided on an "as needed" basis or for specified tasks such as meal preparation.

Community residences for people who require less supervision are often structured as apartment complexes, with staff members living in units in the complex. Residents tend to work in the community, or take vocational or other educational classes offered in the community, and are integrated into the community as completely and fully as is possible.

Intermediate-Care Facilities. Other group homes are more segregated from the community. These include nursing homes, for those who suffer from serious medical ailments and require supervision by registered nurses and/or physicians, and larger care facilities for people with disabilities, known as intermediate-care facilities or ICFs.

ICFs can be categorized in much the same way as community residences. There are large ICFs that typically consist of a complex of buildings designed to house many people, and smaller ICFs that look very much like community residences. Even in large ICFs with many buildings, each structure will typically house fewer than sixteen people. Residents may have their own bedrooms, or they may share a room with another.

As in a community residence, the level of care provided at an ICF depends on the needs of the residents. ICFs designed for residents who have moderate to severe disabilities provide for more supervision, frequently having live-in house managers, rotating staff, or a combination of the two, much like community residences for people with moderate to severe disabilities. Residents whose disabilities are less severe receive less supervision, generally receiving aid for specific tasks or on an "as needed" basis.

Many of the larger ICFs provide housing both for those needing a great deal of supervision and for those who are more independent. One benefit of this approach is that people who initially require a great deal of supervision can "graduate" to less supervised units as their living skills improve. Residents who have mild disabilities can graduate to an even more independent lifestyle, such as residence in a supervised apartment complex with one or more peers.

Depending on the degree of their disabilities, residents may work in sheltered workshops, take classes offered by the ICF, or take a bus to jobs in the community. Social activities are planned by staff members, with those whose disabilities are less severe doing the bulk of the planning for themselves.

Now that we know about the various types of group homes, which type is best? That depends entirely on you and your child. Jon, the brother of one of the authors, lives in a small community residence with five other people and is very happy. Sam, the brother-in-law of another of the authors, lives in a larger intermediate care facility and is also quite happy.

Some prefer community residences because of the smaller size and the greater degree of integration into community life. However, intermediate care facilities can be quite small, and the residents can be quite integrated into community life as well. Residents may travel to the community for jobs or for social or educational activities. Moreover, even in larger intermediate care facilities with several group homes, the homes themselves may be no larger than typical community residences.

Finally, there are those who question the importance of integration into the community at large, preferring to focus on the quality of life of the residents at the particular facility.

The major benefits of group home living are twofold. First, the residents receive the benefit of professional supervision and organized social, employment, and educational assistance. Second, the residents receive social benefit from peer living arrangements. These benefits can be achieved at both community residences and at intermediate care facilities. The critical factors are the quality of the programming and the concern and dedication of the people involved.

Ultimately, the decision is up to you and your child. It is simply a matter of where you believe your son or daughter will be the happiest.

Independent Living

Independent living typically involves people living by themselves in houses, apartments, or boarding homes. The key characteristic of independent living is limited supervision. Family members, friends, or professionals from adult agencies may visit on a periodic basis, but the distinguishing characteristic is the independence of the resident.

Independent living is more common among those whose disabilities are less severe. For example, if your child has a job in the community and good living and social skills, yet needs assistance with certain tasks like money management, an independent living arrangement may be appropriate. Your child could live in an apartment, perhaps near a friend or family member who could help in those areas where assistance is required.

One potential drawback to independent living as compared to the family-type living arrangements (where your son or daughter lives with a friend or family member) or the group home alternative (where your son or daughter lives with other people who have disabilities) is the potential for loneliness. This can be alleviated by having your child take a roommate (who may or may not have a disability), or by finding an apartment near family and friends.

A recent trend in independent living is to have people with relatively mild disabilities live near one another for companionship and support. In addition, increasing numbers of those with mild retardation and mental illness have been marrying, and independent living with informal supervision by friends, family, or agency officials has been found to be appropriate for many of them. Similarly, people with moderate to severe disabilities have done well living in apartments with roommates who do not have disabilities, although great care must be taken to select a roommate who is willing and able to help the person who has the disability with daily living needs.

In some cases families have even purchased duplexes—one side is rented to cover expenses while the other side is for the person with a disability. Local charities, friends, or relatives then provide regular visitation. There are also various government subsidy programs to help make independent living work, such as Section 8 Housing, in-home support programs, and even meals on wheels.

Where Should My Child Live After I Am Deceased?

As we have stressed throughout this chapter, there is no right or wrong answer to this question. The question of future living arrangements for your child is intensely personal, and the answer depends on the particular needs and desires of your child. What is important is that you consider the alternatives clearly and carefully and that you reach the best possible decision given the particular circumstances of your child and your family.

If your child's disability is relatively minor, an independent living arrangement, perhaps with a roommate or in an apartment complex near friends and family, may be appropriate. Bill, the son of one of our clients, lives in an apartment building next door to his brother. Bill has mild retardation and works at a job in the community. Given Bill's abilities, and his brother's willingness to help, the arrangement works ideally.

If your child has been living with you for his or her entire life, it may be desirable to continue a family-type living arrangement and have your child live with friends or relatives. This is probably the most common approach nationwide and is very common among our clients as well.

If your child is now living in a group home, or if you believe your child would benefit from the companionship or structure of group living, such an approach is probably the way to go. As we discussed above, there is a great deal of variation in approach among group homes, and it is important that you select the right home given your child's own particular needs and desires.

The best way to begin the investigation process is to make a list of the factors in a group home that you consider to be most important. Does the age of the other residents matter to you? How about the nature of their disabilities? The size of the home? Its location—for example, its proximity to you or the quality of the surrounding neighborhood? What is the cost? Are government benefits sufficient to cover expenses? Will your child have a private room? What types of recreational facilities are available? What type of food is served? What are the policies on visitors, telephone usage, or vacations? Will your child have access to a television or a stereo? What types of employment or educational opportunities are available? What types of punishments are used, and what types of behavior give rise to such punishments?

The list will help you narrow your search and provide a framework for questions when you actually begin visiting potential residences. However, you should be careful not to become too rigidly tied to your criteria. You will probably find that some factors you initially thought were important become less so as you observe actual procedures in the homes.

After making your list, you can begin contacting the organizations mentioned in the beginning of this section such as your local advocacy organizations, the National Information System and Clearinghouse, the National Information Center for Children and Youth with Disabilities, and appropriate state and local agencies to get a list of group living facilities in your area. Other organizations listed in the Directory of Organizations in Appendix III can also be helpful. You should then contact those facilities to receive whatever information is available regarding their operations.

Homes that appear promising should be visited so you can gain an appreciation for what day-to-day life in the home is like. It is important that you schedule your visits when residents are present so you can see how the homes actually operate. It is also important that you take your child with you on as many visits as possible. After all, your child may be living in the home, and it is critical that he or she be comfortable there. You may even want to contact relatives of current residents in order to get their opinions.

In making your decision, you will probably find that it is your "feel" for the home that is most important. Do the other residents appear happy? How do they interact with the staff? With each other? What was your child's reaction? Was the staff enthusiastic? Did they appear to like what they were doing?

After all, the entire purpose of the life planning process is to make your child's life as happy and complete as possible, and your "feel" for the home is probably the best way to determine whether your child will be happy there. When you do find a home you like, be patient because the waiting list almost certainly will be quite long. Almost every town in America has a severe shortage of housing for people with disabilities, and extremely long waiting lists are typical. If you think a group home will be appropriate for your child, find out what homes are available and get on the waiting list as soon as possible. It is advisable to consider applying to more than one home to increase the chance that a suitable arrangement will be found.

What Options Are Available To My Child In the Way of Education?

Special Education

According to provisions in the Education for All Handicapped Act, state and local school districts must provide an appropriate elementary and secondary education for your child from ages 6 through 21. States that mandate public education for children age 3 to 5 are also required to educate children with disabilities of this age, if possible in classes with children who do not have disabilities.

Educational services are also available through private schools that are specifically designed to educate children with specified types of disabilities. You can obtain information regarding private schools from local advocacy organizations, the National Association of Private Schools for Exceptional Children, the Department of Education for your school district, or from many of the organizations listed in the Directory of Organizations found in Appendix III.

Public school education is typically free of cost. In fact, the law requires states that provide free education to children who do not have disabilities to provide free education to children with disabilities as well. The cost of private schools varies and usually is paid by families. However, if a state or local education system places a child in a private school because it lacks the facilities to educate children who have disabilities, the cost of the private school must be borne by the state or local educational system, although this is becoming rare as a result of recent changes in educational policy. Other services provided by public expense include transportation and special educational aids. To obtain further information on special education programs in your state or community, contact your state, county, or local education office or your local school district.

Another educational program for young children is Project Head Start. Although the main purpose of Project Head Start is to provide educational opportunities to low-income families, the program provides opportunities for children with disabilities as well. For more information, look up Project Head Start in the telephone directory or contact your local school board. Information can also be obtained from many of the organizations listed in the Directory of Organizations in Appendix III.

Vocational Rehabilitation

The federal government provides extensive financial support to the states for vocational rehabilitation. Vocational rehabilitation programs provided by the states help persons with disabilities prepare for and find work by providing a wide range of services, financial assistance, and training. Employment ranges from regular jobs to sheltered workshops and home-making. The definition of "handicapped individual" used to determine eligibility for vocational rehabilitations is

> "any individual who (a) has a physical or mental disability which for such person constitutes or results in a substantial handicap for employment and (b) can reasonably be expected to benefit in terms of employability from vocational rehabilitation."

Vocational rehabilitation programs cannot exclude individuals because of their age or type of disability. However, it should be noted that the definition emphasizes employment potential. Persons with disabilities who do not have employment potential (as determined by vocational rehabilitation counselors) may not qualify for vocational rehabilitation benefits. Recent trends, however, have been to find people who have relatively severe disabilities to be employable and therefore eligible for benefits. Even if you think your child will fail to satisfy the eligibility requirements, you should consider applying to make sure.

The regulations do not require the person with a disability to be in financial need to qualify for the services. In fact, the regulations prohibit states from charging any individual for evaluation of rehabilitation potential, counseling, referral services, and placement. Each state determines whether or not to establish a financial-need requirement and fees for the other services offered.

Your child's vocational rehabilitation plan will vary depending on personal skills, the counselor's evaluation and recommendations, and the state in which you reside. However, the following vocational rehabilitation services must be available to qualified persons "as appropriate":

- An evaluation of your child's employment potential, including diagnostic and related services.
- On-going counseling to determine the type of employment that is most suitable.
- Medical help, to the extent possible, to reduce or remove your child's disability, in order to improve job performance. This help includes medical, surgical, psychiatric, and hospital services, as well as providing artificial limbs, braces, hearing devices, and eyeglasses needed on the job.
- Vocational training at trade schools, rehabilitation centers, or at home, including training materials such as books and tools. Prevocational training is also available for those who need help with academics.
- Educational opportunities, including payment of tuition and expenses for educational efforts necessary to obtain a job.
- Financial assistance during the rehabilitation period for room and board, transportation to and from the job, and other necessary job maintenance assistance.
- Placement in suitable employment.
- Interpreter services for people with hearing impairments.
- Services for those with visual impairments including reader

services, rehabilitation teaching services, and orientation and mobility services.

- Services to members of the person's family to help promote adjustment or rehabilitation of the individual with a disability.
- Any goods and services that can be reasonably expected to increase or maintain your child's employability such as occupational licenses, tools, and supplies.

Vocational rehabilitation is available for those who are employed as well as for those who are unemployed. If you think your son or daughter is working below his or her capability and would benefit from additional training, vocational rehabilitation should be considered.

Adult Service Agencies

Most areas have private or quasi-private agencies known as adult service agencies devoted to providing aid to people who have disabilities. These agencies can be operated by for-profit or not-for-profit corporations, and many are partially supported by federal, state, or local governmental funds or by contributions from charitable organizations. The agencies may charge a fee for services, or their services may be offered free of cost.

The range of services offered by adult services agencies varies widely. Some are very much like the intermediate care facilities discussed previously, offering residential facilities and comprehensive programs in vocational rehabilitation, recreation, and employment services. In fact, such agencies may actually operate intermediate care facilities themselves.

Others are more limited in scope, perhaps providing employment training for specified types of businesses. Still others may limit themselves to clients with specified types of disabilities (for example, the hearing or visually impaired, or those with physical disabilities).

The process for locating and choosing among adult service agencies is very much like the process for locating and choosing among group homes. You can locate the agencies in your area by contacting your local advocacy organizations, state and local agencies responsible for programs involving people with disabilities, and many of the other organizations listed in the Directory of Organizations found in Appendix III.

It is also possible to obtain information from the vocational rehabilitation center in your state. In fact, it will generally be advisable to contact an adult service agency only after you have dealt with the local vocational rehabilitation center. Because vocational rehabilitation centers typically have greater resources than private agencies, you will find the latter most useful if the local vocational rehabilitation center has been unable to help you (perhaps because it found your child to be unemployable).

Because there are so many adult service agencies, and because they offer such widely divergent services, care should be taken to select the agency that is most appropriate for your particular needs and circumstances. Accordingly, it is advisable to phone or write several of them and to visit those that appear most promising. Many of the factors you will want to consider will be similar to the factors to be considered in choosing among group homes, and you should review the section of this chapter relating to choosing residential settings for your child before visiting adult service agencies.

Special Educational Programs for People with Visual or Hearing Impairments

In addition to local school district programs, there are schools located throughout the country specifically for people who have visual or hearing impairments. These schools often accept children from infancy through 12th grade. Other special schools are available for college students and/or adults.

In addition to having a regular academic curriculum, schools for those with hearing impairments will often have special courses in speech therapy, lip reading, use of hearing aids, and sign language. Schools for those with visual impairments generally have a regular academic curriculum as well as special courses in braille, skills of daily living, orientation, and mobility. These schools often develop leaders for the hearing or visually impaired communities.

You can obtain information from the Office of Special Education and Rehabilitation Services at the Department of Education in Washington, D.C. Information can also be obtained from many of the organizations found in the Directory of Organizations in Appendix III.

Many states also have special vocational rehabilitation units for the hearing and visually impaired. You can obtain information from your local vocational rehabilitation office as well as from the organizations listed in the previous paragraph.

What Options Are Available to My Child in the Way of Employment?

Recent times have seen rapid increases in the amount and type of employment opportunities available for people with disabilities. Families and professionals tend to view employment in a positive light, focusing on the positive self-image that work frequently engenders and the increased opportunities for social relationships resulting from interaction with coworkers. In addition, people with relatively mild disabilities can sometimes earn relatively significant amounts of money.

Depending on the type of disability involved, employment may be an option for your child. You should not, however, feel pressured to seek employment for your child if you and your child do not think it appropriate. Remember, employment should be viewed as a means to a goal, as one of the elements in building a happy and fulfilling life for your child.

The following is a summary of some of the types of employment opportunities available for people with disabilities. Different alternatives will be appropriate for different people. As with the selection among possible residential alternatives, the proper choice will depend on the needs and desires of your son or daughter.

Sheltered Workshops

A sheltered workshop is a separate employment entity, all of whose workers have some type of disability. The workshop contracts with private businesses to perform certain tasks for the business at specified contractual rates. In most cases, the workshop will be involved in packaging, assembly, and shipping of products and will be paid based on the amount of work completed. For example, a workshop might contract with a doll-house manufacturer to pack various component parts supplied by the manufacturer into boxes for sale in stores.

Jobs are divided into small, simple tasks so they can be performed, in assembly-line fashion, by people with moderate to relatively severe disabilities. Workers are usually paid according to their productivity, rather than on an hourly basis.

For workers who lack the skills needed to participate in the performance of actual contracts, sheltered workshops often have educational programs known as prevocational training centers to aid in developing skills needed to perform in the workshop setting. For example, workers may practice tasks such as sorting, collating, and assembly and then will move on to sheltered workshop employment if and when these skills are mastered.

Sheltered workshops have been criticized on several grounds. First, the workshops depend on contract work from private businesses, and such contracts can be difficult to find, particularly in hard economic times. As a result, many sheltered workshops may have significant periods when work is simply unavailable. While the better workshops seek to fill this downtime with educational and other activity programs, many workers frequently have too little to do. Second, the nature of the work received by sheltered workshops can limit opportunities to develop more advanced skills. In order to compete in the marketplace, workshops must bid on contracts that private industries are confident they can complete. These tend to be jobs requiring low-skill repetitive-type work. Third, workshops are, by their very nature, sheltered. As a result, opportunities for workers to interact with those who do not have disabilities are limited. Finally, workshops tend to be very low paying.

Despite these criticisms, however, sheltered workshops have a number of defenders. True, these defenders argue, it would be better if we could find higher-paying integrated employment for everyone. However, even with "job coaches" (discussed in the next section), integrated employment is not available or appropriate for everyone. The proper comparison, these people argue, is not always between workshops and integrated employment, but rather between sheltered workshops and unemployment.

Moreover, many workshops do achieve the major goals of employment discussed above, strengthening the worker's sense of self-worth and fostering socialization with peers. Workers in sheltered workshops tend to work at a more relaxed pace than those in integrated employment situations, and many workers with disabilities find this to be beneficial. Finally, the better workshops utilize a variety of methods to combat isolation from the community. Some attempt to locate near other businesses to foster greater integration, and others provide integrated employment opportunities with job coaches for those whose disabilities are less severe.

As with group homes, sheltered employment workshops vary widely in quality. If you are interested in investigating sheltered employment options for your child, you should examine several facilities and select the one that is most appropriate given your child's particular needs and abilities.

Integrated Employment

Integrated employment refers to employment situations that are integrated into the community at large. That is, a person with a disability works alongside those who do not have disabilities. Several different types of integrated employment are available.

In one approach, known as the "supported job model," an individual is hired by a company and trained one-on-one by a "job coach." The amount of training can be quite extensive; the job coach remains with the employee on a constant basis during the beginning of the training, making sure the work gets done and teaching the employee on a step-by-step basis. Employers favor this method because the presence of the job coach assures quality during the learning process. At the beginning of the training period, the job coach may actually do most of the work. As the employee learns what the job requires, the amount of "coaching" is reduced, with the coach disappearing entirely when the employee completely masters the job. Importantly, the job coach remains available if problems develop or if the employee requires additional training.

Job coaches may be provided by not-for-profit agencies, group homes, intermediate care facilities where the worker may reside, or even by a sheltered workshop from which the worker may have "graduated." A recent trend is for the employer to select a trainer from among its workers, perhaps providing bonuses or extra pay in exchange for the added responsibility. This can work quite well, as it speeds the integration of the person with a disability into work life. Care must be taken by the private company to select a trainer who has a good heart and an adequate understanding of the needs of workers with disabilities.

In a second approach, known as "supervised employment," or the "enclave," a company will hire a group of individuals with disabilities to do specified tasks at a particular job site. The workers will interact with workers who do not have disabilities on a daily basis and will be supervised by a trained worker from an adult service agency who is responsible for their performance. In many cases, employment is temporary. The workers are hired for a specific job and are released when the job is completed, although permanent employment is sometimes possible.

Workers whose disabilities are relatively minor are able to work alongside those who do not have disabilities with minimal or no training. This is known as "competitive employment" and is very common in the cleaning and fast food industries.

Finding A Job For Your Son Or Daughter

As already mentioned, a wide variety of methods are available for locating suitable employment for your son or daughter.

The local vocational rehabilitation training center will have extensive information on employment and job opportunities in your area and will help with job training and placement. Similarly, many adult service agencies will have information on local job opportunities for adults with disabilities.

If your son or daughter lives in a group home, the agency that operates the home will hopefully have information about local employment options and may have its own system for providing suitable employment. Even if your son or daughter does not live in a group home, local group homes would probably be willing to help you. Information on local employment options can also be obtained from local advocacy organizations, state and local agencies responsible for aiding those who have disabilities, and from many of the organizations listed in the Directory of Organizations found in Appendix III.

Finally, there are the time honored methods employed by those who do not have disabilities. Perhaps there is a suitable opening at a place where a friend or relative may work. Or maybe you can find something that appears promising in the want ads.

Obviously, you will want to make sure your son or daughter is happy with whatever job he or she ultimately selects. This will require analysis of the type of work involved (Is it something your child will be happy doing?), the work environment (Is it safe and will coworkers be supportive?), the location (Can your child get to work easily?) and the benefit package (Are wages fair? Are hours excessive? Is vacation time adequate and can it be scheduled at the proper times? Will insurance benefits be provided?)

In addition, you will need to assess how the wages received will affect your son or daughter's eligibility for government benefits. As discussed in Chapter Four, many of these governmental programs have strict income limitations, and your child could become ineligible for these programs if the limitations are exceeded. However, in most cases the self-esteem derived from work is more important than any loss in government benefits.

One final point to keep in mind. A vocational decision is not irrevocable. If your son or daughter is unhappy with a job, change is possible. A new workshop can be found. Additional vocational training can be taken to improve job skills. As always, the goal is to increase the quality of life for your son or daughter. If a first effort to achieve that goal proves ineffective, there is nothing prohibiting you from changing your plan.

What Social Activities Are Available for My Child?

As with any other person, your child's social and recreational desires are uniquely individual, and your goal, in preparing a life plan and writing a Letter of Intent, is to correctly identify those desires and make sure the life plan provides mechanisms that will enable your son or daughter to continue to enjoy the activities that provide pleasure in his or her life.

Identifying the things your son or daughter likes to do should not be difficult. You have raised or are raising your child and you, above anyone, know what your son or daughter enjoys doing and what he or she does not. You know which activities your child looks forward to eagerly, which activities are joined in without enthusiasm, and which activities your child must be dragged to, kicking and screaming.

Your job is to make sure your child's desires continue to be respected after your death. For many, this will simply be a matter of communicating your child's desires to future caregivers in your Letter of Intent. You may have already selected another child to look out for the interests of a son or daughter with a disability, and you may have confidence that they will "do what needs doing." (The Letter of Intent will still be important in case the child you select dies or moves out of state.)

For example, you will recall William, the son of one of our clients. He enjoys listening to music, socializing with friends, attending church, going to religion camp, and visiting relatives. William's father placed him in a group home near a church so William would have peers to interact with and a church to attend, and indicated in his Letter of Intent that every effort should be made to enable William to continue his favorite activities. William's two brothers, the people responsible for looking out for him after his father's death, are positioned to make sure William's desires will continue to be respected.

Similarly, Lisa, one of our clients, likes attending church and also likes to bowl. She lives in a group home that features many social programs: art, regular trips to movies and amusement parks, as well as a regular bowling league. Lisa has no relatives, other than her mother, living in the area, but her mother has several friends who have volunteered to make sure Lisa gets to church after she is gone.

If you are unsure what your son or daughter likes to do, or if you would like to offer your child new and different activities, perhaps to expand the range of his or her interests, several alternatives are available. One of the great sources of pleasure in life is a simple get-together with friends, and many communities have loosely organized group get-togethers for people with disabilities. You can probably find out about them through local organizations that advocate for people with disabilities, or you may want to organize one yourself. It may also be possible to participate in recreational activities sponsored by local group homes even if your child is not presently a resident. Methods of contacting local group homes are discussed in a previous section of this chapter on residential alternatives.

Finally, many organizations specializing in recreation, such as the YMCA and various special recreation associations, have programs specifically designed for people with disabilities. Activities include swimming, basketball, and informal get-togethers. Adult service agencies frequently sponsor "day activity programs" that combine social activities with educational programs designed to help those with disabilities improve their daily living skills. Such programs vary widely in content and quality and you should visit several before deciding on one. Methods for contacting adult service agencies are discussed in the section of this chapter devoted to options relating to education.

The Special Olympics programs for people with developmental disabilities also offer a first-rate forum for social enhancement. Participation is open to everyone regardless of ability, and the opportunity to participate with peers in sporting events, and perhaps to develop new and valued friendships, should not be overlooked. Perhaps the Special Olympics oath expresses the goals of the organization best: "Let me win, but if I cannot win, let me be brave in the attempt."

The importance of planning so that your child can continue to enjoy the activities that make life enjoyable cannot be overstated. Too many parents worry about the "big things"—residence, employment, and education—without paying sufficient attention to the "little things," like recreation, that can be the difference between a rewarding life and a neglected one.

Conclusion

Many parents who have a child with a disability do not prepare an estate plan because they feel uncomfortable with the traditional, legal document approach. They choose to do nothing in preference to doing the wrong thing.

For the minority of parents who do prepare wills, there is a typical scenario. An attorney advises them to disinherit their child and leave some resources in trust for their child's benefit. (Trusts for beneficiaries with disabilities are described in Chapter Six.)

The attorney may spend an hour counseling the parents and then have a secretary fill in the blanks of boilerplate documents. For the most part, any resources will be managed by a trustee, who may or may not know the parents' desires. The tragedy is that the parents leave the attorney's office thinking they have done everything—that their estate plan is finished. By the time they reach their car, though, they may stare at the pieces of paper in their hands and wonder just how their child really will be taken care of in the future. They don't feel they have covered all the bases.

One of the greatest illusions in the estate-planning field today is that the average family can guarantee a bright future for a person with a disability simply by preparing a will and a trust. The truth is that a will and a trust rarely carry out the wishes of the family unless the parents build a strong planning foundation by first developing a comprehensive and flexible life plan.

The life planning approach calls upon you to take the following steps:

- Decide what you want for your child in all of the major life areas: residential placement, education, employment, socialization, religion, medical care, final arrangements, and so on. Flexibility is important, so there should be many prioritized options listed under each heading. Your "child" may live another 50 to 60 years, and planning should try to cover the maximum life span.

- Put these hopes and desires in writing by using the nonlegal document known as a Letter of Intent. These letters are discussed in Chapter Two.

- Decide whether your child will need an advocate or a legal guardian. Advocates and guardians are discussed in Chapter Three.

- Decide on the combination of financial resources that will be needed to implement the life plan. The considerations relevant to making this decision are discussed in Chapters Four and Five.

There's a lot to consider, a lot of decisions to make. But plans must be made if you are to give your child the best possible chance to live a happy and rewarding life after your death.

CHAPTER 2

THE LETTER OF INTENT

NOW THAT YOU HAVE PREPARED A TENTATIVE LIFE PLAN FOR your son or daughter, you probably have a fair idea of what you would like his or her life to look like after your death. It is now time to communicate your ideas and knowledge to future caregivers.

In most cases, the future caregivers will be relatives. But even if these relatives are very close to your child, they may not be aware of important personal information. For instance, do the future caregivers know all the pertinent information about your child's medical history? Do they know the names, addresses, and phone numbers of all the professionals who serve your child? Do they know the names of professionals who you think should be avoided?

Moreover, if these relatives die or move away, successor caregivers will need explicit information.

Although not a legally binding document, a Letter of Intent is an ideal format. It allows you to communicate your desires to future caregivers and therefore will prove invaluable to them. The letter assumes even greater importance if these future caregivers are out of state and do not see your child frequently, or if the ultimate caregiver will be a trust officer at a bank.

To write a Letter of Intent, just follow the guide contained in this chapter, which covers vital details about what works well for your child in all of the major life areas: residential placement, education, employment, socialization, religion, medical care, final arrangements, and so on. Flexibility is important, so there should be several prioritized options listed under each heading. Possibly you will want to add some categories of your own to those listed in the guide, and you should feel free to make any adjustments necessary to meet the individual needs of your son or daughter.

Be sure to include enough information. For instance, if you write down a Social Security number, be sure to use the words "Social Security Number" so that someone reading the document after your death doesn't have to guess what those numbers represent. If you list your child's doctor, make sure to include his or her address and phone number. Also, using category headings similar to those in the guide may make it easier for anyone to find particular pieces of information.

If both parents are living, one of you may want to do the actual writing of the Letter of Intent while both of you will want to sign it. The letter can be typed or handwritten. It isn't an essay for school, and perfect grammar, spelling, or style are not the point. Your major concern is to make sure that your child will have a happy and meaningful life. Write clearly enough so that anyone who reads the letter in the future will understand exactly what you meant.

Some of the items we ask you to include in the Letter of Intent are discussed elsewhere in the book. For now, do your best, although you may want to make revisions after you have read the relevant discussions.

We also ask for a fair amount of information about your child's finances. Do the best you can for now, although the information in Chapters Four and Five may be of help for future planning.

We cannot stress too much the importance of reviewing the letter and making revisions as changes in your plans for your son or daughter arise. Each year you should take out the letter and review it to make sure it remains current. Choose the same date each year, perhaps your child's birthday, so you won't forget. Occasionally there will be a significant change in your child's life, such as a new residential placement or a bad reaction to medication, and the letter should be revised immediately if any such change occurs. Many clients keep the letter on a word processor so changes can be made more easily.

The following material is only a guide to writing your Letter of Intent. It is a list of everything we could think of that parents might put in their Letter of Intent. Not every point will apply to your particular situation. Remember, the purpose of the Letter of Intent is to include personal information about caring for your child that you want to communicate to future caregivers.

Letter of Intent

Written by: ___________________________ Date: __________

____

(Relationship to the person with the disability—mother, father or both)

To Whom It May Concern:

Information About ____________________________________

(Father's name)

General information: List the father's full name, Social Security number, complete address, phone numbers for home and work, county or township, date of birth, place of birth, city/town/country where raised, fluent languages, religion, race, blood type, number of sisters, and number of brothers. Indicate whether he is a U.S. citizen.

Marital status: Indicate the father's marital status. If he is currently married, list the date of that marriage, the place the marriage took place, and the number of children from that marriage. Also list the dates of any previous marriages, names of other wives, and names and birth dates of children from each marriage.

Family: List the complete names of the father's siblings and parents. For those still living, list their addresses and phone numbers, as well as pertinent biographical information.

Information About ________________________________

(Mother's name)

General Information: List the mother's full name, Social Security number, complete address, phone numbers for home and work, county or township, date of birth, place of birth, city/town/country where raised, fluent languages, religion, race, blood type, number of sisters, and number of brothers. Indicate whether she is a U.S. Citizen.

Marital status: Indicate the mother's marital status. If she is currently married, list the date of that marriage, the place the marriage took place, and the number of children from that marriage. Also list the dates of any previous marriages, names of other husbands, and names and birth dates of children from each marriage.

Family: List the complete names of the mother's siblings and parents. For those still living, list addresses and phone numbers, as well as pertinent biographical information.

Information About ________________________________

(Your son or daughter's name)

General Information

Name: List the full name of your son or daughter. Also list the name he or she likes to be called.

Numbers: List your child's Social Security number, complete address, county or township, telephone numbers for home and work, height, weight, shoe size, and clothing sizes.

More details: List your child's gender, race, fluent languages, and religion. Indicate whether your child is a U.S. citizen.

Birth: List your child's date and time of birth, as well as any complications. List your child's birth weight and place of birth, as well as the city/town/country where he or she was raised.

Siblings: List the complete names, addresses, and phone numbers of all sisters and brothers. Which ones are closest to the person with a disability—both geographically and emotionally?

Marital status: List the marital status of your son or daughter. If married, list the spouse's name, his or her date of birth, the names of any children, and their dates of birth. Also list any previous marriages, as well as the names, addresses, and phone numbers for the spouses and children from each marriage.

Other relationships: List special friends and relatives that your child knows and likes. Describe the relationships. These people can play an invaluable role, especially if the trustee resides out-of-state.

Guardians: Indicate whether your child has been declared incompetent and whether any guardians have been appointed. List the name, address, and phone number of each guardian and indicate whether that person is a guardian of the person or guardian of the estate, plenary or limited.

If successor guardians have been chosen, list their full names, addresses, and phone numbers. Even if your child has no guardian, it is often wise to state in the Letter of Intent your wishes about who you want to act as guardian if one is needed in the future. Make sure you have spoken with them.

Advocates: List the people, in order, who you foresee acting as advocates for your child after your death. Make sure you have spoken with them.

Trustee: Indicate whether you have set up a trust for your child and list the full names, addresses, and phone numbers of all the trustees.

Representative payee: Indicate whether your son or daughter has or needs a representative payee to manage public entitlements, such as Supplemental Security Income or Social Security.

Power of attorney: If anyone has power of attorney for your son or daughter, list the person's full name, address, and phone number. Indicate whether this is a durable power of attorney.

Final arrangements: Describe any arrangements that have been made for your child's funeral and burial. List the full names of companies or individuals, their addresses, and phone numbers. Also list all payments made and specify what is covered.

In the absence of specific arrangements, indicate your preferences for cremation or burial. Should there be a church service? If the preference is for burial, what is the best site? Should there be a monument? If cremation is the choice, what should be done with the remains?

Medical History and Care

Diagnoses: List the main diagnoses for your son or daughter's condition, such as autism, cerebral palsy, Down syndrome, epilepsy, impairment due to age, learning disorder, mental retardation, neurological disorder, physical disabilities, psychiatric disorder, or an undetermined problem.

Seizures: Indicate the seizure history of your son or daughter: no seizures; no seizures in the past two years; seizures under control; seizures in the past two years, but not in the past year; or seizures currently. Does anything act as a "trigger" for increased seizure activity?

Functioning: Indicate your child's intellectual functioning level (mild, moderate, severe, profound, undetermined, etc.).

Vision: Indicate the status of your child's vision: normal, normal with glasses, impaired, legally blind, without functional vision, etc. List the date of the last eye test and what was listed on any prescription for eyeglasses.

Hearing: Indicate the status of your child's hearing: normal, normal with a hearing aid, impaired, deaf, etc.

Speech: Indicate the status of your child's speech: normal; impaired, yet understandable; requires sign language; requires use of communication device; non-communicative, etc. If your child is non-verbal, specify the techniques you use for communication.

Mobility: Indicate the level of your child's mobility: normal; impaired, yet self-ambulatory; requires some use of wheelchair or other assistance; dependent on wheelchair or other assistance; without mobility, etc.

Blood: List your child's blood type and any special problems concerning blood.

Insurance: List the type, amount, and policy number for the medical insurance covering your son or daughter. What is included in this coverage now? Indicate how this would change upon the death of either parent. Make sure you include Medicare and Medicaid, if relevant.

Current physicians: List your child's current physicians, including specialists. Include their full names, types of practice, addresses, phone numbers, the average number of times your child visits them each year, the total charges from each doctor during the last year, and the amounts not covered by a third party, such as insurance (including Medicare or Medicaid).

Previous physicians: List their full names, addresses, phone numbers, the type of practice, and the most common reasons they saw your child. Describe any important findings or treatment. Explain why you no longer choose to consult them.

Dentist: List the name, address, and phone number of your child's dentist, as well as the frequency of exams. Indicate what special treatments or recommendations the dentist has made. Also list the best alternatives for dental care in case the current dentist is no longer available.

Nursing needs: Indicate your child's need for nursing care. List the reasons, procedures, nursing skill required, etc. Is this care usually provided at home, at a clinic, or in a doctor's office?

Mental health: If your child has visited a psychiatrist, psychologist, or mental health counselor, list the name of each professional, the frequency of visits, and the goals of the sessions. What types of therapy have been successful? What types have not worked?

Therapy: Does your son or daughter go to therapy (physical, speech, or occupational)? List the purpose of each type of therapy, as well as the name, address, and phone number of each therapist. What assistive devices have been helpful? Has an occupational therapist evaluated your home to assist you in making it more accessible for your child?

Diagnostic testing: List information about all diagnostic testing of your son or daughter in the past: the name of the individual and/or organization administering the test, address, phone number, testing dates, and summary of findings. How often do you recommend that diagnostic testing be done? Where?

Genetic testing: List the findings of all genetic testing of your child and relatives. Also list the name of the individual and/or organization performing the tests, address, phone number, and the testing dates.

Immunizations: List the type and dates of all immunizations.

Diseases: List all childhood diseases and the date of their occurrence. List any other infectious diseases your child has had in the past. List any infectious diseases your child currently has. Has your child been diagnosed as a carrier for any disease?

Allergies: List all allergies and current treatments. Describe past treatments and their effectiveness.

Other problems: Describe any special problems your child has, such as bad reactions to the sun or staph infections if he or she becomes too warm.

Procedures: Describe any helpful hygiene procedures such as cleaning wax out of ears periodically, trimming toenails, or cleaning teeth. Are these procedures currently done at home or by a doctor or other professional? What do you recommend for the future?

Operations: List all operations and the dates and places of their occurrence.

Hospitalization: List any other periods of hospitalization your child has had. List the people you recommend to monitor your child's voluntary or involuntary hospitalizations and to act as liaison with doctors.

Birth control: If your son or daughter uses any kind of birth control pill or device, list the type, dates used, and doctor prescribing it.

Devices: Does your son or daughter need any adaptive or prosthetic devices, such as glasses, braces, shoes, hearing aids, or artificial limbs?

Medication: List all prescription medication currently being taken, plus the dosage and purpose of each one. Describe your feelings about the medications. List any particular medications that have proved effective for particular problems that have occurred frequently in the past and the doctor prescribing the medicine. List medications that have not worked well in the past and the reasons. Include medications that have caused allergic reactions.

OTC: List any over-the-counter medications that have proved helpful, such as vitamins or dandruff shampoo. Describe the conditions helped by these medications and the frequency of use.

Monitoring: Indicate whether your child needs someone to monitor the taking of medications or to apply ointments, etc. If so, who currently does this? What special qualifications would this person need?

Procurement: Does your child need someone to procure medications?

Diet: If your child has a special diet of any kind, please describe it in detail and indicate the reasons for the diet. If there is no special diet, you might want to include tips about what works well for avoiding weight gain and for following the general guidelines of a balanced, healthy diet. You might also describe the foods your child likes best and where the recipes for these foods can be found.

What Works Well for ______________________________

(Your son or daughter's name)

Housing

Present: Describe your son or daughter's current living situation and indicate its advantages and disadvantages.

Past: Describe past living situations. What worked? What didn't?

Future: Describe in detail any plans that have been made for your son or daughter's future living situation. Describe your idea of the best living arrangement for your child at various ages or stages. Prioritize your desires. For each age or stage, which of the following living arrangements would you prefer?

- A relative's home (Which relative?)
- Supported living in an apartment or house with ____ hours of supervision
- A group home with no more than ___ residents
- A state institution (Which one?)
- A private institution (Which one?)
- Foster care for a child

- Adult foster care
- Parent-owned housing with ___ hours of supervision
- Housing owned by your child with ____hours of supervision, etc.

Size: Indicate the minimum and maximum sizes of any residential option that you consider suitable.

Adaptation: Does the residence need to be adapted with ramps, grab bars, or other assistive devices?

Community: List the types of places that would need to be conveniently reached from your child's home. Include favorite restaurants, shopping areas, recreation areas, libraries, museums, banks, etc.

Daily Living Skills

IPP: Describe your child's current Individual Program Plan.

Current activities: Describe an average daily schedule. Also, describe activities usually done on "days off."

Monitoring: Discuss thoroughly whether your son or daughter needs someone to monitor or help with the following items:

- Self-care skills like personal hygiene or dressing.
- Domestic activities like housekeeping, cooking, shopping for clothes, doing laundry, or shopping for groceries and cleaning supplies.
- Transportation for daily commuting, recreational activities, and emergencies.
- Reinforcement of social and interpersonal activities with others to develop social skills.
- Other areas.

Caregivers' attitudes: Describe how you would like caregivers to treat matters like sanitation, social skills (including table manners, appearance, and relationships with the opposite sex). What values do you want caregivers to demonstrate?

Self-esteem: Describe how you best reinforce your son or daughter's self-esteem, discussing how you use praise and realistic goal setting.

Sleep habits: How much sleep does your son or daughter require? Does he or she have any special sleep habits or methods of waking up?

Personal finances: Indicate whether your son or daughter needs assistance with personal banking, bill payments, and budgeting. If so, how much help is needed?

Allowance: Indicate whether you recommend a personal allowance for your son or daughter. If so, how much? Also, list your recommendations about supervision of how the allowance is spent.

Education

Schools: List the schools your child has attended at various ages and the level of education completed in each program. Include early intervention, day care, and transition programs.

Current programs: List the specific programs, schools, and teachers your son or daughter has now. Include addresses and phone numbers.

Academics: Estimate the grade level of your son or daughter's academic skills in reading, writing, math, etc. List any special abilities.

Emphasis: Describe the type of educational emphasis (such as academic, vocational, or community-based) on which your son or daughter currently concentrates. What educational emphasis do you think would be best for the future?

Integration: Describe the extent that your child has been in regular classes or schools during his or her education. What are your desires for the future? What kinds of undesirable conditions would alter those desires?

Day Program or Work

Present: Describe your son or daughter's current day program and/or job.

Past: Describe past experiences. What worked? What didn't? Why?

Future: Discuss future objectives. Prioritize your desires.

Assistance: Indicate to what extent, if any, your son or daughter needs assistance in searching for a job, in being trained, in becoming motivated, and in receiving support or supervision on the job.

Leisure and Recreation

Structured recreation: Describe your son or daughter's structured recreational activities. List favorite activities and the favorite people involved in each activity.

Unstructured activities: What are your child's favorite means of self-expression, interests, and skills (going to movies, listening to music, dancing, collecting baseball cards, painting, bowling, riding a bicycle, roller skating, etc.)? List the favorite people involved in each activity.

Vacations: Describe your son or daughter's favorite vacations. Who organizes them? How often do they occur, and when are they usually scheduled?

Fitness: If your son or daughter participates in a fitness program, please describe the type of program, as well as details about where and when it takes place and who oversees it.

Religion

Faith: List the religion of your son or daughter, if any. Indicate any membership in a particular church or synagogue.

Clergy: List any ministers, priests, or rabbis familiar with your son or daughter. Include the names of the churches or synagogues involved and their addresses and phone numbers. Also indicate how often your child might like to be visited by these people.

Participation: Estimate how frequently your son or daughter would like to participate in services and other activities of the church or synagogue. Indicate how this might change over time. Also describe any major, valued events in the past.

Rights and Values

Please list the rights and values that should be accorded your son or daughter. Here are some examples of what you might list.

- To be free from harm, physical restraint, isolation, abuse, and excessive medication.
- To refuse behavior modification techniques that cause pain.
- To have age-appropriate clothing and appearance.
- To have staff, if any, demonstrate respect and caring and to refrain from using demeaning language.

Other

Give an overview of your child's life and your feelings and vision about the future. Describe anything else future caregivers and friends should know about your son or daughter.

Finances, Benefits, and Services for ____________________

(Your son or daughter's name)

Assets: List the total assets your child has as of this date. Indicate how those assets are likely to change—if at all—in the future.

Cash income: List the various sources of income your son or daughter had last year. Include wages, government cash benefits, pension funds, trust income, and other income. This might include Social Security, Social Security Disability Income (SSDI), or Supplemental Security Income (SSI).

Services and benefits: List any other services or benefits your child receives. These might be services for children with physical impairments, developmental disability services, clinics sponsored by support groups, early periodic screening, diagnosis and treatment, employment assistance, food stamps, housing assistance, legal assistance, library services, maternal and child health services, Medicaid, Medicare, Project Head Start, special education, Title XX service programs, transportation assistance, or vocational rehabilitation services.

Gaps: Indicate whether any services or benefits are needed but are not being received by your son or daughter. Indicate whether plans exist to improve the current delivery of services or to obtain needed benefits.

Expenses: List all expenses paid directly by your child in various categories, such as housing, education, health care, recreation, vocational training, and personal spending. List all expenses paid directly by parents, guardians, or trustees in various categories. List estimates of all expenses paid by third parties, such as insurance companies paying doctors directly or Medicaid paying for residential services.

Changes: Indicate how your child's financial picture would change if one or both parents died. Be sure to list any additional cash benefits to which your child definitely would be entitled. Also list any cash benefits for which your child might be eligible.

Sample Letters

The following sample Letters of Intent may be useful when you write your own letter. All of them were written by clients of ours and have been reprinted with their permission. Names have been changed, and information regarding medications has been omitted. Otherwise, the letters are completely authentic.

Sam, the subject of the first, has cerebral palsy that was caused by brain trauma resulting from electrocution. James, the subject of the second, has mental retardation that was probably brought on by seizures that began at age 3. Lisa, the subject of the third, has schizophrenia that first appeared at age 21.

You may want to skim the letters or read them in their entirety. If your son or daughter has a physical disability, you should not assume that only the sample letter relating to physical disabilities will be of use to you. The same is true if your child has a mental illness or mental retardation. You may find any or all of the letters to be useful.

Sample Letter for Physical Disability

To Whom It May Concern:

I, Jane Doe, am writing this letter on behalf of my husband, Fred Doe, and myself to explain the intentions of our estate plan and to give future caregivers as much information as possible about our son, Sam Doe. It is our hope that this information will be used to provide the best possible care for Sam and is done with his knowledge and input.

Father: Fred Doe

Social Security Number: 000-00-0000
Residence: (Address & Phone number)
Business: (Name, Address & Phone number)
Blood Type: O+
Religion: Roman Catholic

Fred is a male Caucasian born (date) in (city, county & state). He was baptized and confirmed at (name, address of church). He graduated from (name of high school) and received a B.S. degree in Financial Management from (name of college). He served in the U.S. Army Reserve Corps from which he received an Honorable Discharge on (date).

Fred married Jane Deer on (date) at (name of church). They have a daughter, Sara Doe, born (date) and a son, Sam Doe, born (date).

Relatives: Frank Doe (father) is deceased.

Helen Doe (mother) is deceased.

Steve Doe (brother)
(Address & Phone number)

Steve is married to Jacqueline and they have 7 adult children, all living on the West Coast. He is retired but still does some work for his sons' businesses and also does some carpentry work. He moved to California in the early 1960's but comes back to Illinois for a visit every year or so.

Arnold Deer (father)
(Address & Phone number)

Arnold is a pediatrician with a practice in (name of city). He was born September 7, 1917 in (city & state) and raised there. He married his wife on (date) in (city & state) and moved to (city & state) in 1943 to do his residency at (name of medical center). He and his wife raised 4 children (list of their names). He has not had any major illnesses and is in excellent health. He is very involved in (name of church), especially their mission outreach program to Haiti. He also loves working in his yard and always has some household project going. Other hobbies include downhill skiing, fishing, and walking.

[The letter goes on to list and describe 9 other relatives.]

Sam Doe—General Information

Social Security Number: 000-00-0000
Residence: (Street address & Phone number)
School: (School address & Phone number)
Blood Type: unknown
Religion: Episcopalian
Height: 5'7"
Weight: 85 lbs.
Shoe size: 7
Shirt size: boys 16-18 adult medium
Pants size: boys 16 waist size 27"
Hands: small

Sam is a male Caucasian born (date) at (hospital name) in (city, state & county) at 9:00 a.m. He weighed 6 lbs. 3 oz., and delivery was normal. He lived with his family first at (address) and since 1980 at (address). On (date) when Sam was 7 months old, he was electrocuted by a pole lamp with faulty wiring. The shock stopped his heart, which caused trauma to his brain resulting in cerebral palsy. He was hospitalized at (hospital name) for 26 days.

Sam was baptized at (name of church) on (date). He attended Sunday School there and at (name of church) from 1980 to 1988. Currently he attends church only 2 or 3 times a year.

Sam is a U.S. Citizen. Sam is not currently receiving any government benefits. Sam is an unemployed, full-time student being supported by his parents.

Relatives:

(Name & Address of grandparents)

Sam has a close relationship with his grandparents. They have often cared for Sam. He normally sees them a couple of times a year, both here and in (name of city). They are very comfortable with him and enjoy him tremendously, and Sam loves being spoiled by them. They understand Sam's wants and needs and are very supportive. Their home is well set up for Sam to stay with them, but physically both of them need to be available for any lifting or transferring.

(Name and Address of Aunt & Uncle)

Sam and his aunt have a special relationship and share a unique sense of humor. (name of aunt) has physically cared for Sam often. Sam has also become very fond of his uncle, who is very comfortable with him. His cousins (names) are also comfortable with Sam. They interact very naturally with him and enjoy his company. Sam spends a lot of time with this family when he is visiting in (name of city). They have also visited us a number of times.

[The letter goes on to describe Sam's relationships with 7 other relatives.]

Close Family Friends who know Sam well and with whom he has a good rapport:

Name, Address & Phone number

List of children & their current addresses

Sam has an extremely close relationship with the whole family. He has grown up knowing them, spending vacations and holidays together, etc. (Wife's name) has often cared for Sam and is very comfortable and inventive with him, although she is no longer able to lift him by herself. (Husband & Wife's names) understand Sam and also know our hopes and expectations for Sam. (Husband's name) owns and operates a rubber manufacturing plant in (city). (Wife's name) works for the (school district name) and is an aide in a special education classroom. She is currently taking classes at (name of college) and working towards a teaching certificate. The family is totally at ease with Sam and interacts very appropriately with him.

[The letter includes descriptions of 3 additional neighbors and friends.]

Peers:

Jenny Doe (Jerry & Jesse Doe, Parents)

(Address & Phone number)

Jenny is a friend of Sam's who also has cerebral palsy. They have been going to school and camp together since grade school. They have a unique relationship and can talk to each other about things they do not discuss with anyone else. They share many problems and frustrations, but mainly they enjoy making each other laugh.

Mary Doe

(Phone number)

Mary is a social worker in the (City name) school system. She has worked for North Suburban Special Recreation Association (NSSRA) in their summer camps, which is where Sam met her. She also volunteers time to NSSRA during the school year to help run programs for the orthopedically handicapped. A couple of times a year she will set up "dates" with Sam and Jenny to go to a movie or out for ice cream or pizza. She understands Sam and has helped him determine what is inappropriate or immature behavior with contemporaries.

Guardians: Not at this time

Trustees: *(The letter lists 3 individuals and one bank official, with their addresses and phone numbers.)*

Advocates: *(3 individuals, their addresses, and phone numbers are listed.)*

The above people have been consulted and are willing to act as advisors to the trustees for any decisions that have to be made regarding Sam and are willing to act in his behalf to aid the trustees with the execution of the trust. I expect the trust to reimburse them for the time they spend acting as Sam's advocates and for any travel expenses they incur in carrying out this function.

Power of attorney: Not at this time

Final Arrangements: We would choose to have a memorial service and have Sam buried at the (name of church), which adjoins our property in (city and state). We have a plot there and the certificate is in the strong box.

Medical History and Care

Sam has severe mixed spastic athetoid cerebral palsy with quadriplegic involvement, which resulted from a prolonged period of cerebral anoxia secondary to cardiorespiratory arrest due to accidental electrocution at age 7 months. His brain damage was mostly motor, so his disabilities are mainly physical although he has a lot of learning disabilities. He is totally dependent for all his physical needs. Sam does have some muscular control. His right side is less involved than his left, so he uses his right hand to drive his electric wheelchair, type, pick things up, etc. He can stabilize things with his left hand, but that is about all.

Seizures: Sam had some seizures when he was still in a coma after his accident, but has had none since.

Functioning: Sam is developmentally delayed but functions at a near normal level intellectually. He has severe learning disabilities.

Vision: With his glasses Sam has normal vision. His prescription is for far-sightedness but his glasses also aid in fixation. Sam is much less fatigued when doing school work or when working on the computer if he wears his glasses.

Hearing: Sam's hearing is normal.

Speech: Sam's speech is impaired but usually understandable. Sam is very patient and good at giving clues as to what he is talking about if he is not being understood. His speech therapist at (school name) is (therapist's name). She feels that Sam's articulation is the best that he is physically able to achieve, so she is concentrating on language skills.

Sam has experimented with different communication devices, but so far speech is much more efficient for him, and more natural.

Mobility: Sam is nonambulatory and uses an electric wheelchair. Because of his poor postural control, he needs special supports built into the chair to be able to sit. When not in the chair he spends his time prone on the floor, lying over a special wedged support we had made. This wedge, or some similar object, is necessary as Sam needs to stretch out during the day to relieve muscle contractures, backaches, and cramping.

Sam's wheelchair is very heavy and not very portable, so we have a van with a lift to transport him. Sam cannot sit in his chair for extended periods of time, so the van also has a fold-out seat that he can lie on. We also have collapsible ramps (one for each wheel) for places that are not accessible. These work if the entrance is not too high.

Blood: (type not listed)

Insurance: Sam is covered on our health insurance policy, which we have through (name of firm). The coverage is very comprehensive. They pay 80 percent of all physician and therapist charges, except the pediatrician's routine physical; 100 percent of most tests and X-rays; 100 percent of almost all dental charges and then 80 percent; 80 percent of most devices that you can get a prescription written for; they do not cover eye exams and glasses. Basically I just submit everything.

[The letter then lists the name of the insurance company, with its address, phone number, and plan number.]

There are two different forms. The medical coverage is with (name and address of company). The dental coverage is with (name, address, and phone number of company).

As long as my husband is alive, Sam will be covered by our insurance. After his death, the insurance will remain in force for 6 months. It can then be renewed for only 2 years.

Physicians: see separate listing

Nursing Needs: None needed

Mental Health: Sam has never seen a professional except through the school system for psychological testing. He does participate in a program at (school name) called "Peer Group." This is a kind of confidential "rap session" conducted by the school psychologist in which the kids can discuss any subject they want. Sam participated in a similar program in grade school.

Therapy: Sam receives O.T., P.T., and speech therapy at (school name). The goals of these therapists are stated in Sam's I.E.P., which is attached to this letter. Older I.E.P. reports and other therapy evaluations would be found in the file cabinet in the basement.

Diagnostic testing: None done

Genetic testing: None done

Immunizations: Diphtheria, Pertussis, and Tetanus (list of dates shots given) Measles, Mumps, and Rubella (date shot given). TB skin test (date and result of test)

Diseases: Chicken pox (date)

Allergies: None

Other Problems: Sam has had a few ear infections from water that did not drain out of his ear. This happened during swimming and bathing. Sam is aware right away when this occurs and responds immediately to the drops prescribed by his pediatrician.

Sam wears adult diapers and sometimes gets a rash on the inside of his thigh from the plastic. We treat this with Desenex, or any other diaper rash medication, but it is sometimes hard to get rid of. This condition has improved drastically since Sam has become more conscientious about telling us when he needs to be changed.

Sam is sensitive to poison ivy. He got it twice when the dog rubbed against him after coming in contact with the plant. We used

Cortaid and have an advantage because Sam simply isn't able to scratch.

A few times Sam has gotten burned or scraped himself badly. I feel this happened because he has lost some of his pain sensors as a result of his brain damage, but no professional will confirm this.

Procedures and General Care

All hygiene procedures have to be done for Sam by a caregiver and are done at home.

Toileting: Sam wears adult diapers. We started this about 4 years ago when positioning him on any kind of toilet became difficult. He was simply too uncomfortable to effectively use it. We use Depends in size regular, which can be purchased at most drug stores and some grocery stores. We have found the best prices at PharMor, Castle Drug, and on sale at Osco or Walgreen's.

Bathing: We purchased a special shower wheelchair and had the seating adapted at the Rehabilitation Institute of Chicago. This chair can be wheeled into the walk-in-shower we had built. I use a hand held sprayer that can be hung on the wall. Sam does not like the water spraying on his head but tolerates it long enough to have his hair washed. After he is cleaned he likes to just sit in the shower for a while with the water aimed at the lower half of his body.

Teeth: Sam does not like having his teeth brushed, so he forgets to remind me to do it. He likes Aim gel toothpaste the best. I use an Interplak electric toothbrush on the lowest power.

Hair: I use Head & Shoulders shampoo because I only wash Sam's hair about every 3 days, but I'm not sure it makes any difference. I have Sam's hair cut about every 6 to 8 weeks. He enjoys going because he knows a lot of the beauticians and likes to visit (tease) with them. [The name of the beautician who cuts his hair is listed, as well as the name of the shop, the address, phone number, and cost of the hair cut.]

Shave: He just started. I am using a Remington Electric Razor. I started out doing it once a week, but I'm noticing that may not be enough.

Nails: Sam's finger and toenails need to be cut about once a month. He will let you know if a nail is bothering him. I use fingernail scissors.

Deodorant: I use Old Spice every morning when I dress Sam.

Nose: Sam needs to have someone wipe his nose for him. He wears a terrycloth wristband to wipe his chin and nose but is not very efficient with it. I try to keep a cloth (I have been using cloth diapers for this and for wiping his mouth during feeding) or Kleenex in the backpack of his wheelchair for this purpose.

Clothing: At this time almost all of Sam's clothing is ready-made, but I have purchased a few mail-order items especially made for people confined to a wheelchair from a company called Everest & Jennings Avenues, 3233 E. Mission Oaks Blvd., Camarillo, California 93012. I can foresee using this type of resource more in the future. I have a file folder with some information on this company and a few others in the file cabinet in the basement. Sam is most comfortable in casual clothing like T-shirts, sweatshirts and sweatpants, or elastic waist pants or shorts.

Shoes: Shoes are very hard to get on Sam because his toes curl and he has ankle contractures. He also has a startle reflex that causes him to stiffen. I buy shoes that are oversized and have purchased some specialty dress shoes from Avenues (see Clothing). He gets sores on his heel if the shoes are too stiff. He usually wears slippers or socks around the house.

Startle Reflex: Sam has a startle reflex when touched in a sensitive place that causes him to stiffen his body. This occurs most noticeably when putting on shoes, changing diapers, cutting his nails, etc. He can usually reduce this tension when told to relax.

Drooling: Sam has a real problem with this. He is working on it, but we constantly have to remind him and wipe his chin and mouth area. He wears a terrycloth wristband on his right hand so that he can wipe himself, but he is not always efficient with it.

Sneezing: Sam has a sneeze reflex when his nose is stimulated and when eating. He often sneezes several times first thing in the morning. When he does sneeze, he sneezes with his mouth open so it goes everywhere.

Snoring: Sam snores very loudly, which might be a problem if he shares a bedroom.

Feeding: I feed Sam most of his food. He can finger feed himself, but it takes him a long time. I will give him snacks to feed himself. We have a plastic dish with a nonskid bottom that I put food in, or I place it directly on his tray.

Sam has trouble chewing, so I have to cut up meat in very small bites. He does best with small bites of everything. He also has a hard time with liquid foods, like soup. I crush several saltine crackers in the soup and feed it to him that way. Sam does not like the taste of very spicy foods. They create a lot of saliva, making it harder for Sam to swallow.

Drinking: Sam drinks everything with a straw. I use flexible straws. He has a glass holder with handles for drinking by himself.

Operations: Sam had an aductor myotomy (release of the aductor muscle in the groin area) in October, 1978 at (name of hospital). The surgery was performed by (name of doctor). After the cast was removed, Sam spent a month in the hospital for intensive physical therapy.

Hospitalizations: The only other time Sam was hospitalized was when he was electrocuted and was in a coma. That was in October of 1973. If Sam ever does need to be hospitalized and needs someone to monitor his care and act as liaison with the doctor I would recommend (person's name) or (person's name). I would also want my parents consulted because of their medical background.

Devices or Special Equipment

Electric wheelchair: Sam is in a slim, narrow adult Rolls Arrow Power Drive wheelchair with a joystick control. The seating system was made by the Rehabilitation Institute of Chicago, Seating and Positioning Center.

Jay Cushion: This special seat is being used in Sam's wheelchair to alleviate pain in his buttock and back and cramping in his right leg. Extra gel packs have been inserted, plus a wedge on the left side.

Prone Wedge This was designed for Sam by the Rehab. Engineering Department at the Rehabilitation Institute of Chicago. It is a wedge he uses to lay on the floor with straps to prevent him from rolling off.

Shower/Commode Chair: Sam uses the Guardian chair from Sunrise Medical. The seating system was redone by the Rehabilitation Institute of Chicago to provide enough support for Sam.

Lift: We purchased a Braun semiautomatic wheelchair lift for our van so that we could transport Sam.

Phone: Sam has a GTE speaker phone in his bedroom. It has 12 programmable phone numbers.

Computer: Sam has an Apple II GS to do any homework or other writing. He can use the regular keyboard and a mouse with his right hand. We have the computer plugged into a power strip so that Sam can turn it on and off himself. Sam approaches the computer from his right side and uses only his right hand on a regular keyboard. If he is using the mouse we usually set it on his tray, and in that instance Sam sits facing the computer.

Bed: We purchased an extra high bed for Sam because this is where I change his clothes, diapers, etc., and it is much easier on me than bending over. It is also easier to transfer Sam to his wheelchair or shower chair or just pick him up from this raised position.

Medications: none

OTC Medications: Sam does not take liquid medications very well but has no difficulty swallowing a pill. I always buy coated ones, and he swallows them easily if you place them way back in his mouth. I give him a drink after he swallows.

[A list of OTC medications which Sam uses and the conditions for which they are needed is included here.]

Monitoring: Sam will always need to have someone give him any medication or apply ointments, etc.

Procurement: Sam will need someone to buy medications for him or take him to buy medications.

Diet: Sam does not require a special diet. He is so slender that I do not worry about him eating too much. He eats a very balanced diet because he is dependent for feeding and doesn't eat a lot of junk food. He is capable of telling you what he likes and wants, but being a typical teenager, he prefers McDonalds or pizza to home cooking.

Dairy: Sam is not fond of milk, but I give him a large glass of chocolate milk with dinner. He loves cheese, especially American or Velveeta. He likes cottage cheese and I often crush potato chips in it. He also likes yogurt but only the thick kind (like Yoplait, custard style) with fruit—strawberry or blueberry.

Bread & Cereal: Sam likes bread and crackers of any kind. Pretzels are a favorite snack. He loves garlic bread. Sam is not very fond of cereal and had trouble eating it because of the liquid. He will eat Rice Crispies with just a little milk and sugar. He also likes it when I mash some banana in it or some strawberries. He likes pancakes, waffles, and French toast. He doesn't like muffins but will eat banana bread or zucchini bread. Sam loves any kind of pasta, with or without sauce. If I fix a plain pasta, he likes butter and salt on it.

Fruits: Sam has difficulty eating most fruits because of their juiciness. It is easiest for him if they are cut up and spoon fed to him and, if they are tart, with some sugar on them. He likes bananas, strawberries, peaches, applesauce, blueberries, and grapes without seeds. He likes cherries, but I've always taken the pits out. He will tolerate pears and melons but no citrus fruit, juice, or pineapple.

Vegetables: Sam likes most vegetables but will not eat green beans, cabbage, or squash, although he will eat canned green beans. He cannot eat tossed salads or fresh tomatoes. In fact, he cannot eat any raw vegetable. He likes his vegetables with butter or cheese on them. Fresh corn has to be cut off the cob.

Meat & Fish: Sam likes meat. Again, it has to be cut up in small bites and the more tender it is, the easier it is for him. He does not like liver, sausages, or bacon but loves hot dogs. Sam likes fish and really loves shrimp and lobster.

Desserts: Sam likes dessert but usually prefers to have it later and doesn't eat it on a regular basis. He loves chocolate in any form. His favorite cookies are chocolate chip, sugar wafers, or Oreos.

Drinks: Sam prefers to drink Pepsi, lemonade, or Kool-aid (especially grape flavor). I do have him drink a glass of milk a day (chocolate).

Breakfast: Sam does not like to eat first thing in the morning. Since he starts school at 7:45 and I insist he eat something, we have come up with a breakfast of 2 tablespoons of peanut butter mixed with 2 tablespoons of strawberry or grape jam. He also drinks a Pepsi. This was at the suggestion of one of the staff because he was having so much trouble staying awake during classes. It helped and is now a habit, like coffee.

Soup: Sam loves soups. His favorites are vegetable, Lipton's chicken noodle, split pea, tomato, navy bean and ham, and broccoli with cheese. I thicken the soup with several crushed saltine crackers; in some soups, like tomato or chilli, he likes cheese.

Favorite Dishes: Cheeseburgers, hot dogs, spaghetti, pizza, lobster or shrimp dipped in butter, macaroni and cheese with ketchup on top, grilled cheese, grilled cheese and ham, broccoli with cheese, fried, grilled, or roasted chicken, turkey with gravy, pork roast, deep fried perch or walleye, fried shrimp dipped in ketchup, mashed potatoes and gravy or baked potatoes with sour cream, asparagus, corn, chocolate pudding, chocolate ice-cream or vanilla with chocolate sauce, strawberry shortcake, brownies.

I have been considering consulting a nutritionist about Sam's diet to see if any vitamins are recommended.

What Works Well for Sam

Housing: Sam currently lives with us in our home in (name of city). The first floor has a very open floor plan that is easily accessible to Sam. He has access to his bedroom, the bathroom, the living room where he keeps his computer, the family room, and the kitchen. Sam enters the house through the patio door in the back. The patio door is flush with a deck and the deck is ramped at the side of the house. The disadvantages are that there are no sidewalks in our immediate neighborhood so that when Sam goes out he is in the street. Fortunately the streets are very quiet. We are within "wheeling" distance of some shopping, but again there is a problem with sidewalks and some very busy streets.

For the immediate future we would like to see Sam finish the vocational program at (name of school), which will take 2 to 3 years, and then give a fair chance to the work program that they and the Department of Rehabilitation Services come up with for him. I would say a fair chance would be at least a year. In order to do that Sam would have to remain in the (name of area). The people I have listed as Advocates above have said they would be willing to help make arrangements for such a transition period. The most logical thing, it seems, would be to hire full-time help to live with Sam in our home in (name of city). Optimally Sam would qualify for the Illinois Supported Employment Program, which would place him in a public setting. At that time the Department of Rehabilitation

Services or Access Living could aid in finding suitable living arrangements. Access Living specializes in setting up supported living in private settings or group home situations. Since this would be a large part of Sam's social life, we would suggest a group situation as best, but he would be able to make that determination. The group situations are never larger than 16 people so as not to lose SSI support. They are federally subsidized. The Ray Graham Association in Elmhurst and ELIM Christian School in Palos Heights, Illinois offer some similar arrangements and Miseracordia in Chicago has a project in the planning stages, but I have not investigated these programs thoroughly yet. These organizations also have programs for people on public aid.

If this type of program did not work out for Sam, and Sam's sister or another relative would want to house Sam, then we would want the trust to pay for any equipment, remodeling, or additions that would be needed to make the facility accessible to Sam and comfortable for the relative.

Another alternative would be for Sam to live on our property in (city and state named) with full supervision. Wisconsin also has state employment programs for the disabled. One program is run by The Opportunity Center in Madison, Wisconsin. I will investigate this more thoroughly in the next year. I want Sam to try every resource available to him because I feel some kind of employment would make his life more meaningful. If these resources do not work out we feel we have funded this trust to the extent that it would cover Sam's living expenses and full-time care for Sam in (city name). In such an instance, Sam's sister or one of the Advocates would need to supervise this situation on a regular basis. They could do that personally or hire someone from (city name) to do it; probably a combination of these two options would be best. The following people would be good sources of information about (city name) and are well acquainted with Sam. [A list of three couples, their addresses and phone numbers follows.]

Adaptations: Sam's living space does not have to be large, but it needs to be large enough and open enough to accommodate his wheelchair.

He needs a private bedroom but not a private bath. He needs enough living space for a T.V. and a computer. His physical disabilities prevent him from using a kitchen, so that does not have to be accessible; in the bathroom, only the shower needs to be accessible. Someplace, bed or bathroom, needs a mirror so that he can see himself. The entrance to the living quarters needs to be wheelchair accessible.

Favorite Possessions: Sam's favorite possessions that he should be able to keep with him wherever he lives are: a remote control T.V.; his Apple II GS computer, or whatever computer he has at the time; his Walk-man radio with preset stations; his speaker phone; his Wedge pillow; his shower chair; his Bulls hat; his books about space exploration and the solar system.

Sam is not very fussy about community. He likes to go to shopping centers and out to eat. He enjoys going to the movies and to the Bulls games, but other than the Bulls he is not very interested in sports. I would hope that any community in which Sam lives would have some type of recreational program available because that is an excellent source of social contact for him and because sometimes he needs motivation in this area.

Daily Living Skills

Current Activities: Sam is in school full-time and in the summer goes to day camp through North Shore Suburban Special Recreation Association (NSSRA). In his free time he likes to watch TV and play games on his computer. He is interested in anything about space. He likes to visit in the neighborhood and go to shopping malls. He loves the beach, but it is very hard to take him there now. He actively participates in recreation programs run by NSSRA. For example, this summer he is attending day camp; a Thursday night sports camp; Friday Night Comrades, which is a group outing in the community or just hanging out with friends; and a sailing field trip.

Monitoring: Sam needs help with all physical activities. He is totally dependent for self-care skills, all domestic activities, and transportation. Although he can maneuver his wheelchair himself, sometimes he likes help in tight situations. Socially he is very independent and self-confident.

Caregivers' Attitudes: We would want any caregiver to keep Sam reasonably clean and physically presentable. His relationships and social skills are appropriate, and we wouldn't expect a caregiver to have to be involved in these areas unless Sam asked for advice. We would expect any caregiver to be honest, compassionate, and amiable. A high energy level also would help!

Self-esteem: Sam has an outgoing personality and a good sense of humor. He is very adaptable and gets along in most situations. He is very self-confident and actually proud of being handicapped most of the time. He says he will fight for the rights of the handicapped.

Sleep Habits: Sam requires 8 to 9 hours of sleep a night. He prefers to stay up late and sleep late, so he gets to do that on the weekends. During the week I try to have him in bed by 10:30. He sometimes has trouble falling asleep, so I try not to give him any Coke in the evening. He is very good about just lying in bed until he does fall asleep.

Sam sleeps on his stomach with a couple of cloth diapers folded under his face instead of a pillow. He likes to sleep with socks on because his feet get cold; he likes his feet tucked in. He likes his arms pulled up above his head. If he wakes up in the middle of the night, he usually needs a new diaper under his face because he has drooled too much, his feet covered, or his arm (right) pulled up.

Because Sam likes to sleep late, I don't get him up until the last minute. I usually get him up about 6:00 and change and dress him on the bed. Then I put him in his wheelchair and feed him right away, which only takes about 10 minutes. Then I brush his teeth and wash his face. The bus picks him up at 7:10. He "wakes up" during the half hour bus ride to school.

Personal Finances: Sam would need a lot of guidance with personal finances, as he has never had his own resources. He understands the basics of banking, credit, bill payments, etc. but has not had much practical experience in these matters. Also, Sam is not physically capable of signing his name by himself. I have always helped hold a pen in his hand and guided it with him.

Allowance: Sam is very capable of handling a personal allowance on his own. We would expect him to use this for personal entertainment and extras like going to a movie, out to eat, buying new computer games, books and magazines, candy, some special or novelty piece of clothing, gifts for relatives or friends on birthdays, Christmas, etc., special outings to a sports event or concert.

At this time these things are paid for by us. Sam is pretty active in special recreation programs. Excluding those programs, Sam spends about $50.00 a month on luxuries.

Education

Sam's school placement has been determined by NSSED (North Suburban Special Education District). This is a cooperative program that both (names of two nearby towns) belong to. We have had a very good relationship with it, and they have been responsive to us.

Schools Sam has Attended: [A list of six schools, their addresses, and the dates Sam attended them is included.]

Academics: Sam's academic skills are very poor. He functions at the 2nd to 3rd grade level in reading and math, but his verbal comprehension is much higher. He has a lot of learning difficulties and problems with memory retention. He is also somewhat immature and had taken a very casual attitude toward school, although he made great strides in these areas this year. He is especially interested in working with computers and works very hard on this subject. He is finally beginning to show some real pride in his work. His social maturity has also improved dramatically this year.

Emphasis: Sam has just started some vocational classes this year and will continue with that program for the next 2 years. He became a client of DORS this last semester, and they will try to assist with some vocational placement. The goal is to see if Sam could do some data processing; he is very motivated to do this.

Integration: All of Sam's basic academics have been in self-contained classes of the physically handicapped program. Some of these classes have also included kids identified as developmentally delayed and multiply handicapped. In the younger grades he was mainstreamed for classes like art, music, social studies, and science. He enjoyed these classes, and they helped tremendously with his social skills. Sam learns best in small groups or one-on-one situations. I would expect that (school name) will continue this type of program with Sam to finish up his academics and then concentrate on vocational skills.

Leisure and Recreation

Structured Recreation: Most of Sam's structured activities are programs conducted by the North Suburban Recreation Association. They run a summer day camp program that Sam has attended since he was 3 years old. During the winter they also run programs like teen clubs, bowling, swimming, special field trips. Sam enjoys participating in these programs because they allow him to spend time with his peers without parents around. The adults who run the programs are young enough to seem almost like peers to Sam, and Sam has always related well to them. Sam also enjoys spending time with and helping younger kids. He gets a chance to do this at summer camp.

Sam has also been a part of a Special Education Floor Hockey team and has attended dances, plays, and other programs at his school. He views these activities mainly as social. He loves to dance and has no inhibitions about it. He is also self-confident about going places on his own. Sam has also attended (camp name), a privately funded overnight camp for physically disabled kids. [The camp address is listed.]

Unstructured Activities: Sam's main form of entertainment is the TV and his computer. He likes games he plays on the computer but will also work at copying things into the computer just to improve his skills. Sam loves the Bulls and will watch wrestling or football on TV but doesn't have an interest in any other sports. Sam likes video games but it is hard for him to work most of them. He even enjoys watching someone else do it. Sam likes to go to movies. He likes action films and is fascinated by animation and special effects more than story. He also loves comedy. Sam likes to swim but is hard to get into a pool. He uses an oversized inner tube that he hangs onto; he needs someone to stay with him.

Religion

Faith: Sam was baptized at (name of church) in (name of city) on (date). He currently is a member of (name and address of church). He has attended Sunday School and services there in the past but currently goes very rarely.

Sam is acquainted with Rev. (name). His phone number at the church is (phone number). The Reverend has always been very receptive to Sam. Sam has been made to feel very welcome at church, but it is a very small facility and not easily accessible. Sam has resisted participating in church at this time but does have a background that may be a good source of social interaction and support for him in the future.

Rights and Values: Sam should be kept free from harm, physical restraint, isolation, abuse, and excessive medication.

With the guidance and advice of the trustees and advocates, Sam should be given the freedom to decide where he wants to live and work and under what circumstances. Sam should be encouraged to give input into decisions that are made about his lifestyle.

Sam should be provided with age-appropriate clothing, and his appearance should be well-groomed; clean, shaved, and hair cut. His surroundings should be pleasant and sanitary. Any caregiver should demonstrate respect and caring for Sam and refrain from using demeaning language. Sam should be allowed as much privacy as he wants and be given respect for his personal possessions.

General Comments

Once Sam has completed the vocational training program at (school name) and participated in a work program, both we and he will have a better idea of what kind of work program he will be capable of. Our hope is that he will be capable of placement in a public setting, but we realize that this would probably have to be some type of supported work program and that he would not be capable of a full-time position because of his physical limitations. Things like toileting, positioning, and eye strain will be a problem for him for extended periods of time. We do feel that some type of employment is important for Sam's sense of well-being and will also be important for him socially.

In Sam's work situation and private life we would wish for the least restrictive environment possible given his severe limitations. We are in the process of exploring alternate living arrangements now and will keep a file on this in Sam's file drawer. I will be updating this letter with specific suggestions as I discover appropriate options. Our plan is to continue to keep Sam at home until he finishes the vocational program and then to explore various living options. We feel that emotionally he would benefit from some form of independence and that socially a group situation might be best for him. His personality is such that he could easily fit into a variety of situations as long as his physical needs were taken care of.

It is our intention in setting up this trust that Sam be taken care of in the least restrictive environment that he can handle and that is emotionally and physically supportive to him. We want Sam to have input into decisions that are made concerning his living arrangements and how funds from the trust are spent. We have picked the trustees and advocates for their competence and their concern for Sam and his well-being. We have made his sister a joint trustee so that she can be as involved as she wants to be in helping make decisions. We have assigned advocates who are willing to give advice and, if needed, to help carry out the trust with visits to Sam, overseeing living arrangements, paying bills, etc.—whatever the trustees might like help with.

It is our intention that the trust funds be used to enhance Sam's life and give him as much financial assistance as he needs to live comfortably. If no other living arrangements are suitable to Sam and he has no other means of satisfying his financial requirements, it is our feeling that we have funded the trust so that Sam could be provided for in a private home in (town name) with live-in assistance. Should it become obvious that Sam will never use the property in (town name), then we would expect the trustee to make a decision as to whether to dispose of it or not, to the trust's benefit, according to the provisions stated in the (trust name). If (current trustee's name) is not then the acting trustee, he would be an excellent advisor on this subject.

If some other private situation should arise that Sam would prefer, such as living with a relative or his sister, we would want the trust to cover any expenses incurred in making the facility accessible for Sam and convenient for caregivers. Some examples would be: ramping; remodeling a bathroom to make it accessible; building a room addition to give Sam his own room; installing an intercom system that Sam could work; purchasing special furniture and equipment that works well for Sam or makes things convenient for the caregiver (examples would be Sam's high bed, a remote control TV, a remote control system for other electric appliances like lights, radio, etc.). If Sam is living with someone, we would expect him to pay rent and the caregiver to receive financial support and respite care.

Sam should have at his disposal a van with a lift so that he can be transported by the caregiver and visit friends or relatives; and so that anyone visiting Sam can take him out.

We would expect the trust to pay for special recreational activities for Sam. Some examples would be: tickets to a sporting event or concert; dining out with friends or relatives occasionally; participation in special recreation programs similar to those he currently joins now with NSSRA; going to a movie. We also would like the trust to pay for any vacation, within normal bounds, that Sam could take and the transportation and expenses of his traveling companion/caregiver. We would like to have Sam keep in contact with his relatives. If it would make more sense for them to visit him, and they are traveling with the express purpose of visiting Sam, then the trust may pay their traveling expenses. If there are any special devices that could be purchased to make an activity that Sam is interested in possible for him—such as a specialized life jacket, adaptive seating in a boat or sled, adaptive equipment like a fishing pole he could hold—and they are not covered by insurance, then we would want the trust to pay for them.

We expect the trust to pay the advocate and the trustee for their time involved in administering the trust and for any time they spend following up on what is being done—for instance, if they have to travel to check up on Sam or his caregivers, or research options for Sam, etc. It is also acceptable for the trust to pay the spouses of the trustee or advocate for any assistance they give in administering the trust or any visits they make to Sam.

Finances, Benefits, and Services

Assets: At this time Sam's only asset is his savings account (Account number and amount—name address and phone number of bank)

Cash Income: Sam has no income at this time, although we have recently applied for Supplemental Security Income. Sam will receive about $90 at the end of summer, 1991, for computer work he will have done during summer camp with NSSRA.

Services or Benefits: Sam is in the special education program at (name of school).

Sam recently became a client of the Department of Rehabilitation Services. His representative is (name). Initially his contact with them will be through (school name).

Sam is currently part of the Audio Visual Service at the (name of local library), through which he receives Talking Books on cassette tapes.

Expenses: Currently most of Sam's expenses are paid by us. When he receives Supplemental Security Income, he will begin paying rent to us. His education and vocational training are covered in the public education program he is receiving at (school name). His health care is covered under my husband's insurance program. His clothing, food, and most recreational activities are paid by his parents.

The Paper Trail

Will: Sam does not have one at this time.

Safe-deposit Box: None for Sam. We have a safe-deposit box that we keep in the basement, on top of the file cabinet, in which are kept birth certificates, titles, school degrees, etc.

Life Insurance: None

Burial Papers: The cemetery certificates will be in our safe-deposit box. No other arrangements have been made at this time.

Health Insurance: [The name, address, phone number, plan number, and name of the company through which insurance is held is listed.]

There are two different forms. The medical coverage is with (name of company). The dental coverage is with (name of company). As long as my husband is alive, Sam will be covered by our insurance. After my husband's death, the insurance will remain in force for 6 months. It can then be renewed for only 2 years. Copies of these policies are in the file cabinet in our bedroom in the top drawer under the heading "Insurance."

There is a $300 yearly deductible ($500 for retired employees); then the medical plan pays 90 percent of the excess reasonable and customary medical expenses incurred for the year. After the insured has paid $2,000 of the excess, excluding the deductible, the policy pays 100 percent. This policy covers physical therapy, speech therapy, vision therapy, occupational therapy, chiropractic care, and ambulance service when the above are rendered by licensed or certified professionals or on outpatient basis. They do not cover routine eye care, physicals, private rooms in the hospital or TV, nonprescription drugs or preventative medicines, etc.. The insurer has been very good about covering devices, such as the wheelchair at 80 percent, as long as we have a doctor's prescription. The dental insurance covers all cleaning and most reasonable procedures at 80 percent.

Employee Savings Plans: None

Income Tax: None

Real Estate: Current real estate documents concerning our house and property in (name of state) are in our file cabinet in the bedroom. This would include real estate taxes, plat of survey, mortgage papers, etc. The deeds or certificates of title are in the safe-deposit box in the basement. We also have an appraised listing of some of our more valuable possessions in the file cabinet in the bedroom under "Valuables." Receipts for improvements and maintenances are in the file cabinet in the basement.

Advisors: [A list of the names, addresses, and phone numbers of the family's tax, financial, insurance, trust, and legal advisors is included.]

Other: All of Sam's current, 1991, school, medical, recreational, and dental records are in the file cabinet in our bedroom in the top drawer under the corresponding headings. All past records are in the file cabinet in the basement in the top drawer under the corresponding headings. Also in that drawer are the manuals and warranties on any of Sam's equipment; information on housing and work programs; information I've collected on devices or equipment that have been used for Sam or might someday be useful; information on recreational programs; and any other resource materials I have saved. The second drawer of the file cabinet contains manuals and warranties for our property, receipts for home improvements, and other household information. The bottom two drawers contain copies of our income-tax records and related materials. All Sam's valuable papers such as birth certificate, baptismal records, social security papers, etc. are in the safe-deposit box kept on top of the file cabinet.

Sample Letter for Mental Retardation

This Letter of Intent is written by William E. Smith and Wendy H. Smith, the parents of James A. Smith.

To Whom It May Concern:

Information about Father:

William E. Smith
(Social Security Number)
(Mr. Smith's current address, including county)
(Mr. Smith's current home and office phone numbers)
Date of birth (including county and state)
Raised in ___________, __________
Roman Catholic religion
Caucasian Race
Blood type - A positive
One half-brother —(name)
U.S. citizen
Married to Wendy H. Smith on (date) in Chicago, Illinois
4 children (names listed)
Father: (name, address and phone number)
Mother: (name, address and phone number)
Stepmother: (name, address and phone number)
Half-brother: (name, address and phone number)

Information about Mother:

Wendy H. Smith

(Social Security Number)
Current address, including county
Current phone number including area code
Date of birth (including county and state)
Raised in ____________, ______________
Roman Catholic religion
Caucasian Race
Blood Type - unknown
No siblings
U.S. Citizen
Married to William E. Smith on (date) in Chicago, Illinois
4 children (names listed)
Father: (name, address and phone number listed)
Mother: (name, address and phone number listed)

Information about James A. Smith:

James is 5 ft. 10 inches tall, weighs 195 pounds, wears size 12 shoes, has a 36" waist, and wears large size shirts and coats. He is of the Caucasian race, has been baptized in the Roman Catholic Religion, has made his Communion, and has been Confirmed. James is a citizen of the United States. He was born on June 9, 1965, in ____________, Illinois and was raised in ____________, Illinois the first 19 years of his life. Since 1984, he has resided at the Somewhere, Illinois address.

Siblings: Marlene Smith (name address, phone number)
Jeffrey E. Smith (name address and phone number)

Other Relationships: Walter Lock-Friend (name address and phone number)

Representative Payee: William E. Smith
Wendy H. Smith

Successor Payee: Jeffrey E. Smith

Power of Attorney: None, other than parents as guardians.

Final Arrangements: Burial in a Catholic cemetery. (Parents' intention is to purchase a family plot to include James.) There should be a Catholic church service. A monument should be erected. No cremation.

Medical History: Onset of petit mal seizures was at 3 years of age. Hospitalization and testing took place to try to find an appropriate drug and treatment program. Various drugs were tried over several years. They were not successful because James couldn't tolerate the particular drugs or their side effects. Grand mal seizures were first noticed at age 15. Tegretol was introduced at that time and is still being used as the drug of choice. Between the ages of 15 and the present time, attempts have been made to introduce additional anticonvulsants and/or behavior-modifying drugs. The additional attempts were not successful. In the years 1989, 1990, and 1991, tests were administered to evaluate and review his current neurological, physiological, and behavioral status. The University of Chicago and Northwestern University administered EEG's (1 1/2 hour, full night's-sleep, and 6-hour-daytime-awake EEG) and an MRI test. Current drug program is to discontinue all other drugs except Tegretol and to raise its daily level to ____ mg/day. Tegretol is administered as follows:

[A chart showing James's medication schedule and dosages is included.]

James also is prescribed Maltsupex to counter a side effect of Tegretol. He receives __ tsp. dissolved in half a glass of water at bedtime. The Maltsupex relieves extreme constipation. James also receives the following liquid vitamins daily.

[A chart showing vitamins and dosage taken is included.]

The vitamins are needed to prevent a deficiency that causes severe cracking and bleeding at mouth corners due to long-term high dosage of Tegretol.

James has been tested for allergies since age 4. See attachment A for description of allergies and treatment on a monthly basis.

Functioning Level : Severely developmentally disabled; trainable level; I.Q. approximately 50-55.

Vision: Normal —does not use any eyeware.

Hearing: Normal

Speech: Verbal. Makes needs and wishes known. Uses words, phrases, and simple sentences. Uses a communication "break" card. Program was developed by a speech therapist. See attachment B. Program was recommended by Dr. ____________________, Institute for Applied Behavior and Analysis, Los Angeles, California. Consideration is currently being given to the use of the facilitated communication program that uses the Cannon computer.

Mobility: Normal

Blood: Type not currently known - to be obtained at next blood test.

Insurance: See data provided. Upon death of father, all insurance coverage for James ceases. James would need insurance at that time. Plan to be developed by parents and/or others using the manual: "Health Care Financing for Severe Developmental Disabilities," by Arnold Birenbaum, Dorothy Guyot, and Herbert J. Cohen.

Regular Physicians: [A list of physicians, their addresses, and phone numbers as well as most recent fees is included.]

Previous Physicians: [The name, address, and phone number of James's pediatrician is provided.]

Dr. _______ is deceased, but his records from birth to age 23 are kept at the offices of: ________________________.

Dental: [The name, address, and phone number of James's current dentist is provided.]

James uses a removable partial-upper dental appliance. Expected life of appliance is 5 years. A new appliance recently cost $700 (in 1991). Molds of upper and lower teeth are located in fireproof cabinet containing James's binder. If Dr. _______ is unavailable, we suggest contacting one of the local university dental schools to obtain a reference to a dentist that serves the disabled.

Nursing Needs: James does not currently need nursing care.

Mental Health: James is currently not involved with any psychiatrist, psychologist, or mental health counselor.

Therapy: James has had an occupational evaluation in 1990 performed by (name, address, and phone number).

It was their recommendation that he have periodic reviews and progress reports on an annual basis, or more often if the need is indicated, to be supportive of his other services or programs (vocational, recreational, residential, community, etc.)

Speech evaluation was performed in 1990, but because the clinician was not going to be available, our intention is to pursue speech evaluation in Facilitated Communication or as part of the Continuance of Augmented Communication. Over the course of years, James has participated in speech and occupational evaluation and therapy programs. In the future, occupational and speech therapy evaluations, progress reviews, and/or therapy should be performed at the advice of a professional advisor or case manager. If certain devices or materials are suggested to assist James, they should be provided.

Diagnostic Testing: [A list followed of 14 individuals or testing organizations which performed diagnostic tests on James. Each one of these organizations' reports was bound in a binder as an appendix to this Letter of Intent.]

Genetic Testing: None

Immunizations: To be provided

Diseases: Chicken pox in 1969

Allergies: See attachment B

Other Problems: Skin irritation on either side of nose. Follow-up visit to skin specialist recommended. Condition less severe in summer months. At other times, an ointment such as (name of ointment) should be used.

Procedures:

- Check ears for wax buildup. Cleanse ears approximately every 3 months with peroxide. Can be done at home.
- Should be given a complete physical yearly. Remove wax at that time, if necessary.
- Toenails should be trimmed once a month.
- Can trim his own fingernails (with assistance) approximately twice a month.

Operations:

Tonsillectomy, 1970, ___________Hospital
Myringectomy and tubes in ears, 1968, ___________Hospital

Hospitalizations:

Tonsillectomy, 1970, ___________Hospital
Drug testing and monitoring, 1969, _____________Hospital

Birth Control: None

Devices: Uses a partial upper dental appliance (removable).

Medications:

1. Tegretol according to the following schedule:
   [Schedule shows times and dosages of this medication.]

2. Maltsupex: (Dosage listed) dissolved in a glass of water at bedtime.
3. Vitamins:
   [List of vitamins and dosages is included.]

OTC: The following are prescribed but are not paid for by public aid. Needed to prevent vitamin deficiency, which causes severe cracking and bleeding at mouth corners due to long-term high dosage of anticonvulsants. [The list is included.]

James needs to use a medicated shampoo (such as _________) to control a severe dandruff condition.

Monitoring: Medications listed above must be monitored.

Procurement: Someone must procure James's prescription, vitamins, and OTC medications for him.

Diet:

No caffeine products (chocolate, tea, coffee, or colas). Only clear soft drinks such as 7-Up, Sprite, etc. Food items should be low sugar, no preservatives or additives. Use cooked cereals, bran, oat, or whole wheat cereals and bread.

Except for items specifically mentioned above, a normal, well-balanced diet would be appropriate. Desserts should be fruit related. Muffins or donuts can be used as rewards after running exercise periods. Some exceptions can be made for "special" occasions or treats.

James enjoys almost all foods, but his favorites are cheeseburgers and fries, spaghetti, lasagna, pizza, fried chicken, roast beef, and blue cheese salad dressing. Strawberry cheesecake is a favorite dessert.

What Works Well for James

Housing

Present: James currently lives at home with his parents. He has his own room with the usual bedroom furniture plus an upholstered rocker. His room has calendars, program charts, and behavior management charts. He enjoys having stories read to him several times a week from his book collection in his room.

Past: James has always lived at home.

Future: Our choices for James's future housing are:

1. Supported living in an apartment or house with 24-hour coverage.
2. A group home with no more than 4 residents.
3. Housing owned by James's trust with 24-hour supervision.

James should live in an area that has established programs or provides access to reciprocal programs in other communities (such as SEASPAR, WEDSRA, a Place in the Sun, etc.).

Size: It is preferred that James live in one-half of a two-flat or duplex so that he has access to a yard. His unit should have 2 bedrooms that can be shared by James and up to 2 additional clients or staff. The building should be in close proximity to bus routes, work opportunities, and community resources. It should also be close to a running track James can use or a parklike area that has walking or running paths. This is necessary because James has been running 3 times per week, approximately 5 miles per time, since age 14.

Adaptation: The stove in the residence should have color-coded operating controls with electrical igniters that emit a "clicking" sound indicating flame ignition.

Favorites:
- An upholstered rocker
- T.V. set with a VCR to play video tapes
- An audio tape player
- Cross country skis and boots
- A large "bean bag" cushion with large support pillow and covers
- An AM-FM radio

- A storage cabinet or unit containing the following to be located in James's bedroom. This unit will be used to store: a library of picture books to look at and story books to have read to him, simple puzzles, coloring books and crayons, and arts and crafts materials
- Schwinn exercise bike kept in an accessible area and used on days when James doesn't run. Should be used in A.M.
- Schwinn conventional bicycle (no gears)
- A large inflated ball to be used to bounce as relaxation
- Softball and frisbee to be used to play catch with others

Community facilities that should be convenient:

- Family type restaurants
- Pizza restaurants
- Bakeries
- Fast-food restaurants
- Grocery stores—supermarkets and neighborhood markets
- Shopping areas and malls
- Drugstores
- Running track or park paths for running 3 times per week
- Facilities that provide programs and activities for people with mental disabilities
- Library
- Parks and/or recreation areas
- Barber shop
- Theaters and museums

Individual Program Plan

- Behavior Management Program (DRO - use of penny holder and coins)—see binder for program.
- Behavior intervention procedures to be used when James is exhibiting irritability, agitation, and sensory or stress overload. In a nonharsh manner, he should be told to go to his room and sit in his rocker. Using a timer, set an interval of time. When the time rings and he has regained control, he may leave his room and resume his activity.

- Behavioral charts to control outbursts of aggression. Use of coupons as incentive and reinforcement plan—see binder for program.
- Communication and/or break card—see binder for details.
- Vocational Competency Evaluation Report—to be added when completed.
- Facilitated Communication Evaluation and Report and device description will be added when available.

Current Activities: See summary and analysis of James's activities in binder.

Monitoring:

In order to help reduce James's hyperactivity, reduce levels of irritability, and to enhance the effect of his anticonvulsant medication, James engages in 3 early morning (before breakfast) runs per week. This activity was prescribed by one of James's previous neurologists. The runs should be conducted as follows on Sunday, Tuesday, and Thursday:

1. Run for a 10-minute-period
2. Take a 5-minute break, during which time he takes a drink of water or Gatorade
3. Run for a 10-minute period
4. Take a 5-minute break for another drink and to wipe off perspiration
5. Walk for 5 minutes to cool down

Because James is prone to seizures, he should use the following items:

1. Athletic supporter
2. Running shoes
3. Bicycle helmet
4. Visor (under the helmet)
5. Gortex running suit in winter months
6. Elbow pads

For self-help skill and domestic activity information, refer to the Summary and Analysis of James's activities in binder. James has had experience in using and paying for public transportation, but only in the company of his parents. James needs a program to reinforce his social and interpersonal skills when interacting with people across environments. James has utilized a chart that specifies self-help skills, striving for independence. Stars are used for a reinforcement on a daily basis.

Caregivers' Attitudes: We want caregivers to help James maintain set levels of expectation in his own personal cleanliness and grooming and the order and cleanliness of his environment. Caregivers should be kind and nonharsh, but they should expect James to comply with established behavioral requirements and see that he shares in chores and related activities. They should be firm but understanding. People that are easygoing and have a good sense of humor bring the most favorable responses from James.

Self-Esteem: The following statements can be used to keep him motivated, attentive, on target, and compliant:

"Good job."
"I like the way you're doing (or did) that."
"Much better, let's try that again."
"You worked very hard at that."
"Thank you for your help."
"Would you please do ________________? Thank you."

When James has regained control of himself, say "Thank you, we can continue now."

Sleep Habits: James usually goes to bed at 10:00 p.m. and rises between 6:30 and 7:00 a.m. He usually sleeps all night except when he wakes to use the bathroom. Sometimes after a particularly exciting day, he may wake up during the night and talk to himself for a period of time and then fall back to sleep.

Personal Finances: James needs total supervision of his money management. He is able to sign his checks, fill out deposit and withdrawal slips, identify money denominations, and carry out money transactions—with direct supervision—during activities such as simple shopping. James should have a savings account in a bank. He should be supervised to make indicated withdrawals for his allowance approximately once a week. James has an envelope with materials and stencils to help him fill out his banking documents.

Allowance: James currently gets $17 in coins (1 roll of quarters, dimes, and nickels) every month. His behavioral reinforcement program usually results in $40 monthly dinner expenditures for James and a staff person ($20 for dinner for 2 twice a month). James usually spends $10 per month for a haircut. Nonprogrammed entertainment such as movies should take approximately $20. James should receive $6 per month to be used to "save" for more expensive items or entertainments at a later date. James needs total supervision in the expenditures stated in this section. Treats that are used as reinforcement in James's behavior-management program (items such as mixed nuts, peanuts, sesame sticks, yogurt covered raisins, California fruit and nut mix, and pretzels) should be purchased monthly for approximately $10 to $12 per month. These items are best purchased in bulk food stores. Approximately $20 should be used to purchase ice cream cones, potato chips, and 7-UP used as reinforcement at the special events James attends. These reinforcements of snacks or treats are part of the behavior management charts covering behavior at swimming, basketball, ice skating, etc. Sometimes French fries purchased at McDonalds can be substituted. James's current usage of vitamins is costing approximately $35 per month. See Medical History section for details.

Name Brands: When replacing James's personal items, or when buying new things for him, only brand name products should be considered because of quality, durability, and longevity. James's size and strength and the "wear and tear" pressure he puts on things require good quality. For instance, buy Schwinn for stationary and conventional bicycles, Zenith for electronics, London Fog and L.L. Bean for outer wear, and Levi for pants.

Education

Schools: [A list of the schools attended by James, and the dates of attendance, is included.] James started in a preschool program at the age of 2 1/2. He progressed through various special education programs until he graduated in ______.

Current Programs: James is not currently enrolled in any educational programs.

Academics: James is considered trainable and has tested out at the kindergarten level in some academic skills.

Emphasis: All of James's education was in the area of special education, with only one year of vocational training prior to graduation. We would like to see James participate in a functional skills program that would review previous skills and teach new skills necessary for maintenance and survival across varied environments such as residential, work, community, and recreational.

Integration: James was not in any mainstream classes, but he was located in a self-contained classroom in normalized settings.

Day Program or Work

Present: James is not in any current day program or work situation. At home, with parents' supervision, James does the following: cuts grass with power mower, sweeps sidewalk, helps wash cars, takes out garbage, wipes and puts away dishes, unloads dishwasher. While shopping, James selects items, bags items, and carries the bags to the car. See "A Summary and Analysis of James Smith" in binder for more details.

Past: In James's last year at __________ High School he: unloaded dishwasher in cafeteria, stacked chairs on tables, mopped floors, put chairs in place, vacuumed carpet in girls' gym, and picked up trash outdoors on school grounds.

Future: Our objective is to have James placed in a supported employment position in the community following a vocational competency evaluation.

Assistance: James's placement in a supported employment position will likely require a permanently assigned job coach.

Leisure and Recreation

Structure Recreation:

- A Place in the Sun Special Recreation Program provides open gym, organized games, camping activities, parties and dances, vacation trips, and participation in community-based activities and outings. Usually takes place on one evening a week (Tuesday) and some weekends.
- Ice Skating lessons at local ice arena on Wednesday evenings.
- Western DuPage Special Recreation Association Swim Team participation one evening a week (Thursday) and whenever meets are arranged. James also participates in basketball activities on Saturdays.
- Friday night Special Recreation Program that includes dinners out, dances, parties, and community-based activities and outings conducted by South East Special Parks and Recreation.
- Periodic special events and activities on weekends, conducted by the above mentioned organizations.

Unstructured Activities: James enjoys going to movies he can understand, bowling, dances, riding his bicycle, engaging in simple arts and crafts, and cross country skiing.

Vacations: James's vacations have been with his family or special recreation groups. James has gone to Florida's Disney World twice,

California, Ohio, Indiana, Michigan, Wisconsin, and other places that have vacation attractions such as theme parks.

Fitness: James participates in a one-hour-per-week fitness program sponsored by A Place in the Sun that is conducted by a Chicago Health Club fitness instructor. Parents oversee James's running program. See Monitoring section above for details. On nonrunning days, James rides an exercise bike for approximately 45 minutes to an hour.

Religion

Faith: James is a member of the Roman Catholic Church.

Participation: James has been involved in a SPRED program for approximately 15 years. See "A Summary and Analysis of James Smith" in binder for details. He does not now regularly participate. He attends SPRED masses about 5 times per year. We would strongly recommend he participate in a similar program if available because he enjoys the activity. We would not be opposed to James participating in other denominational religious activities because he likes to sing, and enjoys music and "hospitality" activities. Weekly participation would be recommended.

Rights and Values

We believe James should be accorded the following rights and values:

- To be free from harm, physical restraint, isolation, abuse, and excessive medication.
- To refuse behavior modification techniques that cause pain.
- To have age-appropriate clothing and appearance.
- To have staff, if any, demonstrate respect and caring and to refrain from using demeaning language.

Other

In our experience with James, we have found that he wants to comply and please the people he interacts with, but because of his autistic attributes, he appears to withdraw and be aloof. With gentle intrusion and persuasion and nonpushy or nonharsh tactics, you can generally get James to go along with almost anything. He would rather be involved (even from the sidelines) than be left behind to sit and be inactive. James always shows enthusiasm for activities such as gift buying for birthdays and holidays, gatherings of people to celebrate events, and involvement in preparing food, etc.

In the event James should exhibit irritable or disruptive behavior, causative factors may be known or unknown. Some of the tactics we have found to be helpful in the home or out in public are:

- Indicate to James that we see he is angry or upset and remove him temporarily from the particular situation for a short period of time (perhaps 15 to 30 minutes). After attempts have been made to "give James some space" by sitting in a room alone, standing outside, taking a walk, or listening to some music, and it appears that James is getting himself under control, James should be asked if he has himself under control and if he is ready to come back and join the activity he left. If he is in control, he should be allowed to rejoin.

Measures we have used with James at home to soothe him during periods of irritability or extreme excitement with hyperactivity or loud vocalization:

- Have James sit in his room in his rocker for a specific period of time measured by a timer.
- Taking a warm soaking bath for 45 minutes.
- Ride his exercise bike and listen to soft music.
- Use a vibrator on his shoulders, scalp, temples, and palms of his hands.

The above practices have been useful in resuming the ongoing caring relationship with James.

Gifts for James

At each observance of James's birthday and at Christmas, a gift should be purchased for him. An appropriate card should be purchased to accompany the gift. The card should be signed "From Mom and Dad." The gift should be approximately $50 to $75 in value.

Sample Letter for Mental Illness

Written by: Gary and Susan Jones, parents of Lisa Jones

To Whom It May Concern:

The goal of the Jones Family Special Needs Trust is to provide our daughter, Lisa Jones, the means to lead a full and comfortable life during her lifetime. This Letter of Intent is a nonlegal document intended to supply information about our daughter in order to aid the trustee and other caregivers to make appropriate decisions as needs arise.

Information About Father

General Information

Name: Gary Jones
Social Security No.:
Address:
Telephone No.:
Born: (date and place)
Languages:
Religion: Methodist
Blood Type: unknown
Education: B.A. Chemistry, 1944 (name of school)
Ph.D. Biochemistry, 1950 (name of school)
Employment History: 1949 Univ. of ____________

1950-57 _____ School of Medicine
1957-91 Univ. of ___ School of Medicine
Marital Status: Married to Susan Jones (date and place); two children

Family:

Father: (name) died at age 71 of stroke and heart failure
Mother: (name) died at age 33 from consumption
Stepmother: (name) current address
Brothers: One brother stillborn
(name) died at age 56 of homicide; had depressive disorder in middle age.
Sisters: (name) died at age 61 of pneumonia
(name) current address and phone number
(name) current address and phone number

Information About Mother

General Information

Name: Susan Jones
Social Security Number:
Address:
Telephone No.:
Birth: (date and place)
Languages:
Religion: Methodist
Blood Type:
Education: B.A. Psychology, 1948, ________ University.
Employment: Editor (name of company), 20 years. Retired at age 60.
Marital Status: Married to Gary Jones (date and place); two children.

Family

Father: (name) died at age 70 of accidental fall. No medical problems.

Mother: (name) died at age 87 from heart failure. Had diabetes.
Brothers: One stillborn.
One died in childhood from convulsions.
(name) Current address and phone number.
Sister: (name) Current address and phone number.

Information about Lisa Jones

General Information
Name: Lisa Jones

Numbers: [Social Security Number, address, height, weight, and clothing size are included.]

More Details: Gender: Female Nationality: U.S.A. Race: Caucasian Language fluency: English Religion: Methodist

Birth:
Date: June 10, 1956, 4:00 p.m.
Place: X Hospital, Chicago, IL
Weight: 7 lb. 10 oz.
Childhood years: (name of city)

Sibling: Cheryl Jones (sister)
(address, phone number)

Schools: Lisa attended local grammar and junior high schools, followed by four years at (name of high school). She was a gifted ceramicist in high school. She had a one-woman show at a college and was offered an art scholarship that she did not take. She was always good in art and music; and was a very fine bass guitarist in high school.

She attended one year at (name of school) and the (name of school) before leaving (city name) for (city name) . Then, she went to (state) where she worked and attended many community colleges (list of colleges). She became ill, came home, and years later completed a B.A. degree at (name of school).

Marital Status: Single

Other Relationships: Good friends in or near (city name): (a list of friends names).

Guardians: None

Final Arrangements: None. Preference is cremation; church service; burial of ashes at (name of cemetery), which is where her uncle is buried; no monument, just a simple plaque.

Medical History and Care

Diagnoses: Diabetes mellitus, bipolar disorder

Seizures: None

Functioning: Mild

Vision: Normal with glasses. Date of last eye test (Date)
Prescription: myopia, astigmatism

Insurance: Medicaid

Regular Physicians: Dr. X at (name of clinic) is her current psychiatrist, whom Lisa has seen about once a month during the past year. Lisa is charged $5 a visit. She is presently seeking a psychiatrist at one of the university medical clinics because she feels she cannot afford to pay the $5 per visit. The clinic does not want her parents to pay. She has lately been attended to for other illnesses by various physicians at the clinics at (names of hospitals); these have accepted payment from Medicaid.

Previous Physicians: Drs. (names) are internists who have seen Lisa for general care and diabetes mellitus. (Drs. names, addresses and phone numbers listed).

Dentist: (name, address and phone numbers).

Mental Health: While working and living alone in (city) at age 21, Lisa first exhibited psychotic symptoms that led to a diagnosis of schizophrenia. She returned home to (city) to recuperate and was seen by (Dr.'s name). After a few months she felt well enough to consider going back to (city) and received permission from her psychiatrist to do so, as long as she continued to receive psychiatric attention. However, several months later, she experienced another psychotic episode and returned home again. During the following four years, she was hospitalized on three separate occasions for episodes related to her psychiatric condition, which was now diagnosed as a manic-depressive disorder. Each hospital visit was relatively short, none longer than three weeks. She was seen by (Dr.'s names) during this period.

Over the past five years, Lisa has slowly improved and has not required hospitalization. She has primarily remained at home and has looked for employment or tried to learn a new skill that she hoped would lead to a job. More recently, she spent a period of approximately one year and a half attending classes at (name of schools). She received a B.A. degree in Theater Arts from (name of school) in 1989. She was supported by her parents all during this time. She felt confident that she could find a permanent job after graduation and went to (name of city) once more in 1990 to pursue this goal. During the 11 months she spent in (name of state), she found a few jobs that did not pay very well. She did not seem to be functioning well. She was not eating and sleeping well and, at the advice of a psychiatrist, changed her dosage of calming medicines and became very hyper and "on edge." In December, 1990, she agreed with our suggestion that she return to (state) to recoup from her endeavors and to take a fresh view of her vocational pursuits.

Lisa does not outwardly appear to be seriously ill. However, following the development of her psychiatric illness approximately 12 years ago, she has not been able to find a part-time or full-time job that has lasted for more than a few months. She did work at a part-time clerical job at (name of college) for a longer stretch because she enjoyed her work and her boss and co-workers were easy to work with. Lisa has had problems working at most jobs because she feels the boss and others do not like her or her way of working. She is often paranoid about this, and if we (or the psychiatrist) try to convince her otherwise, Lisa will often get very angry to the point of shouting. She has become very sensitive to the fact that she has not been able to work, although she wants to very much. She becomes agitated and angry if she believes anyone is questioning her about going to work. She imagines that relatives and friends deride her because she doesn't work and that even strangers on public transportation know she doesn't work and are talking about her.

The subject of work has to be approached carefully. Lisa should be allowed to bring up the subject first. She has tried so often to find a job. She looks for help-wanted ads daily in major and local newspapers and often applies for work she is not suited to or capable of. It has been a heart-wrenching experience for her to endure and for her parents to watch.

A major obstacle to finding and keeping a job has been a side effect of the drug, lithium chloride, that increases urine output, which causes her to go to the lavatory frequently. As a consequence, she becomes extremely thirsty and drinks gallons of liquids. She is also a heavy smoker.

Therapy: Lisa has not seen a physical therapist at any time. She saw occupational therapists while hospitalized. Lisa had a minor speech problem in elementary school and saw a speech therapist for a time. She has no problem with speech at this time.

Diagnostic Testing: We are not aware that this procedure has been performed on Lisa.

Genetic Testing: We are not aware that this procedure has been performed on Lisa.

Immunizations: She has received all of the standard immunizations.

Diseases: Lisa had measles, mumps, and chicken pox during childhood.

Allergies: As a child, Lisa suffered from allergies but seems to have outgrown them. She has some mild hay fever during the autumn ragweed season. She also has a mild allergy (unknown cause) at other times.

Other problems: Lisa has gotten kidney stones that were painful on two separate occasions. She apparently passed these stones in the urine in each instance. She also noted their presence five other times when they obstructed flow but were not painful. She feels she ought to avoid dairy products, since she finds that after ingesting them she seems to form stones. At least, she suffers discomfort.

Operations: After a bout of measles when she was 6 years old, she had abdominal pain that was diagnosed as appendicitis. An appendectomy was performed, but the removed organ was normal.

Hospitalization: When Lisa was 14 months old, she was dehydrated after a bout of diarrhea and had to receive fluids at (name of hospital). As an adult, she was hospitalized for psychotic episodes at (name of hospital). These were relatively short stays (no longer than 3 weeks each time).

Devices: Lisa wears glasses for her myopia.

Medications: Lisa takes Lithonate (dosage) to stabilize her bipolar disorder and Trifluoperazine (dosage), an antidepressant. Klonopin (dosage) and valproic acid (dosage) have been tried as substitutes for Lithonate, but they did not appear to be suitable replacements. She takes (dosage) of insulin each morning. Since her fasting blood sugar levels were very low, she has been reducing her insulin intake.

OTC: Aspirin has been useful.

Monitoring: No assistance from another individual has been necessary for the taking of medications or the application of ointments.

Procurement: Lisa usually obtains her own medications with her green card at (pharmacy).

Diet: Lisa is a diabetic and should watch her food intake with respect to time, amount, and kind of food, but she is not conscientious. Her haphazard eating habits were developed over years of an irregular lifestyle. She has no obvious dislikes with regard to food.

What Works Well for Lisa Jones

Housing

Present: Lisa is currently living with her parents. The greatest advantage is that she gets free room and board. Living at home, she gets a lot of care and attention. The disadvantage is that she is not becoming accustomed to living independently, which she will need to do when her elderly parents are no longer living.

Past: She has previously lived alone, as well as in a cooperative arrangement. Living alone is unsatisfactory for her since she does not eat well and her housekeeping is slovenly. She tried living in a group situation in 1989. This was better in that meals were provided, but there were certain disadvantages such as irregular meals, a shared bathroom among too many residents, and some residents who had problems that were disturbing to Lisa. This was not a healthy situation, and Lisa was right in leaving. We were hoping that she could find another room-and-board situation, but nothing was available.

Future: No definite plans have been made for Lisa's future living arrangements. The best plan may be for Lisa to live in an apartment managed by a group such as Thresholds. A communal eating arrangement may be the best for her. An apartment of her own does not seem to be an easy situation to find.

a. A relative's home might be a satisfactory solution, although no particular candidate comes immediately to mind. All of her relatives live in (name of state), and Lisa is not particularly close to any of them. Moreover, since it is difficult living with Lisa, it would probably not be a good idea to have her live in the same household with a relative.

b. A group home could be satisfactory, but we are not aware of the availability of a particular home at this time. We have a few leads which we will investigate.

Size: A studio apartment may be the minimum size that would meet Lisa's requirements, while an extra room may allow for more general comfort.

Adaptation: No devices that assist individuals with limited mobility are needed.

Favorite Recreation: Cassette player, radio, ethnic drums which she owns, writing poetry.

Community: Shopping areas, library, public transportation.

Daily Living Skills

Individual Program Plan: Lisa is devoted to either finding a job or to preparing herself to be eligible for a particular position. She seeks out help wanted ads and goes to interviews but almost always finds the position impossible, e.g., hours, location, etc., and fails to follow through. Her mother feels that she is actually afraid to go to work. Looking for a job is a way she fills her time. When she is at home, she engages her mother in constant conversation to the point where both feel it cannot continue. At times Lisa realizes that talking at her mother every waking moment is not a good thing, so she tries to leave the house to "get out of the way."

Current Activities: On a typical day, Lisa looks into want ads and makes phone calls. Sometimes, she goes to community colleges and the local library to look into requirements and courses for the jobs she has found in the paper. For a while, she thought of taking courses to become a teacher in English as a Second Language, which was suggested to her by a friend's wife. She was also interested in printing, but she learned that in printing she'd have to repair the machine. She says she doesn't want to do repair work, so she has checked that job off her list. She enrolled in a Spanish class recently but subsequently dropped out. She has asked the schools she attended to send transcripts and made some effort to enroll in graduate classes in order to teach.

Speech or English. She tries to convince herself that she should do these things but finally admits she doesn't want to study, read, or go to classes. One of her problems with work is that she doesn't want to do menial labor. She is too intelligent for such menial labor, but she doesn't have the emotional stability to do the things she thinks she'd like to do.

Monitoring: Lisa could use help with self-care skills such as hygiene and dressing and domestic activities such as housekeeping and cooking. Her mother keeps after her to pick up after herself, but she cannot seem to do so.

Caregivers' Attitudes: Caregivers could emphasize general standards of cleanliness, appearance, and social graces.

Self-esteem: We try to praise Lisa when she does do something well and to downplay apparent setbacks or feelings of inadequacy. She has a problem with self-esteem. We seem to have to treat her as a young adolescent in this regard rather than as the 35-year-old woman that she is.

Sleep Habits: Sleep habits are poor, since she goes to the bathroom often. When she has little to do, she often sleeps during the daytime. This undoubtedly disrupts her sleep pattern at night. When depressed she sleeps long hours, but this may also be due to poor management of her diabetes.

Personal Finances: She does not manage money well. She tends to spend without budgeting and therefore needs to borrow before the month is up and her check comes from Social Security. Certain habits, such as drinking soft drinks and smoking, use up a large portion of her funds. She does try to roll her own cigarettes in order to save money. We have suggested that she keep records of her spending and budget her money.

Allowance: Lisa needs an allowance to keep within certain limits of spending. Clothing and other expenses are currently special requests. At the present time, we are providing her with clothes, shoes, and glasses. Whenever Lisa sees a doctor who does not accept Medicaid, we have paid her fees. When she lived in (name of city), we bought an old used car for her and paid for insurance and other expenses. We often sent money to her because she didn't have enough, although she received more aid from welfare there than she did in our state.

Plans for Further Education

Current Programs: Lisa has spoken of taking courses in English as a Second Language and/or in Speech at (name of university), but she changes her mind constantly.

Academics: Lisa's attainments in reading and writing are about a B-C grade at the college level. Mathematics was at a D level. In certain courses she did get A grades, but her average grade point in college was about 3 on a 5 point scale.

Emphasis: Lisa has said at one time that she was hoping to be able to teach at a community college. However, she seems to have given this up after some thought. Her mother thinks that this was her father's understanding and believes that her father does not understand Lisa since he does not spend the hours with Lisa that her mother does. When she was at (name of college) and did some practice teaching, it was too stressful for her and she quit school. She then went to (name of college) and got her degree in theater arts. In other words, she transferred colleges and changed her major in order to complete her B.A. A highly academic course is something she doesn't seem to be able to handle. We encouraged her to get a degree primarily because it would keep her busy. We were surprised and pleased that she was able to get her degree: this indicated that she could complete her work. We were proud of her achievement but do not think she should tackle any rigorous graduate program. She does not enjoy reading and does not read books or newspapers. Her attention span is short: she is impatient and cannot seem to concentrate on anything other than her emotional and mental state. Mother, at least, does not think she is suited to a full graduate program. At present, Lisa says she does not want to go to classes but may change her mind later. Lisa dreams of a better life, earning respect as well as income. We hope her aspirations may be realized. But, unless she changes drastically, we realistically think she should only take one course at a time so as not to cause her stress.

Integration: Lisa has been in regular classes and schools during much of her education. She may have a chance at succeeding in her goal, but it is a very small one. She should consider other, less stressful options. She is presently hoping to learn silk screening from a friend, so that she can design and print T-shirts to sell. Perhaps, if she cannot sell her shirts, she can find a job using this new skill. Lisa is really better suited to a job that uses her artistic skills.

Day Program or Work

Present: She is actively seeking part-time or full-time employment.

Past: The side effect of lithium therapy involving great thirst, drinking, and frequent visits to the lavatory is a drawback in finding a suitable job. She has been easily discouraged. Her tendency to paranoid thoughts also complicates relationships with a boss and fellow workers. In other cases, she may not have been as quick in performing the work involved, compared with others. She can exhibit low self-esteem as well as temper and anger.

Future: Lisa should continue to be supported in her efforts to find some worthwhile occupation, since she appears to be motivated to do so. We are willing to send her to whatever classes/schools she wants to attend, but we feel she should take one class at a time.

Leisure and Recreation

Structured Activities: She had an important role in a play several years ago that was reviewed favorably by [name of newspaper]. She is no longer very involved in theater, though she has tried to find jobs as a theater tech. She likes to hear both popular and classical music and goes to free concerts alone. She has friends with whom she plays music, but she does this infrequently. Her parents have invited her to the theater, but she feels her frequent need to go to the bathroom makes it impossible for her to enjoy a play.

Unstructured Activities: She enjoys writing poetry and has recently gone to poetry readings. She was to read her poems one evening but left without participating or telling anyone. They were unhappy about this. She likes to listen to taped music and the radio. She took a class in folk dancing and enjoyed it, but she has not done this recently.

Vacations: She would probably enjoy vacations with her best friend, an old grammar-school friend, whom she visited in (city) for a week a few years ago. Another friend has invited her to visit, and she would perhaps like to.

Fitness: Lisa has not been involved regularly with a fitness program but she ordinarily walks a great deal. She thinks nothing of walking what others would consider a great distance, e.g., several miles each way to and from shopping malls and train stations.

Religion

Faith: Lisa was brought up in the Christian faith. She is nominally a member of the (church). She has expressed some interest in several other religions, but lately seems to be interested solely in Christian churches.

She believes that guardian angels guide and instruct her through her dreams. She has considered and has tried suicide, but in the last several years she has felt that God doesn't want her to do this. Her mother is partly responsible for this change with long talks against suicide.

Clergy: Reverend _______ of the (church) knows Lisa and is concerned about her. She has not been visited by ministers of any other religion, but she would probably enjoy engaging in conversation with them.

Participation: She would probably enjoy a church relationship if it did not involve extraordinary demands. At the (church) in (city) a member said something cruel and nasty to her and she quit attending.

Rights and Values

1. Lisa should be free from harm, physical restraint, isolation, abuse, and excessive medication.
2. Lisa should have the right to refuse behavior modification techniques that cause pain.
3. She should have the right to have age-appropriate clothing and appearance.
4. She should have health-promoting staff demonstrate respect and care. They should not use demeaning language.

Other

Lisa has had a difficult life. She has had no easy roads to travel. Learning to cope with diabetes at age 16 was a terrible adjustment and limited her activities. Since she did well in art and liked music, she did not study academic areas diligently. She did not want to go to a chiefly liberal arts college. Later in life, she found that job opportunities in fields associated with the arts were limited. She had one exciting job in (city) with a documentary film house. She helped make some films that were prize winners. Because of her diabetes, she could not join the Peace Corps, something that might have allowed her to have a structured existence for a while. As with many of her peers, she tried cocaine and other drugs and feels that she got a bad dose one day and became ill when this experience was "coupled with bipolar genes." This may be an overly simple explanation for the genesis of her illness. In any case, she has suffered long, and we hope to be able to smooth her way as much as possible in the future.

Finances, Benefits, and Services

Assets: She has essentially no assets except for a very few personal belongings. She has sold many possessions such as television set, cameras, film equipment, etc. She has also donated film equipment worth almost $3,000, music and film to various schools and organizations.

Cash Income: She spent most of last year in (city) looking for a job. During 8 months of this period, she received $5,000 from Social Security. Her parents supplemented this with $8,103. This included $2,700 for the purchase of a used car, $824 for car insurance, and $562 for two round-trip air fares. Her earnings were probably about $500.

Services: Medicaid pays for her medications.

Gaps: Lisa needs more money for transportation to get health care at (clinic) and other facilities. She will try to get a special pass so that she can find public transportation at a discount. She should get supplemental funds for room and board to pay her parents so they can put this money into her Special Needs Trust. At the present time, she is getting a bare minimum from Social Security.

Expenses: From her Social Security income, Lisa pays for cigarettes, soft drinks, some fast foods, bus fare, other transportation, and not much else. Her parents have been paying for the remainder of her expenses: housing, board, clothing, education, and health care not covered by Medicaid.

Changes: Lisa's financial picture would not change if one of her parents were to die. When both parents are dead, her trust will become effective.

The Paper Trail

Will: The new wills of Gary and Susan Jones are being drafted by (name of law firm). The principal beneficiaries are the Jones Family Special Needs Trust and Cheryl Jones. Cheryl and the (bank) are likely to be the initial cotrustees of the trust. A reminder to Cheryl is to name some successor trustees after she becomes a cotrustee to assure continuity with people who are close to Lisa.

Real estate: Lisa does not plan to live in her parents' home after both parents are deceased. After her father retires, the family home may be sold and other plans will need to be made.

Advisors: (names, addresses, and phone numbers)

Other: Papers, such as the most recently completed application form and award letter from the Social Security Administration, are located in Lisa's personal file folder, which may be found among her personal effects in her room in her parents' home.

Conclusion

The process of writing a Letter of Intent can be as difficult as it is important. We hope the sample letters provided in this chapter have been helpful to you, and we wish to thank those clients who gave permission to reprint them. There were many other letters we could have selected, and those of you who were not contacted should not feel slighted. Unfortunately, this book must be finite in length, and many caring and helpful letters had to be omitted.

Chapter 3

Advocacy and Guardianship

The single burning issue in many clients' minds is to make sure their child's interests will be protected in the future. They know everything that they do for their child, and they know that whatever they put in their Letter of Intent, whatever they do in terms of residential care, their child will need someone who will look out for his or her interests after they themselves are gone.

Many assume that this means a guardian must be appointed. This is a very controversial issue and ultimately a very personal decision to be made by the family.

Some of our clients shy away from guardianship due to the expense, court involvement, and the need in many states to have their child declared incompetent before a guardian can be appointed. These clients prefer having friends and relatives act as *informal* advocates to deal with personal issues and a combination of trusts and representative payees to handle financial concerns. Other clients prefer the formal, legally binding relationships created in guardianship proceedings.

In this chapter we discuss the factors you will need to consider in making your decision—what guardianship is, what alternatives to guardianship are available, and how you can decide which option is best for your child. Regardless of what decision you make, whether to pursue guardianship or to go with something less formal, far and away the most important thing you can do is to choose the right people to act on behalf of your child. Neither guardianship nor advocacy will work if the wrong people are selected, and in most cases either option will work if the right people are in place.

Why Does My Child Need An Advocate?

No matter how effective a life plan you may develop, no matter how clear your Letter of Intent may be, in practice the plan will work only as well as the people selected to implement it.

This is almost too obvious for words if you expect your child to live with a friend or relative after your death. In such cases the future caregiver is required to step into your role—to cook and clean for your child, monitor school and work situations, drive your child to favorite recreational activities and outings with friends, watch over his or her medical condition and, in the best of all worlds, keep an eye open for new opportunities that will enable your child to lead a happy and rewarding life. In short, the future caregiver is required to do everything that you do currently and hopefully nearly as well.

If you plan on a group or independent living situation for your child, an effective advocate can be equally important. Too many people become intimidated by the structure of the social service system, by the programs, by the professionals who always seem to know what is best for the people in their care. While these professionals are almost always skilled and good-hearted, it is important that your child have an advocate, someone who has the personal knowledge, deep concern, and firm willingness to pursue your child's best interests.

Professionals may not know your child as a person, and their recommendations may be based on what's best for people who have disabilities generally, rather than on what's best for your child particularly. The person whom you select to act as advocate should know your child as an individual—his or her likes and dislikes, needs and capabilities—and should be able to act on that knowledge and communicate it to others.

In a supervised residential setting your child is likely to come across many professionals with different ideas about what is best. Also, many of the people who help your child—the house managers at a residential facility, the supervisors at a sheltered workshop—may not be professionals. The winter 1990 issue of the Arc-Oregon reveals some eye-popping facts about Oregon (which is typical of many other states):

- The average entry-level worker in community DD residential services is paid only $4.54 an hour ($4.85 an hour after six months).
- For a family of three with one wage earner, $5.50 an hour is required just to be at the federal poverty level.
- Workers in community programs are frequently eligible for the same state and federal welfare programs as the clients they serve.
- The average turnover rate of direct-care residential staff was more than 200 percent in 1989. In other words, every position was filled an average of three times in twelve months.
- This means that minimally trained staff, likely to stay on the job only a few months, care for people who have highly individualized, and often very complex, needs.
- People actually do leave residential direct care to work at Burger King, or they work both jobs.

Obviously, then, selecting a person to look out for the interests of your child after your death can be of vital importance, even if your child lives in a supervised residential facility. The person you select may be the one constant in your child's life, the one person your child will be able to count on when the need arises.

What will this person be required to do? Asking questions is a good place to start. If decisions made by professionals appear questionable, your child's advocate will need to ask about them, understand why they were made. If, after speaking with the appropriate people, your child's advocate is not convinced a decision is right; the advocate must be able to push the point and get the decision reversed. A master's degree or Ph.D. in psychology is not required. What is required is basic common sense and a good heart.

To consider a real life example, one of our clients had a relative living in a group home situation. All of a sudden the boy's behavior dramatically changed. He stopped eating and became very quiet. The advocate made inquiries, but the staff said they had no idea what caused the change. Only after relentless investigation was it discovered that the boy was being verbally abused by one of the residential staff members. In short order, the staff member was fired.

Friendship is another important role an advocate must be able to fill. People who have disabilities often find themselves in insular environments, living alone in apartments or with others who have disabilities, isolated from the community at large. It is the advocate who must "break down the barriers"—taking your child to church, the library, the zoo; extending invitations to home-cooked dinners and family and holiday celebrations. A good advocate will work to involve your child in life outside the residential setting.

Finally, as we have continually stressed throughout this book, your Letter of Intent must be revised and updated periodically, because your son or daughter is a living, changing person. As needs and desires change, as new options and opportunities arise, the life plan must be revised as well. After your death, your child's advocate will be the person to make these revisions.

Who Should Be My Child's Advocate After I Am Gone?

As you have read the beginning of this chapter, you have likely had a number of thoughts. First and foremost you will want someone who knows and cares for your child. There is no substitute for love and commitment, and the people you select should have plenty of both.

As a general rule, we ask our clients to select three or four people who care strongly for their child, regardless of their geographic location. That way, if the person with the disability outlives the initial advocate, there will be other people who are prepared to act. Sometimes our clients prefer to have two or three people acting at once, perhaps because the advocates have different strengths and weaknesses. Maybe one of the people you are considering is good with money, while another is more likely to foster your child's social relationships. In such a case, you may want both of them acting, each using their strengths to offset the weaknesses of the other. Other clients prefer the advocates to act in succession, perhaps an older sister acting first and a cousin taking over when the sister is no longer able.

You will probably want to select at least one advocate who lives relatively close to your child. This will better enable the advocate to monitor your child's needs.

The following are some of the factors to consider in selecting future advocates for your child:

- Will one or more of the advocates be able to visit your child frequently and be available in emergency situations?
- Are they free of conflicts of interest and able to act in your child's best interest?
- Can they serve as advocate for a long period of time? If not, can they be trusted to select appropriate successors?
- Do the advocates have good common sense?
- Do they have experience in dealing with everyday legal and financial problems—bill paying, investments, insurance, taxes, and so on? Can you trust them to seek the aid of professionals—doctors, lawyers, and financial advisors—when needed?

Whomever you do select, be sure to discuss your decision with that person in an open and direct manner. That way you can be sure the prospective advocates will be willing to act, and the advocates can gain a clear appreciation of what is expected. You will probably want to let the advocates read a copy of your Letter of Intent.

If you are unable to think of anyone to act as advocate, you should be aware that many areas have public agencies or nonprofit organizations willing to provide such services. You can locate the applicable organizations in your area through the Department of Health for your state, as well as through many of the other organizations listed in the Directory of Organizations found at the end of this book. Some of our clients who do not have friends or relatives living near their child select a trusted friend or relative who lives outside the local geographic area to act as advocate, with the understanding that the advocate will make use of local advocacy organizations.

Finally, a recent innovation in the mental health field is to teach self-advocacy skills to adults with disabilities. There are groups that teach such skills in many communities, and you may consider encouraging your child to join one. You might begin by calling a local group you are affiliated with and inquiring about self-advocacy programs. One of the authors was pleasantly surprised when he ran into his older brother (who has mental retardation) at a National Convention of the Association for Retarded Citizens of the United States. Unbeknownst to the author, his brother was representing a state self-advocacy group.

Often self-advocacy works best in conjunction with other types of advocacy arrangements. You could appoint a friend or relative as advocate to help a child who has developed self-advocacy skills.

In the remainder of this chapter we discuss the concept of guardianship and alternatives to guardianship. Thus far we have used the expression "advocate" in a generic sense, to refer to the person who will look out for your child's interests after you are gone. Mental health professionals generally view advocacy as an alternative to guardianship. A *guardian* is a person who is appointed by a court to look out for the interests of your child; an *advocate* acts without court appointment. In the remainder of this chapter we adopt the more formal usage.

What Is Guardianship?

The law presumes that individuals over the age of eighteen are competent; that is, that they are able to make their own decisions about what is best for them in their daily lives. This means that, as a legal matter, no matter how severe the disability may be, your child will have the right to make his or her own decisions about the future upon reaching the age of majority. If your child is now over eighteen and if a guardian has not been appointed, your child already has that right.

This presumption of competence can be overcome only in what has come to be known as a "guardianship proceeding." The rules governing such proceedings vary by state. Typically, the proceeding begins with a petition filed in probate court by a "petitioner" (often a close friend or relative of a person with a disability) requesting a finding that the person with the disability is "incompetent" and the appointment of a "guardian."

Guardianship is a court-approved legal relationship in which a competent adult (the guardian) has a defined degree of legal authority to act on behalf of a person who is found to be incompetent (the ward). In general, guardians can be classified into categories according to whether they make decisions regarding the personal care of the ward (guardian of the person) or the financial care of the ward (guardian of the estate), whether their authority is limited to very specific types of decisions (limited guardianship) or whether their powers are broad (plenary guardians).

Guardian of the Person

Subject to the specific court order, a guardian of the person is responsible for the personal welfare of the individual with a disability. The guardian's responsibilities may vary greatly. A guardian of the person may have to make decisions concerning the ward's residence, medical care, education, vocational development, food, clothing, leisure activities, need for professional services, and so forth. If the ward has children, the guardian of the person may be given custody over them as well.

Some states require the guardian of the person to submit a report at least once a year. The report form varies from state to state. Normally, the report will briefly discuss the following:

- The current mental, physical, and social condition of the ward.
- The present living arrangement of the ward, and a description and address of every residence where the ward has lived during the period of guardianship and the length of stay at each place.
- The medical, educational, vocational, and other professional services given to the ward.
- A summary of the guardian's visits and activities on behalf of the ward.
- An indication whether or not there is a need for continued guardianship.
- Other relevant information.

Although a guardian of the person may have broad authority, there are some decisions that are too personal for a substitute decision maker to control. For instance, the guardian generally does not have the right to draft the ward's will or decide whom a ward will vote for. In many states a guardian cannot consent to or veto a ward's marriage, though the guardian may be able to bring a suit in court to have the marriage annulled if the guardian can establish that the ward lacked sufficient mental capacity to understand what he or she was doing.

In addition, most states will not allow a guardian (without court authority) to consent to extraordinary medical procedures such as sterilization, abortion, organ transplants from the ward to another person, or experimental treatment. Furthermore, most states provide safeguards against involuntary commitments to a mental facility. These states allow wards to commit themselves voluntarily to mental facilities, but prevent the person with a disability from being involuntarily committed without a hearing. Commitments in these states are treated as "involuntary" whenever the person with a disability protests the commitment. In addition, in some states the guardianship order must specifically grant the guardian of the person the authority to admit a ward into a residential facility.

Guardian of the Estate

Subject to the specific court order, a guardian of the estate is a person or organization appointed by the court to care for, manage, and invest the ward's property, with the duty to protect and preserve the property. The guardian of the estate must apply the principal and income of the estate for the ward's care, health, and comfort. It is the duty of the guardian of the estate to use the assets only for the benefit of the ward and not for the guardian's personal profit. Unlike a trustee, the guardian of the estate does not have legal title to the ward's property; rather, the guardian has a duty to manage the property. The guardian of the estate should not commingle or combine the ward's property or funds with his or her own property.

The legal system has established a standard of competence for the guardian of the estate. To meet this standard the estate guardian must use reasonable care and skill in managing the ward's financial affairs. Reasonable care and skill is normally defined as the care and skill that a person of ordinary prudence would exercise with personally owned property. If the guardian of the estate does the best he or she can do but still performs below the standard of a hypothetical person, the guardian has breached the duty of reasonable care.

There is a major qualification to the standard of care. The ordinary prudent person will take risks with a certain percentage of his or her own assets, but the guardian of the estate is not permitted to take undue risks with the ward's property. The estate guardian is a conserver of assets. For example, a guardian may invest a ward's assets in U.S. treasury securities in order to earn income safely but typically cannot invest the money in assets such as a real estate limited partnership. The estate guardian might even breach his or her duty by investing the money in higher-risk growth stocks.

In many states, to insure that the guardian of the estate manages the ward's property competently and safely, the guardian is not permitted to spend or invest any of the ward's funds without first obtaining permission from the court. If a guardian spends the ward's money without prior court approval, the guardian may be required to repay the money from personal funds.

To obtain court approval, with the help of a lawyer the guardian must petition the court for authority to make expenditures. The petition must state the purpose and amount of the proposed expenditure. The petition may be for one specific expenditure, or the court may approve a number of expected transactions, such as for rent, food, or clothing prior to the time they are actually needed. This procedure for obtaining court permission for expenditures results in considerable paperwork, expense, inconvenience, and possibly delays that in some instances could harm the ward. It is one of the unavoidable disadvantages of having a guardian of the estate.

Similarly, many states require the guardian of the estate to obtain permission before investing the ward's property. In some states, if the guardian allows the ward's money to remain uninvested, the court will charge the guardian interest. Some courts do not require permission to invest the ward's money in securities such as U.S. treasury bills. However, states and judges vary. Many judges prefer that the investment be insured, which would rule out uninsured money market accounts. Some judges forbid a guardian from investing the ward's property in assets such as real estate or stock, even though such an investment may provide a hedge against inflation. Most judges prefer that the invested money yield higher income than it would in a pass-book savings account, preferring investments such as a fund that buys U.S. treasury securities.

Although a guardian of the estate can be helpful in protecting the ward's financial affairs, there can also be some definite disadvantages. Two disadvantages have just been mentioned:

1. The paperwork necessary to obtain court permission for expenditures made on behalf of the ward can be time-consuming, cumbersome, and expensive.

2. Restrictions designed to protect the assets may be too conservative for productive money management. Furthermore, though a relative who becomes a guardian may not charge a fee, an unrelated guardian can be expensive. This expense is paid from the ward's assets unless some other arrangement is made.

Another expense related to the guardian of the estate that most states require is the posting of a bond. A bond is backed up by an amount of money that must be forfeited if the guardian negligently mismanages the ward's estate or steals the ward's property. Such bonds are sometimes called "performance" or "surety" bonds. Certain companies or individuals (bondsmen) specialize in guaranteeing payment of these bonds (for a fee) in case of mismanagement or dishonesty by the guardian. In some states, a judge has discretion to waive the bond requirement. In these states, the bond requirement is usually omitted when the assets of the ward are minimal or the guardian of the estate is a bank.

Finally, most states require a guardian of the estate to submit detailed reports (called "accounts" or "accountings") to the court about the management and expenditures of the ward's money. To account for financial transactions is to provide a written statement of money earned, accrued, spent, and invested and to explain how and why these transactions have taken place. The guardian of the estate must account for every transaction made with the ward's money, and the receipts and cancelled checks sometimes must be attached. Normally the account is submitted to the court once a year, although each state's requirement differs. Furthermore, some courts require oral reports to supplement the written reports.

In light of the cost, reporting, and paperwork requirements of a guardian of the estate, as well as the investment and expenditure restrictions, a trust usually is a better alternative for fulfilling the parents' objectives. However, each family's situation is unique. Some families may want the safeguard of the court's watchful eye on the person responsible for managing their child's finances. The pros and cons of a guardianship of the estate should be measured against the alternatives available, the family's objectives, and the needs of the person with a disability.

Plenary vs. Limited Guardian

The terms "plenary" and "limited" describe the extent or amount of decision-making authority the guardian has under the guardianship order. The terms can be applied to either a guardian of the person or a guardian of the estate.

Plenary guardian. Virtually no limitations are placed on the decision-making authority of the plenary guardian. In many states, a plenary guardian (frequently called a "full" guardian or a "conservator") has decision-making authority over both the personal and financial aspects of the ward's life. However, in other states, the term refers to the decision-making power of a guardian of the person or a guardian of the estate. For example, a plenary guardian of the person could make decisions concerning all aspects of the ward's personal well-being (as opposed to financial well-being)—food, clothing, health, residence, and so forth. A plenary guardian of the estate could make decisions concerning all aspects of a ward's financial well-being—how the ward's money should be invested, how it should be spent. A plenary guardianship is most appropriate for a person with severe disabilities who is completely without capacity to make or communicate responsible decisions about personal care or finances and needs the full protection of a guardian.

Many states appoint only plenary guardians. Because of the extensive powers of these guardians, usually an adult with a disability must be declared totally incompetent before a plenary guardian can be appointed, even though the disability might not justify the declaration.

Limited guardian. Historically, according to most guardianship laws, judges could either declare a person with a disability totally incompetent and appoint a plenary guardian or dismiss the case and leave the person without the protection of a guardian. This "all or nothing" approach failed to recognize the unique needs and abilities of people who have disabilities.

A limited guardianship provides a more realistic alternative to the "all or nothing" choice between a plenary guardian or no guardian at all. Limited guardianship restricts the guardian's decision-making to only those decisions which the person with a disability cannot make alone. Thus, the person with a disability will have responsibility over the decisions he or she is capable of making, while the guardian will be able to assist when necessary. When the person with a disability lacks some, but not all, capacity to make responsible decisions, the court may appoint a limited guardian of the person, or of the estate, or both. In most states, unlike plenary guardianship, a limited guardianship does not constitute a finding that the person with a disability is legally incompetent. The following examples will illustrate how a limited guardianship might work.

Mary has mental retardation and is forty-two years of age. Although Mary is noticeably "slow," she is very independent and stable and has worked at the local library, shelving books, for years. Mary also sells homemade pastries to friends and neighbors. Mary is overweight and has very high blood pressure. After her mother's death, Mary moved in with her sister's family until they could decide on the best community facility for Mary to live in.

They applied to a local community facility from which Mary will be able to take a bus to the library where she works. The executive director of the community facility insisted that Mary's sister become a limited guardian for Mary because of her high blood pressure. Because of Mary's independence, the limited guardian needed to have only the authority to consent to medical treatment. The executive director told the family that there had been an increase in medical malpractice lawsuits at the local hospital, and most doctors were insisting that a guardian sign a consent-to-treatment form for persons with mental retardation. The doctors feared that such persons might lack the legal mental capacity to give "informed consent." Mary was admitted to the community facility after her sister became her limited guardian to consent to medical treatment. Mary retains control over the rest of the decisions in her life.

The second example illustrates a limited guardian of the estate rather than of the person:

Dick has mental retardation and is thirty-five years of age. Dick lives in a local group home and works in the mailing department of a local insurance company. When Dick's uncle died, Dick inherited $50,000. Dick's mother met with mental health professionals, and they decided Dick could competently manage his weekly salary but needed a limited guardian of the estate to manage and properly invest the $50,000 inheritance. Dick's brother, a CPA, petitioned the court to be appointed a limited guardian for this purpose. The court granted the petition, and Dick's brother will manage the $50,000 for the benefit of Dick. Dick can still take pride in managing his own weekly salary from the insurance company.

If the state where Dick lives allowed only the appointment of a plenary guardian, Dick's life might have been different. A plenary guardian would have total control over the $50,000 and Dick's weekly salary. In losing control of his weekly salary, Dick might also have lost some of his self-esteem.

Unfortunately, in many areas of the country the availability of a limited guardianship may be more theoretical than real. As already mentioned, some states do not provide for limited guardians. Even in states that do accept the concept, many judges are reluctant to grant limited guardianship, feeling that the ward either needs a full guardian or no guardian at all. This allows the judge to avoid making a more refined assessment of the ward's functioning level.

Where limited guardianship is available, however, it can be very helpful. It can be flexibly drawn, to grant the limited guardian authority only over those areas where help is required. This avoids the necessity of declaring a ward incompetent and leaves the ward with authority over the areas that he or she can handle. The following list describes some areas in which the limited guardian might be given authority:

- To apply for and enroll the ward in public or private residential facilities, educational programs, or vocational rehabilitation programs.
- To consent to medical and psychological tests and treatment for the ward.
- To examine confidential records.
- To attend confidential professional staff meetings.
- To apply for governmental funds and services for the ward, including:
  Supplemental Security Income (SSI)
  Disability benefits under Social Security
  Title XX Services
  Vocational Rehabilitation Programs
  Medicaid
  Developmental Disability Services
- To contract and make purchases over $_______ for the ward.
- To cancel or negate contracts and purchases made by the ward over $__________. (Note: This provision has questionable legal validity. However, it may be useful in dealing with someone who has financially exploited the ward.)
- To manage the specific properties of the ward.
- To rent or buy real estate for the ward to live in.
- To file federal and state income tax returns for the ward.
- To help the ward attain employment, an identification card, or driver's license.
- To file or defend a lawsuit on behalf of the ward.

The attitude of the law toward limited guardianship varies from state to state and often from judge to judge. If you are considering having a limited guardian appointed for your child, you will need to consult an attorney familiar with guardianship in your area. In establishing a limited guardianship, you should carefully consider your child's abilities to insure that your child retains as much responsibility as is appropriate.

Private Guardianship Agencies

In some states a private agency can be appointed as guardian of a person with a disability. The laws in most of these states require that the agency be a nonprofit organization.

Most of these nonprofit organizations have professional staffs that can act as guardians and also advise family guardians. It is wise to inquire about staff caseloads (the smaller the better), frequency of visits to wards, amount of time spent with the ward and the residential staff at each visit, size of budget, and resources. Interview the staff to insure that they are caring rather than bureaucratic. Often the staff can answer questions about the local mental-health network; about residential, vocational, and school placement; and about finding an attorney to draft an estate plan with your child who has a disability in mind.

If you are considering such a private agency as guardian or future guardian for your adult child, inquire about its budget and ask for an annual statement. You want an organization that will remain solvent during the entire lifetime of your child. Many of these organizations are suffering from a critical shortage of funds and some have gone out of business. Despite the expense, it is best if the organization charges for its services and is not totally reliant on government and charitable funds, which may disappear.

A private, nonprofit guardianship service can act quite effectively as a coguardian or as an advisor, providing professional services and support to the person with a disability and the other guardian. These organizations, if permitted by state law, can be named as coguardians or successor guardian after the parent's death.

Public Guardians

If a person with a disability needs a guardian but has no one to assume the responsibility, the court will appoint either a public official or a public agency, such as a state-administered guardianship service. Often public guardians are guardians "of last resort" and provide care when the person with a disability has no relatives or friends willing and able to serve as guardian. Most public guardianship agencies have professional staffs and do not charge for their services.

What Are the Alternatives to Guardianship?

Before you decide whether your child needs some type of guardian, you should consider the alternatives to guardianship. These include trust funds, representative payees, and citizen advocates.

Trusts

Trusts are a highly recommended alternative to a guardian of the estate. Trusts accomplish the same objective as the guardian of the estate, management of the assets of a person with a disability.

Trusts offer several advantages and have fewer restrictions than guardians of the estate. Chief among the advantages is a solution to the resource problems that might jeopardize the person's eligibility for governmental aid. As we will discuss in Chapter Four, to be eligible for many governmental benefits, your child's total assets cannot exceed certain stated maximum amounts. Amounts held for your child in properly drafted trusts do not count as your child's assets for these purposes, while amounts managed for your child by a guardian of the estate are considered assets of your child. Accordingly, if you think your child may require government benefits after your death, it is better to leave money in trust for your child than to have a guardian of the estate appointed and leave money to your child outright.

Trusts offer other advantages over guardians of the estate as well. In order to secure proper financial management, it is not necessary to declare the person who has a disability incompetent. Nor is there a need for the constant, detailed reports that a guardian of the estate must submit to the court. It is not necessary to get approval from the court for expenditures on behalf of the person. The posting of a bond is not required. (However, with a professional trustee there will be management fees.) The trustee will also have greater flexibility in investing than a guardian of the estate.

Parents can select a trustee without the approval of the court. The trust document containing the duties of the trustee can be written to include all the preferences of the parents. The trust, like a limited guardian of the estate, can provide protection and assistance and allow the person with a disability to make those financial decisions he or she is capable of making.

While family objectives will vary, normally a trust is a better alternative than a guardian of the estate. Further details about trusts may be found in Chapter Six.

Representative Payee

A representative payee is a person or organization authorized to cash and manage public assistance checks such as Supplementary Security Income and Social Security for a person considered incapable of managing the money. The payee is appointed by the agency administering the funds. If the parents want a particular representative payee selected, they must notify the agency. If the representative payee is not a relative, service fees may be required. The representative payee must keep an accurate record of all expenditures made on behalf of the person with a disability. The representative payee can be an alternative to a guardian of the estate when the only money the person with a disability receives is from the government or from a trust.

Advocacy

An advocate is like a guardian of the person, but without court authority or oversight. The advocate looks out for the interests of a person with a disability and provides personal attention, guidance, and representation. An advocate can be either a friend or relative of the person with a disability or a staff professional of a mental health agency. Some mental health agencies advocate or lobby for laws that will benefit people with disabilities as a group, while other agencies lobby for individuals and their families. Agencies that advocate for the individual can be helpful in advising the person with a disability and the person's family concerning services in the local area. Increasingly, private, nonprofit agencies are being created to provide individual advocacy support.

The advocate can help the person with a disability on almost any matter; however, unlike a guardian, the advocate cannot legally make decisions for the person. For instance, the advocate would be unable to contract for the person with a disability, invest money without consent, or sign a medical consent-to-treatment form. In substance, an advocate is like a guardian in terms of commitment and desire to act on behalf of a person with a disability, but the relationship lacks the formality of guardianship, and the advocate lacks the legal standing of a guardian. The advocate's ability to act on behalf of the person with a disability therefore depends on the cooperation of the person as well as the cooperation of service providers.

Power of Attorney

A power of attorney is a written document by which a person (the principal) authorizes another person (the agent) to act on the principal's behalf. The person holding the power of attorney is called an "attorney in fact," thus distinguishing the person from an attorney at law. The purpose of a power of attorney is to prove to a third person or organization that the agent has the authority to act on behalf of the principal. The power of attorney is a simple document to draft and can be written for almost any situation in which the attorney in fact acts on behalf of the principal—buying and selling goods, contracting with third persons, or whatever.

In limited circumstances, a power of attorney can be an appropriate method for acting on behalf of a person with a mild mental disability who does not need a guardian. For instance, many parents of a child with a disability hold a power of attorney to fill out and submit taxes to the IRS. The powers of the attorney in fact are limited to those specified in the document. For the power of attorney to be effective, the person granting the power (your child) must understand its nature and purpose.

Does My Child Need a Guardian?

We have already stated our views about guardianship for financial matters. In general, we prefer the use of trusts for several reasons:

1. Assets held in properly drafted trusts will not be considered owned by your child and therefore will not imperil eligibility for government benefits or be seized for cost-of-care claims by the government.

2. Trusts do not involve the same amount of paperwork as guardianships.

3. Trusts tend not to be as restrictive as guardianships in terms of investment decisions (although, if you prefer to restrict the trustee's investment options, a restrictive trust can be drafted).

Financial guardianship can, however, be beneficial in certain circumstances. For example, some people who have disabilities have significant assets of their own (perhaps from earnings, gifts, or inheritance) and may lack either the mental capacity or the inclination to place those assets in trust. Problems can develop if the person with the disability lacks the skill to manage the assets. Some parents prefer guardianship in such circumstances, although it may not be necessary if the person with the disability listens to advice from friends or relatives who do not have disabilities or is willing to put the funds in trust. (As we will discuss in Chapter Ten, trusts created by people with disabilities for themselves out of their own funds generally will not protect those funds from government claims for cost-of-care liability.)

Financial guardianship can also be beneficial for people who prefer court oversight of their child's funds. Although the degree of judicial attention varies by state, it is thought that the existence of court supervision will act as a deterrent to mismanagement or even theft.

It is, however, possible to build protection against mismanagement or theft into a trust document; many such methods are discussed in Chapter Six. For example, in most cases we suggest that our clients name two people to act simultaneously as trustee of their child's trust. That way, assuming both trustees are vigilant, each can monitor the performance of the other. Where trusts are sufficiently large, we frequently advise a cotrustee arrangement between an individual and a bank. The bank holds the funds to protect against mismanagement and dishonesty, and the individual, who knows the child best, advises the bank about how to spend trust money.

By far, however, the majority of people who seek our advice about guardianship are not concerned about financial matters. Rather, they are worried about the personal issues that will arise after their death or, sometimes, about the personal issues that may arise while they are living. They want to know who will look out for their child, making sure that food, clothing, and shelter are provided, that exploitation is avoided, that service providers do what is best.

We have already discussed the concept of advocacy. Though it lacks the "official" court-recognized status of guardianship, some clients prefer advocacy for at least two reasons. First, as we will discuss in the next section, establishing guardianship necessarily involves a court proceeding that can be expensive. Many clients prefer to avoid involvement with the legal system when possible, particularly if an advocacy arrangement is workable.

Second, the process of establishing guardianship can be quite distasteful. Typically it involves a finding of legal "incompetence" and a stripping away of the ward's rights to make independent decisions. If your child's disability is sufficiently severe, you may not find this to be important; your child's ability to participate in decision making may be almost nonexistent. In such a case, appointment of a guardian may actually provide added protection for your child's legal rights.

However, in cases where the disability is less severe, parents often prefer having their child participate with an advocate in the decision-making process. This can, of course, be accomplished through guardianship as well; there is nothing that prohibits a guardian from consulting the ward, and the best guardians do so. But where there is no immediate need for guardianship, many parents rely on an advocacy arrangement, counting on friends and relatives to look out for their child while recognizing that they (or the advocate, if they are deceased) can commence a guardianship proceeding in the future if the need arises.

Families that decide in favor of guardianship do so for a variety of reasons. Some parents want to make absolutely sure that the person whom they select to act for their child after their death will indeed be able to perform that function. Sometimes they fear that service providers will not pay sufficient attention to the advocate or that a guardianship proceeding will commence after they die and someone other than the person they want will be appointed guardian.

Many states permit parents who are guardians of their adult children to appoint successor guardians by will (guardians appointed by will are called "testamentary guardians"). Parents sometimes commence guardianship proceedings so they can have themselves named as guardians and thereby control the successor designation. Sometimes it is even possible to have successor guardians named in the original court order appointing the parents as guardian.

Often, however, these same objectives can be accomplished without guardianship proceedings. The parents of an adult with a disability who has not been the subject of a guardianship proceeding can make general statements in their wills or Letter of Intent that a particular individual (the person the parents select as advocate) should be appointed if guardianship later becomes necessary. (For example, guardianship could be pursued if service providers ignore the advocate's wishes.) Although these general recommendations are not binding, courts generally pay considerable attention to the wishes of the parents. The person who is selected can petition the court (using the parent's recommendation as evidence) if it is later determined that guardianship is needed.

Parents sometimes pursue guardianship to be prepared for possible medical emergencies. For example, parents may fear that their child might become injured and will be unable to obtain aid from medical professionals because doctors, fearing possible malpractice claims, will doubt the child's ability to give legally binding consent to medical treatment.

It is unclear how legitimate this concern really is. In many areas doctors will provide treatment on an emergency basis without consent where the need is clear. We are unaware of any instances where a person with a disability was denied *emergency care* due to inability to give informed consent, although it is certainly possible that this has happened. You may want to speak with doctors and hospitals in your area to gain an understanding of the local practice in such situations.

Moreover, most states deal with this problem through a legal concept known as *temporary guardianship.* Temporary guardians (called guardians ad litem in some states) are appointed for a temporary period of time (usually not more than 60 days) for persons with disabilities who do not have permanent guardians, in order to handle emergency situations. If needed, the temporary appointment is established quickly and simply, by having a judge sign a guardianship order either with a shortened court hearing or without a court hearing. Any competent adult can be appointed temporary guardian, and often parents themselves are appointed. The temporary guardian must meet the same qualifications as the guardian of the estate or person but has only the authority specifically written in the court order. It is, of course, possible that an emergency could be so severe that there is not time to obtain even temporary guardianship. One would, of course, expect that a doctor would do what was needed in such circumstances, though there are no guarantees.

Guardianship is sometimes obtained in order to enable the person with a disability to receive services on a nonemergency basis. Typically, this is the case when the services are particularly invasive. For example, a doctor may require consent of a guardian before performing nonemergency surgery. If you do pursue guardianship at the behest of a service provider, you should make sure it is for the benefit of your child, not merely for the convenience of the service provider.

Obviously, the question of obtaining guardianship for your child is difficult and will depend on your own particular facts and circumstances. In advising our clients, we tend to adhere to the following guidelines (though of course there are exceptions):

1. If the person who has the disability is under eighteen years of age, the parents are already the natural guardians under law. Legal guardianship through a court proceeding is neither necessary nor typically available. The parents name guardians in their wills to act if they die before their child reaches age eighteen. If the parents do die, the guardianship is effective until the child reaches age eighteen, at which time the guardians can petition the court if it is determined to be necessary to continue guardianship during adulthood.

2. If the person with a disability has reached the age of majority and the parents have not yet seen a need to pursue guardianship, we tend to set up an advocacy arrangement. (That is, the parents name friends or relatives in their Letter of Intent to act as advocates for their child when they die.) The child's inheritance is managed by trustees, typically caring relatives. We also include a general statement in the will or the Letter of Intent expressing the parents' wishes regarding guardians, should guardianship prove necessary after the parents have died. We discuss the pros and cons of guardianship so that parents can decide whether they wish to pursue guardianship during their lives.

3. If the parents have already been named guardians, we have them name successor guardians by will.

Establishing Guardianship

If, after reading the information in this chapter, you decide you would like to pursue guardianship for your child, it will be necessary to begin a guardianship proceeding. The proceeding will determine the level of competence of your child, whether guardianship is needed, and if guardianship is needed, the type of guardian to be appointed and the amount of authority to be granted to the guardian.

Starting a Guardianship Proceeding

To initiate the proceeding, your lawyer will file a "Petition for Appointment of Guardian for a Disabled Person" with the court clerk (the title of the petition may vary slightly from state to state). Although each state provides a different petition form, the following information must be included by your lawyer in most petitions:

- The petitioner's relationship to and interest in the person with a disability. The petitioner is the person who asks the court to appoint a guardian for the person with a disability.
- The name, date of birth, and place of residence of the person with a disability.
- The reasons for requesting a guardianship.
- The name and address of the proposed guardian, and, if an individual, his or her age and occupation.
- The approximate value of the personal property and real estate owned by the person with a disability.
- The approximate amount of the gross annual income and other receipts of the person with a disability.
- The names and addresses of the nearest relatives of the person with a disability.

Notice to the Person with a Disability

A formal notice or "summons" is then given to the person with a disability to show that a guardianship petition has been filed. The summons indicates the time, date, and location of the court hearing. In most states, a summons and copy of the petition must be delivered or "served" on the alleged disabled person not less than 14 days before the hearing.

In some states, the sheriff delivers the summons to the person with a disability. As a parent, if you believe a sheriff, who is a stranger, would frighten your child, ask your lawyer to motion the court for permission to use a "special process server." The special process server is a person other than the sheriff who will deliver the summons to your child. With the approval of the court, the special process server in most states can be anyone over the age of eighteen who is not a party to the guardianship case. Therefore, with court permission you can select a friend of the family to deliver the summons.

Evidence of Incapacity

In most states, a report by a physician must be attached to the Petition for Guardianship. This physician (often a psychiatrist or an expert who has experience with the particular disability involved) must have examined the person with a disability, usually within 90 days of the hearing. The judge reads the physician's report as evidence of the mental capacity of the person, in order to establish the need for guardianship and as an aid in determining the type and powers of the guardian. The physician must fill out a form that usually contains the following information:

- A description of the nature and type of disability.
- An evaluation of the person's mental and physical condition, including educational level, adaptive behavior, and social skills.
- An opinion as to whether a guardian is needed.
- An opinion, with reasons, about the type and scope of guardianship needed.

- A recommendation, with reasons, regarding the most suitable living arrangement and, where appropriate, treatment and rehabilitation plans.
- The signatures of all persons who performed the evaluations on which the report is based. At least one of these persons typically must be a licensed physician.

You should ask your lawyer for the physician's report form, have a doctor fill it out, then show it to your attorney. Your lawyer, after reading the report, will be able to determine how likely the judge will be to grant the guardianship. By determining the potential of the case prior to the court hearing, you can save considerable time and expense that might otherwise be wasted. It may even be advisable to discuss your child's condition with your lawyer before consulting a doctor. That way your attorney can tell you whether guardianship is possible before you incur any medical bills.

In order to justify the need for a guardian, the doctor's report must clearly and accurately demonstrate that the person's disability creates a need for guardianship. The doctor's report must not be vague. For instance, a physician's report stating only "This person is mentally ill and needs a guardian," will not be sufficient to justify the need for guardianship.

The same report written more specifically could probably justify the need for a guardian. Rather than simply stating "this person is mentally ill and needs a guardian," the doctor might write:

This person has had learning and emotional problems, probably related to unknown organic damage. He has had several schizo-affective psychotic episodes in which he was violent toward others. He will require psychiatric supervision, counseling, and psychotropic medication (currently Navone and Lithium). With Navone and Lithium he is free of psychotic symptoms. But he is incapable of independent living or of work because of an inability to make independent judgments in regard to personal care and ordinary social life.

He is in need of a limited guardian of the person. He needs assistance in making personal, financial, and medical decisions. He is capable of making daily decisions of personal care within a stable, protected, nonchallenging environment. He will need guardianship authority to make decisions about residential placement through his lifetime.

He also needs medication for heart problems and may need hospitalization in the future. [Note: If your child does need help in making decisions in regard to residential placement, it is wise to have the doctor comment on this. Most judges are understandably reluctant to give this authority to the guardian unless absolutely necessary.]

OR

Miss Doe has borderline mental retardation with intellectual scores in the 60 to 70 range. She is working at the Work Center, a sheltered workshop. Miss Doe is partially incapable of making personal and financial decisions. I do believe she is entirely incapable of handling financial affairs. She also needs help in making decisions in regard to her health.

Most states require at least one of the persons who performed the evaluation to testify at the hearing, unless excused by the court.

Appointment of a Guardian Ad Litem

A guardian ad litem (GAL) is a person appointed by the court to act as attorney for a person who is alleged to be disabled in the guardianship petition. Your child, therefore, becomes the GAL's client.

The GAL examines the case and determines the rights of your child, defends him or her if necessary, and writes a report for the court indicating whether or not a guardian is needed and, if so, what type of guardian should be appointed. Acting as an investigator, the GAL visits your child in his or her normal living environment. If it is a residential facility, the GAL also meets with the staff and discusses the long-term prognosis for your child. The GAL must inform your child (often, orally and in writing) of the guardianship proceeding, the contents of the petition for guardianship, and the various procedural rights available.

In the report to the court the GAL will discuss your child's medical records, functional level, and long-term prognosis. The GAL will indicate to the court whether your child will need the help of a guardian in personal and/or financial matters. If, in the opinion of the GAL, a guardian is needed, the GAL will also recommend the type of guardian that would seem to be most appropriate. The GAL might communicate to the court your child's preference for a particular individual to be appointed guardian.

In many states, one must pay a GAL for his or her services. If you cannot afford a GAL, in some states the court will require the state to pay the GAL's fees. Moreover, in some states the judge may waive the requirement of a GAL and thus substantially reduce costs. If state laws permit such a waiver, the judge will most likely waive the requirement for a GAL when a close family member seeks guardianship and the medical report on the person with a disability appears conclusive and accurate. Sometimes the judge will agree to visit with the person with a disability in his or her chambers rather than appoint a GAL. To avoid the cost of a GAL, ask your lawyer whether the laws in your state and the circumstances of the case warrant a waiver of a GAL.

Hearing and Appointment

Usually, the actual guardianship hearing can be completed in about a half hour or less. It is the prehearing documentation that takes the time. The judge will examine the petition for guardianship, the physician's report, and any other documents. Your lawyer will explain the need for and type of guardian requested and answer any questions asked by the judge. The judge will talk with the person with a disability.

If the judge believes the evidence justifies the need to appoint a guardian, he or she will sign a court order appointing a guardian. Remember, the guardian's powers are restricted to those granted by the court. The guardianship order will specify the exact responsibilities and powers the guardian will assume.

Additionally, a case number will be on the guardianship order. The case number identifies the court case. If a question arises in the future, the guardian can give the case number to a court clerk, who can look up the case for clarification.

The formal document issued by the court indicating the appointment of a guardian is usually called the "Letters of Office." The guardian can use this document to prove guardianship.

After the guardian has been appointed by the court, the guardian should notify the ward's contacts such as hospitals, stores, and relatives. These people and institutions should be informed who the ward's guardian is, so they can contact the guardian if they become aware of any problems. Also, this notification might protect the ward from someone's unscrupulous actions.

Modification or Discharge of Guardianship

By petitioning the court, the ward, the guardian, or any interested person can seek an alteration or termination of the guardianship. A hearing on the petition is required. If you want to change the authority the guardian has, the petition must list the reasons for seeking the modification. Most modifications involve a change of guardian or an alteration in the guardian's authority—decreasing or increasing it.

Usually a guardian continues until granted permission to resign. However, a guardianship will terminate if a court determines the ward no longer needs a guardian, the guardian is no longer willing or able to continue as guardian, or the guardian does not do a competent job.

Rights of the Person with a Disability

Laws in all states entitle the person with a disability to rights at the guardianship hearing. These include the usual rights afforded to a defendant in a lawsuit: the right to an attorney, the right to a jury trial, the right to present evidence (including doctors' reports), and the right to confront and cross-examine witnesses.

The rights are granted to insure that a guardian is not appointed when a less-restrictive alternative would be sufficient, and to insure that, if guardianship is appropriate, the proper type of guardian is appointed. In most instances, these rights are not exercised because a parent or a concerned person is properly being appointed guardian. However, they can provide a safeguard against exploitation.

Checklist of Procedures for your Lawyer

(Note: Each state will vary slightly in procedure.)

- Obtain evidence of incapacity of the person with a disability to be submitted at the guardianship hearing. The physician's report should be filled out in detail.
- Prepare a petition for guardianship and file it with the court clerk.
- Prepare a summons to be served on the person with a disability. Obtain hearing date and place from the court clerk. Give the summons to the sheriff for service, or prepare an order to use a special process server and an affidavit.
- Prepare a court order appointing a guardian ad litem (GAL), or prepare an order to waive the GAL.
- Prepare the mailing of notice to relatives and other persons named in the petition.
- If necessary, prepare a petition and order for a temporary guardian.
- Prepare a court order waiving the presence of the person with a disability or the physician if either cannot attend the hearing.
- Prepare a court order appointing a plenary or limited guardian.
- If necessary, prepare a petition and order to deposit the ward's funds in an account.
- If necessary, prepare a petition and order for authority to make expenditures on behalf of the ward.

Conclusion

Whether you decide to pursue a guardianship or not, it will be important for you to name someone to look out for your child's personal and financial interests after you are gone. The key is to name the right people.

As a practical matter, parents trust a finite group of people to serve as their child's future caregivers. We generally ask our clients to rank these people in order of preference. Often these people act as advocates and trustees, and guardians if the client decides a guardianship is necessary. This is sensible because these are the people who are most likely to do a good job.

For instance, let's say Mom and Dad trust Bob (their son) first, then Carol (their daughter) second, then Uncle Don third, then niece Sandy fourth, to look out for the future interests of their son, Jon. Mom and Dad may name Bob and Carol to act as cotrustees to manage Jon's inheritance, with Don or Sally acting if something happens to Bob or Carol. These same people would act as Jon's advocates or as guardian if one was appointed.

Often a relative who acts as trustee to manage the child's inheritance lives out of state. In this case, we feel it is vital that parents recommend local advocates in their Letter of Intent, to serve as the "eyes and ears" of the out-of-state trustee. These local advocates might be friends of the family, neighbors, or professionals who know and care about the child. The out-of-state trustee can even pay the local advocate from trust funds to visit the child and report to the trustee about the child's needs.

CHAPTER 4

PLANNING YOUR CHILD'S FINANCIAL FUTURE:

THE ROLE OF GOVERNMENT BENEFITS

FINANCIAL PLANNING FOR FAMILIES WITH MEMBERS WHO HAVE disabilities is fundamentally different from financial planning for other families. In the usual case, financial planning involves making sure resources are adequate to take care of children before they are old enough to "go it on their own." Later, concern shifts to making sure the parents themselves are adequately taken care of. For example, in many cases young families will be concerned primarily with making sure their financial resources will be adequate to fund their childrens' educational requirements. As the parents grow older, they begin to think about retirement.

Except in the case of the very wealthy, planning for the requirements of adult children tends not to be a major factor. If money is left to pass on to children after the parents die, that is all well and good, but ensuring the financial future of adult children is not a primary planning goal. Children are usually expected to be able to take care of themselves, as the parents have done.

Families with children who have disabilities require a different focus: in many cases, the children cannot be expected to earn enough to meet their financial needs. Therefore, as a parent, you will need to "take the bull by the horns" and develop a financial plan that will enable your son or daughter to meet his or her lifetime needs.

For most families, government benefits will play a very important role. The cost of lifetime care for a person with a disability can be quite high, particularly when the effects of inflation are factored. Few families have the resources to provide for children with disabilities through private means alone. We have "run the numbers" many times and, taking into account inflation, housing, the possible need for supervision, medical costs, and the huge assortment of other living expenses, the cost of providing for a child with a disability through private means alone can require a privately funded trust of more than a million dollars. This figure will be considerably lower if your child lives with friends or relatives on a cost-free basis, in your own home or the home of the friend or relative. The cost will also be lower if your child's disability is less severe, and less supervision is required. Cost is also heavily dependent on the age and life expectancy of the child.

Whatever the actual costs, you need to be very wealthy to rely exclusively on family dollars. That is why it is absolutely essential for most families to create an estate plan that will assure eligibility for government benefits. Even many of our wealthy clients, who expect to use private housing, leave money for children with disabilities in the types of trusts described in Chapter Six so that, if public housing or Medicaid should prove necessary in the future, government benefits will be available to them.

What Types of Government Benefits Are Potentially Available to My Child?

Many people who have disabilities are eligible for benefits under one or more of several government programs. These programs are designed to protect the person with the disability by making sure that the person's financial resources are sufficient to provide the basic necessities of life—food, clothing, shelter, and health care.

In general, the programs can be grouped into two categories. There are *needs based programs*, such as Supplemental Security Income (SSI) and Medicaid, that are available to individuals with disabilities who satisfy certain needs based requirements relating to income and assets. That is, to be eligible, your child cannot receive too much income or own too much property.

There are also programs classified as *social insurance programs*, such as Social Security and Medicare, that are potentially available regardless of how much income or property your child may have. Your child becomes entitled to benefits under these programs by virtue of the *premiums* that you or your child may have paid into the program. Although you may not know it, the premiums have been paid in the form of Social Security tax that has been withheld from your paycheck or, if you are self-employed, in the form of self-employment tax that you have been paying to the government on a quarterly basis.

Some of these programs are operated by the federal government, and others are run by the various states. Still others are jointly financed by state and federal governments and operated by the states in accordance with federally mandated guidelines.

Unfortunately, the rules relating to these programs are very complicated and you may have to read each section in this chapter several times before you understand it. It is not necessary that you understand everything, the basics are enough. The key points are these:

- If your child had a disability before reaching age 22, your child will likely be entitled to Social Security benefits when you or your spouse die, reach retirement age, or become disabled. If your child developed a disability after age 22, Social Security will be available *only* if your child had a significant employment history before becoming disabled.

- If your child has limited income and assets, he or she will likely be entitled to Supplemental Security Income benefits upon reaching age 18. It does not matter when your child first became disabled. For lower-income families, children under age 18 may also be eligible.

- If your child has limited income and assets, he or she will likely be eligible for a place in a government-funded residential setting (assuming space is available). Your child may be eligible for a place even if your child has significant assets, but the government will not pay.

- If your child resides in a residential setting that is funded by the state or federal government, Social Security or Supplemental Security Income benefits will be reduced substantially (to between $30 and $70 a month).

- If your child is eligible for Supplemental Security Income benefits, he or she will likely be eligible for Medicaid.

- If your child has been eligible for Social Security benefits for at least two years, he or she will likely be eligible for Medicare. It does not matter if your child actually received the benefits, just that the eligibility requirements were satisfied.

In order to qualify for benefits as a *person with a disability*, your child will need to be considered to have a *disability* by the particular governmental program involved. Under the rules of the Social Security Administration (which are used by most, if not all, governmental agencies), a person is considered to have a disability if the person is unable to engage in any *substantial gainful activity* by reason of any medically determinable physical or mental impairment that can be expected to result in death or that can be expected to last for a continuous period of at least 12 months. To Social Security, a job will generally constitute substantial gainful activity if the pay is $500 or more per month, after deducting the cost of impairment-related work expenses and disregarding the value of earnings subsidies. The rules are less strict for people with visual impairments.

What Is Social Security and How Can It Benefit My Child?

Most people understand the basic principles behind the Social Security system. Workers pay premiums into a *Social Security trust fund* that is used to pay *Social Security benefits* when the workers reach retirement age. Premiums are withheld from the workers' paychecks (the so-called FICA withholding tax) or are paid on a quarterly basis by the self-employed in the form of self-employment tax.

The amount required to be paid is a specified percentage of each worker's *earnings* up to a *maximum earnings base*. The amount of earnings subject to the tax increases each year to account for inflation.

For 1996, the FICA withholding tax paid by each employee is equal to 7.65 percent of the employee's first $62,700 of wages and 1.45 percent of additional wages. FICA tax is also paid in an equivalent amount by employers —7.65 percent of each worker's wages up to $62,700 and 1.45 percent of additional wages. Self-employed individuals pay both the employer's and the employee's share—for 1996, 15.3 percent of the first $62,700 of self-employment earnings and 2.9 percent of additional earnings.

Social Security benefits are based on the worker's *earnings history*. The Social Security Administration keeps detailed records on the earnings history of all workers. It is possible to receive estimates of what your Social Security payments will be at your local Social Security office. Social Security benefits increase on January 1 of each year to account for inflation.

It is possible to begin receiving benefits as early as age 62 although, in general, the longer you wait before receiving benefits, the larger the amount of your check. There is no benefit in delaying receipt of checks beyond age 70.

Benefits can also be reduced in each year (before age 70) that your *earned income* exceeds the Social Security *earnings limitation*. For 1996, Social Security benefits for people from ages 65 to 69 were reduced by $1 for every $3 of earned income over $11,520.

Social Security benefits for people under age 65 were reduced by $1 for every $2 of earned income over $8,280. There is no limitation on the earnings of Social Security recipients who are age 70 or over; they can earn any amount without a reduction in benefits.

For most people, Social Security benefits are not subject to tax, although a portion of the benefits are taxable if the recipient's *gross income* exceeds a specified amount. For 1996, you could have gross income of $25,000 ($32,000 if you filed a joint return) without subjecting your benefits to tax. If your gross income exceeds the applicable amount, up to 85 percent of your benefits could be taxed, depending on the actual amount of gross income. You can obtain information on the taxation of your Social Security benefits from your local Social Security office.

The foregoing represents a general summary of the rules governing the Social Security retirement system. These rules are probably generally familiar to you, although you may not have been aware of some of the specific details of the program.

Less well understood, although equally important in the case of families with children who have disabilities, are the rules relating to Social Security Disability Income and Social Security Dependents' and Survivors' Benefits.

Unfortunately, the rules are very complex. We will summarize them very briefly.

- The Social Security Disability Income program, known as SSDI, is designed to provide worker's protection in the event they become disabled. In general, a worker is considered to be disabled if the worker is unable to engage in substantial gainful activity because of a mental or physical impairment that has lasted or can be expected to last for at least twelve consecutive months. Benefits are based on the worker's earnings history and are payable for as long as the worker is disabled.

- The Social Security Dependents' Benefits program is designed to continue financial support for a worker's *dependents* after the worker reaches retirement age or becomes disabled. Benefits are based on the worker's earnings history and are generally equal to one-half of the worker's retirement or disability benefits, although benefits may be reduced if more than one family member receives payment under the Dependents' Benefit program.

- The Social Security Survivors' Benefits program is designed to provide support for a worker's *dependents* after the worker has died. Payments begin at the death of the worker, and the amount depends on the *category* of the survivor. For example, spouses age 65 or older are generally entitled to the entire amount the worker would have received. Children generally receive a 75 percent share. As in the case of Dependents' benefits, Survivors' benefits may be reduced if more than one family member receives them.

- Survivors' and Dependents' benefits are available to unmarried children under age 18 and to unmarried children of any age who were disabled before age 22. A child with a disability who marries another Social Security recipient generally will not lose benefits if the disability occurred before the child reached age 22. If you are concerned about the effect of a child's marriage on the child's Social Security benefits, you should check with the local Social Security office before the marriage takes place.

- Survivors' and Dependents' benefits may also be available to spouses who are caring for children under age 16 or children who had disabilities before reaching age 22.

- Dependents' benefits are available to spouses age 62 or older. Survivors' benefits are available to spouses age 60 or older, and generally to spouses who are age 50 or older and have severe disabilities.

- A person who receives Dependents' or Survivors' benefits may not receive retirement or disability benefits based on their own earnings record. Thus, a spouse eligible to receive both Dependent or Survivor benefits based on their spouse's earnings record *and* retirement benefits based on their own earnings record, will typically make the selection that results in the largest check.

- If your child's earned income exceeds $500 a month (after deducting the cost of impairment-related work expenses), your child likely will not be considered disabled and therefore may not be eligible for benefits. People with visual impairments can earn greater amounts of income and still be eligible for benefits. Because Social Security is not needs based, unearned income, ownership of property, and earned income of less than $500 a month will not affect eligibility or the size of your child's benefit.

The following examples will help illustrate how these rules work and will enable you to apply them to your own family situation. Examples One and Two illustrate the rules as they apply to the most common situations involving people who have disabilities. Examples Three, Four, and Five illustrate how the rules work in common situations involving the family as a whole.

These examples are not meant to cover all possible situations, and it is possible that you may have questions that are not discussed. If so, you should contact your local Social Security office.

Example One

John and Marlene have worked for many years and are contemplating retirement. They have one child, Mary, who has had mental retardation since birth.

- Because Mary had her disability before age 22, she will be entitled to Dependents' benefits based on her parents' earnings records when the first of them reaches retirement age or becomes disabled. Mary will also be entitled to Survivors' benefits when her mother or father dies. Her monthly check will be equal to approximately one-half of the larger of her parents' checks under the Dependents' Benefit program or three-fourths under the Survivors' Benefit program.

- If Mary lives in a government-funded residential facility, most of her Social Security check will likely be used to pay for room and board. Government-funded residential facilities are discussed below. In the typical case, Mary will be allowed to keep about $30 a month for her personal needs.

- If Mary's Social Security check is below the Supplemental Security Income minimum, Mary may be entitled to Supplemental Security Income as well. As with her Social Security benefits, most of Mary's Supplemental Security Income will be used to pay for room and board (assuming she stays in a government-funded residential facility). The Supplemental Security Income program is discussed below.

Example Two

John and Marlene have worked for many years and are contemplating retirement. They have one child, Fred, who has severe depression. Fred first showed signs of depression at age 22.

- Fred will not be entitled to Social Security Dependents' or Survivors' benefits based on his parents' earnings records because he did not have his disability until after his twenty-second birthday.

- Fred may be entitled to Social Security based on his own earnings' record if he has worked for a long enough period to qualify for Social Security Disability Income benefits. Fred may also be entitled to Supplemental Security Income (discussed below).

Example Three

John and Marlene have worked for many years and are in the process of deciding whether to apply for Social Security benefits. John is 70 years of age and Marlene is 65.

- Both John and Marlene are eligible for Social Security based on their own earnings records. Because John has reached age 70, he should immediately apply for benefits. He can now earn any amount without a reduction in benefits, and further delay will not increase the size of his check.

- Although Marlene is eligible for benefits as well, she has a difficult decision to make. Because she is not yet 70, but is over age 65, her earnings will reduce her benefits by $1 for every $3 by which her earnings exceed the Social Security earnings limitation. In addition, if she waits until age 70 before taking benefits, her monthly check will be higher. She can call her local Social Security office to get an estimate of what the difference will be.

Example Four

John and Marlene have been married for many years. John has earned a substantial living, and Marlene has worked primarily as a homemaker. They have 2 adult children: Mary, who has had severe auditory and visual impairments since birth, and Bob.

- John will be entitled to Social Security based on his earnings record when he reaches retirement age or becomes disabled.

- Mary is entitled to Social Security based on her father's earnings record when her father dies, reaches retirement age, or becomes disabled—exactly as described in Example One.

- Marlene will be entitled to benefits based on John's earnings record if she cares for Mary. If Marlene does not care for Mary, she will be entitled to benefits on John's retirement or disability only when she reaches age 62. She will be entitled to benefits on John's death when she reaches age 60.

- Marlene will be considered to be caring for Mary if she exercises parental control and responsibility for Mary's welfare or if she performs personal services for Mary.

Example Five

John and Marlene have 2 young children: Fred, who has autism, and Julie. John dies in a car accident.

- Fred is entitled to benefits for as long as he has his disability based on his father's earnings record, as described in Examples One and Four.

- Julie is entitled to benefits based on her father's earnings record for as long as she is a minor (under age 18, or 19 if she is still in high school).

- Marlene is entitled to benefits based on John's earnings record if she cares for Fred. If Marlene does not care for Fred, she will be entitled to benefits if she cares for Julie until Julie reaches age 16. Marlene's benefits will be reduced if her earnings exceed the Social Security limitation. (This is true for all people under age 70 who receive Social Security benefits.)

- Marlene will be entitled to benefits based on John's earnings record whether or not she cares for Fred or Julie when she reaches age 60. If Marlene works outside the home, she will develop her own Social Security entitlement record.

Chapter 4

What Is Supplemental Security Income and How Can It Benefit My Child?

The Supplemental Security Income Program, known as SSI, is a *needs based* program designed to supplement the income of people who are elderly, blind, or disabled and lack sufficient resources to provide for their own needs. As with Social Security, it is administered by the Social Security Administration. However, unlike Social Security, it is funded out of general revenues and not from Social Security taxes specifically earmarked for the Social Security program.

Because SSI is needs based, strict income and resource limitations (discussed below) must be satisfied. Disability is defined in the same manner as for the SSDI program. A person is disabled if he or she is unable to engage in substantial gainful activity because of a mental or physical impairment that has lasted or can be expected to last for at least 12 consecutive months or is expected to result in the person's death. Unlike the requirement for Social Security Survivors' or Dependents' benefits, there is no need that the disability occur before age 22.

The SSI Income Limitation

Under the rules of the SSI program, a person who has a disability is denied benefits for any month in which the person's income exceeds the allowable SSI limitation. The limitation is reset each year and is generally equal to the maximum federal benefit under the SSI program ($470 per month in 1996). Importantly, however, certain items of income are excluded from the calculation, including significant amounts of *earned income*. This exclusion is designed to encourage SSI recipients to enter the work force. (See Examples Seven and Eight below.)

SSI defines income very broadly to include anything your child receives, in cash or otherwise, that can be used to provide food, clothing, or shelter. Thus, *income* for SSI purposes includes earned income such as salary, unearned income such as Social Security benefits, pensions, state disability and unemployment benefits, and *in kind* income such as free food, clothing, and shelter.

The following items are specifically excluded:

- The first $20 of most income received in a month.
- The first $65 of earnings received in a month, and one-half of earnings over $65.
- Amounts of earned income used to pay for certain work expenses a person has because of a disability, such as special equipment or transportation costs.
- Income (earned or unearned) that is used to fulfill a plan for achieving self-support. The plan must be written specifically for the individual and must be approved by government authorities.
- The value of food stamps.
- Assistance based on need funded by a state or local government.
- Income tax refunds.
- Small amounts of unearned income (up to $20) received irregularly or infrequently.
- Small amounts of earned income (up to $10) received irregularly or infrequently.
- Food, clothing, or shelter based on need provided by private nonprofit agencies.
- Cash that is loaned and must be repaid.
- Money someone else spends to pay expenses for items other than food, clothing, or shelter. (For example, someone pays your child's telephone bills, airplane tickets, medical bills.)

SSI Limitation Relating to Resources

To qualify for Supplemental Security Income benefits, your child must also satisfy a strict *resource* limitation. For 1996, the limitation for a single person was $2,000 ($3,000 for couples). That is, SSI benefits were denied to anyone whose resources exceeded $2,000 ($3,000 for couples).

SSI defines resources to include cash, liquid assets such as stocks and bonds, and any other items of property that the individual owns and can convert to cash to use for food, clothing, or shelter. The following items are specifically excluded:

- Resources that a person with a disability uses to fulfill an approved plan for achieving self-support. As with the related income exclusion discussed above, the plan must be written specifically for the individual and must be approved by the government.
- A home owned and occupied by the person with a disability.
- Household goods and personal effects with a total market value of less than $2,000 and equipment required because of a recipient's physical condition, regardless of value
- A car up to $4,500 of its current market value. The entire value is excluded if the car is necessary for employment or medical treatment, or if it is modified for your child's use. In some states the car is excluded regardless of value.
- Cash value of life insurance policies up to a death benefit value of $1,500; and burial policies, burial plots, and term insurance policies, regardless of the death benefit.

Deeming of Income and Resources

In determining the resources and income of your child, a portion of your income and resources will generally be considered available to your child if your child lives with you and is under age 18. This process is called deeming and generally disqualifies children who live in families with income above the poverty line from receiving SSI benefits.

Thus, in many cases, children with disabilities who themselves satisfy the income and resource requirements for SSI eligibility are denied benefits because their parents have too much income or too many assets. However, once the child reaches age 18, the parents' assets are no longer considered available to the child; the child then qualifies for benefits so long as he or she has less than $2,000 in resources and less than $470 in monthly income. Remember, these are 1996 figures and may be revised in future years. In addition, significant amounts of earned income are excluded from the calculation.

Calculating Your Child's SSI Benefit

SSI payments vary from state to state; the amount of your child's check will therefore depend on where you live. The basic federal SSI payment for 1996, which is the minimum the states can pay, was $470 a month. The payment is, however, subject to potential reduction by a variety of factors.

- Your child's SSI check for each month will be reduced by one dollar for every two dollars the child earns over $65 during the month. The reduction does not apply if the income is used to pay for work-related expenses attributable to your child's disability or is used to fulfill an approved plan for achieving self-support.

- Your child's SSI benefit will also be reduced for every dollar of unearned income (such as Social Security) the child receives over $20 during any particular month. If your child does not have $20 of unearned income, he or she is allowed to keep an additional $20 of earned income.

- If your child lives in a private household (for example, your home) and doesn't pay a proportionate share of household expenses, the SSI payment is generally reduced by one-third. The theory is that the child needs less since free room and board are available. If your child pays fair rent and a proportionate share of household expenses, the one-third reduction rule generally does not apply. Some parents charge their children rent and a proportionate share of expenses in order to avoid a reduction in benefits. The portion of the payment attributable to rent could, however, be taxable income to the parents.

- If your child lives in a public or private institution where bills are paid from Medicaid funds, monthly SSI benefits will be *substantially* reduced (typically to around $30).

- If your child lives in a public institution that is not funded by Medicaid, SSI is generally available only if the home is designated as an educational or vocational school or a community residence for 16 or fewer individuals.

Example Six

Fred is 15 years old and has cerebral palsy with epilepsy. Fred is enrolled in special education classes at the local high school and lives at home with his parents. Fred's father earns a good living, and Fred's mother takes care of Fred and Fred's brothers and sisters.

- Fred is not entitled to Social Security benefits currently, but he will be entitled to Social Security benefits based on his father's earnings record when his father dies, becomes disabled, or reaches retirement age, as discussed earlier in this chapter.

- Fred will not be entitled to Supplemental Security Income benefits because he will not satisfy the income and resource requirements. Remember, because Fred lives at home and is under 18, a portion of his parents' property is considered to be his under the deeming rules.

- Assuming Fred does not have substantial income or assets of his own, he will likely be entitled to Supplemental Security Income benefits when he reaches 18; the deeming rules will no longer apply.

- If Fred continues to live at home and fails to pay his share of household expenses, his Supplemental Security Income check will likely be reduced by one-third. If Fred lives in a public or private residential facility that is funded by Medicaid, his check will likely be substantially reduced (probably to around $30). If Fred lives in a public residential facility that is not funded by Medicaid, SSI will not be available unless the home is designated as an educational or vocational school or a community residence for 16 or fewer individuals.

Example Seven

Fred is 25 years old and has a moderate cognitive impairment due to head trauma resulting from a motorcycle accident at age 23. Fred has earnings of $510 per month.

- Fred will not be entitled to Social Security based on the earning records of either of his parents because he did not have his disability before attaining the age of 22. Fred will be entitled to Social Security based on his own earnings record when he retires or becomes disabled.

- Fred likely will not be entitled to Supplemental Security Income because he probably will not be considered disabled since his monthly earnings exceed $500 a month. If Fred spends more than $10 per month on impairment-related work expenses (for example, medication to help him work), he will likely be entitled to benefits. Remember, impairment-related work expenses can be subtracted from Fred's earnings for purposes of determining whether Fred earns the $500 threshold amount. Similarly, amounts set aside under an approved plan for achieving self-support will not count.

- If Fred earned just $490 per month, he would be entitled to benefits, though his earnings would result in a reduction in the benefit level. The first $85 of earnings would result in no reduction, and every dollar over $85 would result in a reduction of 50 cents. The reduction would equal $202.50 ($490 minus $85 divided by two). Based on 1996 numbers, Fred's federal SSI benefit, calculated without regard to any state supplement, would be $267.50 ($470 minus $202.50). Fred's benefit would not be reduced to the extent his earnings were used to pay for impairment-related work expenses or to fulfill an approved plan for self-support.

- If Fred lives in a private residence and fails to pay his share of household expenses, his Supplemental Security Income check will be reduced by one-third. If Fred lives in a public or private residential facility that is funded by Medicaid, his check will likely be substantially reduced (probably to around $30). If Fred lives in a public residential facility that is not funded by Medicaid, SSI will not be available unless the home is designated as an educational or vocational school or a community residence for 16 or fewer individuals.

Example Eight

Mary has schizophrenia and has been receiving Supplemental Security Income for many years. Mary is on medication and recently began working at a job that pays $600 per month after a long period of unemployment.

- Mary would not be entitled to receive benefits under the Supplemental Security Income program if she earned $600 at the time of her application, because she would not be considered disabled. However, earnings of more than $500 after Mary has already been receiving benefits under the SSI program will not render her ineligible. (We agree that it makes no sense that you can earn more than $500 after you've been receiving SSI, but not before. But the law is what it is. Work is encouraged after you begin receiving benefits, but apparently not before.) Mary's earnings may trigger a *disability review*, which would be designed to determine whether Mary continues to meet the Social Security disability definition (that is, whether her medical condition has improved).

- Mary's wages will cause a reduction in her benefits of $257.50. The first $85 will result in no reduction, and the remaining $515 will result in a reduction of 50 cents for each excess dollar received. Based on 1996 numbers, Mary's federal SSI benefit, calculated without regard to any state supplement, will equal $212.50 ($470 less $257.50).

- Mary's wages will not result in any reduction to the extent they are used to pay for work-related expenses attributable to her disability or to fulfill an approved plan for self-support.

- If Mary lives in a private residence and fails to pay her share of household expenses, her Supplemental Security Income check will likely be reduced by one-third. If Mary lives in a public or private residential facility that is funded by Medicaid, her check will be substantially reduced (probably to around $30). If Mary lives in a public residential facility that is not funded by Medicaid, SSI will not be available unless the home is designated as an educational or vocational school or a community residence for 16 or fewer individuals.

Example Nine

Fred has Down syndrome and lives in his own apartment, near his brother. He earns $265 a month working as a bagger at the local grocery store. Fred also receives a Social Security check based on his father's work record of $150 a month.

- Fred's SSI check will be reduced by $130 as a result of his receiving Social Security. Remember, unearned income reduces SSI benefits for every dollar over $20. Because Social Security benefits are considered unearned, the first $20 will have no effect on Fred's SSI benefits; the next $130 will cause a reduction.

- Fred's wages will cause a reduction of $100. The first $65 yields no reduction; the next $200 causes a reduction of $100.

Remember, the first $65 of earned income causes no benefit reduction; every dollar over $65 results in a reduction of 50 cents.

- Based on 1996 numbers, Fred's basic federal SSI benefit (not including any state supplement) would therefore equal $240—the $470 basic benefit, less $130, less $100.

- Fred's wages will not result in any reduction to the extent they are used to pay for work-related expenses attributable to his disability or to fulfill an approved plan for self-support. Fred's Social Security check will not cause a reduction in SSI benefits to the extent it is used to fulfill an approved plan for self-support.

- You may have noticed that in Examples Six, Seven, and Eight it was earnings in excess of $85 that resulted in a reduction in benefits, while in Example Nine it was earnings in excess of $65. The difference in this example is that $20 was used to offset the reduction due to receipt of Social Security benefits.

What Is Medicare and How Can It Benefit My Child?

Medicare is a federal health insurance program run by the Social Security Administration. It is designed to pay the cost of health care for people over the age of 65 and for people with disabilities who are under the age of 65 and have been eligible to receive Social Security benefits for at least two years, or who need kidney dialysis treatments or a kidney transplant. It is not necessary that your child actually receive Social Security benefits for two years, only that the eligibility requirements were satisfied.

As with the Social Security programs discussed above, Medicare is non-needs based. Eligibility is based on premiums that the recipient (or a family member) has paid into the program in the form of payroll tax deductions and does not depend on financial need.

The program consists of two parts:

Part A ***(Hospital Insurance)*** provides hospital insurance benefits that help pay for care in hospitals and for related health-care services after leaving a hospital, including skilled nursing or rehabilitation care at facilities that have been certified by Medicare. No premiums are required; benefits are available to eligible persons regardless of ability to pay. However, Medicare generally does not pay the entire cost of a hospital stay, and Medicare beneficiaries are generally required to finance a portion of each hospital bill from a non-Medicare source.

Part B ***(Supplemental Medical Insurance)*** helps cover the cost of medical services such as physician's services and outpatient hospital treatment. To be eligible for Part B, a person must be enrolled in Part A and pay monthly premiums. The government announces the premiums that apply for each year in September of the prior year. For 1996, the premium was $42.50 per month. Premium rates may be increased if program costs rise.

Under Supplemental Medical Insurance, Medicare generally pays 80 percent of the approved charges for doctors' services and the cost of certain other services that are not covered by Part A, after the insured pays a $100 deductible. Many individuals purchase supplementary insurance from another source to pay the 20 percent that Medicare Part B will not cover.

The charts on the following two pages will demonstrate which medical services are covered by Medicare and how the benefits are paid. Further information on Medicare is available from your local Social Security Office.

TABLE OF MEDICARE BENEFITS

Effective after January 1, 1996

MEDICARE BASIC PLAN: HOSPITAL INSURANCE—COVERED SERVICES PER BENEFIT PERIOD (1)			
Service	**Benefit**	**Medicare Pays**	**Person Pays****
HOSPITALIZATION Semi-private room & board, general nursing, & misc. hospital services & supplies.	First 60 days	All but $736	$736
	61st to 90th day	All but $184/day	$184/day
	91st to 150th day*	All but $368/day	$368/day
	Beyond 150 days	Nothing	All costs
POST-HOSPITAL SKILLED NURSING FACILITY CARE In a facility approved by Medicare. A person must have been in a hospital for at least 3 days and enter the facility within 30 days after hospital discharge. (2)	First 20 days	100% of approved amount	Nothing
	Additional 80 days	All but $92/day	$92/day
	Beyond 100 days	Nothing	All costs
HOME HEALTH CARE	Unlimited visits as medically necessary	Full cost of services, 80% of equipment	Nothing for services, 20% for equipment
HOSPICE CARE	Two 90 day periods, one 30-day period (and extensions as necessary)	All, but limit on cost for out-patient drugs & respite care	Limited cost for outpatient drugs & respite care
BLOOD	Blood	All but first 3 pints	For first 3 pints

* 60 Reserve days may be used only once; days used are not renewable.

(1) A Benefit Period begins on the first day a person receives service as an inpatient in a hospital and ends after he or she has been out of the hospital or skilled nursing facility for 60 days in a row.

(2) Medicare and private insurance will not pay for most nursing-home care.

MEDICARE SUPPLEMENT PLAN: MEDICAL INSURANCE—COVERED SERVICES PER CALENDER YEAR

Service	Benefit	Medicare Pays	Person Pays
MEDICAL EXPENSE Physician inpatient & outpatient medical visits, physical & speech therapy, supplies, ambulance, etc.	Medicare pays for medical services in or out of the hospital	80% of approved amount after $100 deductible	$100 deductible plus 20% of balance
HOME HEALTH CARE	Unlimited visits as medically necessary	100% of approved services, 80% of approved amount for durable medical equipment	Nothing for services, 20% for approved amount durable medical equipment
BLOOD	Blood	All but first 3 pints per calender year	For first 3 pints (or replace)

* Once a person has $100 of expense for covered services in 1996, the deductible does not apply to any further covered services for the rest of the year.

** A person pays for charges higher than the amount approved by Medicare unless the doctor or supplier agrees to accept Medicare's approved amount as the total charge for services rendered.

In addition to the copayments and deductibles discussed above, the Medicare program has several limitations that you should be aware of. First, Medicare does not cover the cost of catastrophic health care (that is, the cost of hospitalization for periods outside the normal 90- or 150-day coverage periods). In 1988, Congress enacted the Medicare Catastrophic Coverage Act, which would have greatly expanded coverage for catastrophic conditions. These expanded Medicare services would have been financed by mandatory premiums and taxes to be paid by Medicare recipients themselves, with Medicaid picking up the cost for low-income Medicare recipients. The legislation received a great deal of criticism because of the cost to Medicare recipients and was repealed shortly after enactment.

Second, the Medicare program provides less reimbursement for expenses incurred in treating mental illness than it does for other types of illnesses. Under the Basic Hospital Insurance Plan (Part A), benefits for psychiatric hospital care are subject to a lifetime limit of 190 days. Under the Supplementary Medical Insurance Plan (Part B), out-of-hospital psychiatric services are reimbursed at a 50 percent rate (as opposed to the 80 percent reimbursement rate applicable to other types of medical services).

Finally, Medicare does not pay for the cost of nursing homes, other than for certain skilled nursing facilities.

Despite these limitations, however, the Medicare program can be a valuable financial resource for your son or daughter. In addition, it is possible to purchase supplemental insurance in the private sector to fill certain of the "gaps" in the Medicare program. Before purchasing such insurance, however, you should make sure the gaps covered by the policy you are considering are the ones you are concerned about. You should also consider whether the Medicaid program, in conjunction with Medicare, will be sufficient to meet your child's medical insurance needs. As we will discuss, this depends on the laws in the state in which your child resides.

What Is Medicaid and How Can It Benefit My Child?

Medicaid is a federally sponsored program, administered by the states, to pay medical expenses of low-income individuals. If your child is eligible for both Medicare and Medicaid, Medicaid can be used to supplement the coverage provided by Medicare. For example, Medicaid can be used to pay for expenses that are not covered by Medicare, such as nursing homes, catastrophic illnesses, and the copayments and deductibles required by Medicare.

Because Medicaid is operated by the states, the rules regarding eligibility and the range of services covered vary by state. However, in most states your child will be eligible for Medicaid if he or she qualifies under the SSI program. In addition, even if your child does not initially qualify for Medicaid because of the state's income or asset test (discussed in the section dealing with SSI eligibility), your child may qualify if medical expenses, when subtracted from personal income and assets, would bring the income and assets down to the state's eligibility level. (This is known as the Medicaid "spend down" rule. If medical expenses cause your child to "spend down" resources, your child becomes eligible for the program. The rule has been adopted by most, but not all, of the states.)

Finally, if your child receives SSI but loses eligibility because of an earnings increase, your child generally will retain eligibility for Medicaid until the government determines that he or she can afford private medical insurance. The required amount varies from state to state. Your local Social Security office can tell you what the amount is in your state.

By federal law, Medicaid is required to cover at least the following services:

- Necessary medical services provided by physicians.
- Hospital or skilled nursing-facility care.
- Home health-care services.
- Outpatient or clinical services.
- Independent laboratory and X-ray services.

In many states, Medicaid will also pay for some or all of the following:

- Dental care.
- Medically necessary drugs.
- Eyeglasses.
- Prosthetic devices.
- Care from state-licensed practitioners (such as chiropractors, optometrists, podiatrists, and acupuncturists).
- Physical, speech, and occupational therapy.
- Private duty nursing.
- Diagnostic, preventive, screening, and rehabilitative services.
- Inpatient psychiatric care.

Because the range of available services is different in each state, it is important that you contact the agency responsible for administering the program in your sate. To obtain further information about applying for Medicaid, or to get information about eligibility requirements, contact your local Medicaid office, usually through your state's Department of Public Aid.

What Are Cost-Of-Care Programs and How Can They Benefit My Child?

As mentioned in the first chapter of this book, all states provide funding for group-living facilities for people who have disabilities and lack sufficient funds to provide for their own housing. These facilities, variously known as group homes, or intermediate-care or habilitation facilities, can be funded by the states themselves, by the federal government through the Medicaid program or, as is generally the case, by some combination of state and federal funding.

The rules vary by state. You can obtain information about the facilities in your state by contacting local advocacy organizations, the local governmental agency responsible for dealing with people who have disabilities, or from many of the organizations listed in the Directory of Organizations at Appendix III.

In many cases, the facilities are open to anyone who has a disability that is considered to be sufficiently "serious." However, state or federal funding is generally available only for people who meet certain "needs-based" tests relating to income and assets. These tests are substantially similar to the limitations under the SSI and Medicaid programs (although some states set a higher income level for Medicaid eligibility for people living in Medicaid-funded facilities). People who fail to qualify for state or federal aid are required to pay for room and board from their own funds. The cost can be quite high, sometimes as much as $30,000 per year. People who initially qualify for state or federal aid can sometimes be held liable for current *and* past cost of care if they later receive funds of their own, perhaps through inheritance or as a result of being a beneficiary of a parent's life insurance.

For example, ill-advised parents have willed money to children who have lived in state-funded facilities for many years. More often than not, the state "attaches" the money under a cost-of-care claim. In effect, the parents have made the state a beneficiary under their wills. As discussed in Chapter Six, it is possible to avoid this problem by leaving money to your child in a properly drafted trust.

As mentioned previously, if your child receives SSI before being admitted to a state-funded facility, the SSI payment will be reduced substantially (typically to about $30 a month). This is generally true of Social Security as well. Your child will generally be permitted to keep wages earned in the facility (for example, wages earned at a workshop that is connected to the facility). Wages earned at a job that is not connected to the facility can be claimed by the facility as a cost-of-care liability.

CHAPTER 4

What Other Government Benefits Are Potentially Available To My Child?

State and federal governments also operate certain other programs that can be of help to people who have disabilities. Under the food stamp program, people who lack sufficient resources to provide for their own nutritional requirements are given stamps that can be exchanged for food at the local supermarket. In most cases, people who are eligible for SSI qualify for food stamps as well. Information about the food stamp program can be obtained from your state's Department of Public Welfare or from the Food and Nutrition Service of the United States Department of Agriculture. Your child can apply for food stamps at the local Social Security office.

Your child can also qualify for housing assistance under various programs sponsored by the United States Department of Housing and Urban Development (HUD). One such program, known as Section 8, provides rental assistance for individuals with disabilities who satisfy certain needs based criteria. To qualify, your child must apply for benefits and live in a building that qualifies for Section 8 rental subsidies. This means that the landlord must agree to participate in the program, the building must pass an inspection by the local housing authority, and the landlord cannot charge more than is considered to be "fair" by the government. Rent is then subsidized; your child pays what the government says he or she can afford, and the government pays the rest.

A second HUD-sponsored program, known as Section 202, provides loans directly to organizations that are interested in building residential facilities for people who have disabilities. The homes tend to be small—they're typically built to accommodate from 6 to 8 residents—and the organizations that build them must be operated on a not-for-profit basis and must satisfy the government that the loans will be repaid. Many group homes have been built with assistance under the Section 202 program.

Information about Section 8 and Section 202 can be obtained from the United States Department of Housing and Urban Development or from your local housing authority.

Applying for Benefits

You can apply for benefits under a particular governmental program with the agency responsible for administering the program. For Supplemental Security Income, Medicare, and Social Security, you will need to contact your local Social Security Office. You can obtain the phone number and address of the office closest to you in your telephone directory. To apply for Medicaid, you will need to contact your state's Department of Public Aid.

It is probably a good idea to call the local office before you visit so you can get an idea of what supporting documentation you will need to bring to complete the application. The process can be long and exasperating. Remember, you will be dealing with a huge governmental bureaucracy that is not known for its efficiency, and you should not be too surprised if you have to make several trips or telephone calls before obtaining benefits. You should probably call every couple of weeks after the application is submitted to make sure it doesn't get lost in the bureaucratic maze.

In general, you will need documentation supporting all aspects of a claim for benefits. In applying for Social Security on behalf of your child, you will probably need to bring:

- Your Social Security card (or the number if it is lost).
- Your child's Social Security card or number.
- Proof of your child's age, such as a birth certificate.
- Your child's medical records. If records are not available, you will need a listing of the names and addresses of doctors, hospitals, and clinics that have provided care, and the names and addresses of social workers who have provided assistance.
- Papers showing admission into a residential facility at any time.

- Your income-tax W-2 statements for the previous two years, so your earnings records can be updated.
- A copy of your child's tax W-2 statements (if any) for the last two years.

For Medicaid and Supplemental Security Income, in addition to the documents listed above, you will also need to bring a detailed listing of your child's financial assets, such as bank books, insurance policies, and stock certificates.

You will need to be persistent and patient. If someone at the Social Security office tells you that your child is not eligible for a benefit that you think he or she is entitled to, proceed with the application in a formal, written fashion to get an official determination. Remember, while the people who work for Social Security can be helpful and knowledgeable, they can make mistakes like anyone else.

If your application is initially rejected, you have the right to request that Social Security reconsider your claim. Many people who are initially denied benefits are later granted benefits during the appeal process.

Generally, you have 60 days after you receive a notice of denial to file an appeal. If you miss the appeal deadline, file it anyway. Sometimes the Social Security Administration will waive the deadline if there is a compelling reason for the delay. The appeal must be submitted in writing, either by letter or on a special request form available from your local Social Security office.

There are four stages of hearings:

- Reconsideration (review by the Disability Determination Services staff).
- Administrative Hearing (review by the Social Security Administrative Law Judge).
- Appeals Council (review by the Social Security Appeals Council in Arlington, Virginia).
- Federal Court (review by an independent Federal District Judge).

During the Reconsideration stage, it is a good idea to solicit the advice of a social worker or other advocate who knows the Social Security Act. If you go to an Administrative Hearing, you will probably want to have an attorney represent you. Frequently a denial of benefits will not be reversed until the Administrative Hearing stage, and it is often advisable to appeal up through that level. Some attorneys will handle appeals on a contingency basis (you pay only if they win, and you pay a percentage of what they win).

If you are appealing a reduction or termination of benefits (Social Security conducts periodic reviews to make sure that people who receive benefits remain entitled to those benefits), you can ask to retain your child's current benefits up through the Administrative Hearing stage if the reduction or termination of benefits was medically based (that is, if benefits have been reduced or terminated because Social Security believes your child has recovered from a disability). You must apply in writing to retain benefits within 10 days of hearing from the Social Security office. If your child loses the appeal, your child may have to repay any benefits that were denied. However, you can request that the Social Security Administration waive collection of this money if certain conditions have been met that prove the facts were reported truthfully and that repayment would be detrimental to your child's welfare.

Incomplete documentation is a major cause of denial of benefits. Make sure that your doctor is familiar with the *impairments* as defined by Social Security. If not, send your doctor a copy of the regulations covering "Listed Impairments." Always make photocopies of all the documents you submit to the Social Security office or to any other governmental agency.

Conclusion

As is apparent, the rules relating to government benefits are complex. If, after reading this chapter, you are unable to determine whether your child qualifies under a particular program, go ahead and apply; the worst that can happen is that you will be turned down. You can obtain answers to particular questions that you may have by contacting the Social Security Administration, your state's Public Welfare Department, or a social worker or attorney familiar with governmental benefits.

CHAPTER 5

PLANNING YOUR CHILD'S FINANCIAL FUTURE:

BEYOND GOVERNMENT BENEFITS

EVEN ASSUMING YOUR CHILD MAKES MAXIMUM USE OF THE government benefit programs described in the previous chapter, in most cases government benefits will not be enough to provide the kind of life you will want your child to have. This is because government benefits pay for "eats and sheets" and little else. That is, the government will provide your child with room and board, but it will not provide funds for many of the activities that make life enjoyable and meaningful—vacations with friends and relatives, a meal out, recreational programs at the local YMCA, and all the other activities you listed when you prepared your child's life plan way back in the first chapter of this book.

Moreover, some parents do not expect government programs to be major contributors to their children's financial futures. While these parents tend to keep open the possibility of using government benefits in the future (by leaving money to their children in the types of trusts described in the next chapter), they require a realistic estimate of the cost of private care.

In this chapter we will give you the tools you need to calculate your child's lifetime financial requirements over and above government benefits, and we will provide you with some ideas about how you can arrange your own financial affairs to enable your child to meet those needs.

This is not to say that the amount you leave in trust should necessarily equal the amount you calculate to be required to meet your child's financial needs. None of us are omniscient; the calculations can be only estimates. It is possible that your child's financial needs will grow in the future or that government benefits will be reduced. Either circumstance would likely result in a substantial increase in your child's need for private funds.

Moreover, if you have other children, you will want to be fair to them as well. This is particularly true if your other children will be expected to act as their sibling's advocate in the future. You will not want to create a resentment that could affect a brother or sister's willingness to be helpful. In fact, when parents do decide to leave a disproportionate share of their estate to a child with a disability, we frequently advise the parents to explain their reasoning to their other children in order to avoid resentment. Some parents leave an explanatory note in their Letter of Intent.

Calculating your child's financial requirements can, however, be quite instructive. It not only gives you a sense of what your child will need when you are gone, but it also helps shape your decisions regarding the disposition of your estate and helps you to decide among various investment alternatives. For example, if you find that your estate will not be sufficient to meet your child's needs, you may decide to purchase additional life insurance.

One mistake to avoid. Some parents disinherit a child with a disability, leaving everything to other children with the informal understanding that the other children will look out for their sibling. This can be a disastrous choice.

The relative who receives the extra money to look after the person with a disability might enter a nursing home and be required by the government to spend the money on his or her own care. The person might go bankrupt and be required to give the money to creditors, or get a divorce and be required to split the money with his or her spouse, or die and will the money to others, or simply refuse to spend it on the person with a disability.

It is far better to leave money in trust for the child who has the disability so that a separate fund of guaranteed money is available to the person who really needs it.

Calculating Your Child's Financial Needs

The process is less mysterious than it sounds. Begin by simply calculating the amount you currently spend on your child over and above government benefits. If your child is very young, you will need to estimate what you will be spending when your child is older. You then have to build in a reserve to pay for things that you currently do for free, but which your child may need to pay for after you have died.

The following are examples of some of the major items you will want to think about:

- Advocacy and guardianship costs. Will your child need the services of a professional advocate? If so, you will need to include the cost. If your child will rely on family members, will you want to reimburse them for their time? If not, how about their expenses? For example, a brother or sister may need to travel to visit a sibling; you may want them to be reimbursed for gas or airfare. Such payments may encourage a sibling to take the responsibility more seriously.

- Emergency expenses for medical needs. What kind of reserve will you need to provide for emergency medical and dental needs? Dental care can be a major expense. In some states, Medicaid does not pay the cost of dental care, and adults can incur substantial expenses for items such as root canals, crowns, or periodontal work.

- Capital items. Here we mean infrequent big-ticket items such as a television, VCR, a CD player, or some nice furniture.

The following is a form that we often ask our clients to complete to gain an understanding of the types of expenses that their child's trust may need to finance. You may wish to complete it yourself.

PROJECTED SUPPLEMENTARY COSTS PER MONTH (Current Dollars)

These are expenses that the individual or family normally pays each month after the government benefit programs have paid the basic items.

$ ______ Housing

______ Rent/Month

______ Utilities

______ Maintenance

______ Cleaning Items

______ Laundry Costs

______ Other

$ ______ Care Assistance

______ Live-in

______ Respite

______ Custodial

______ Guardianship/Advocacy (approx. $50-$75 per hr.)

______ Other

$ ______ Food

______ Meals, snacks-home

______ Outside of home

______ Special foods/ gastric tube

______ Other

$ ______ Clothing

$ ______ Furniture

$ ______ Medical/Dental Care

______ General medical/ dental visits

______ Therapy

______ Nursing Services

______ Meals of attendants

______ Evaluations

______ Transportation

______ Medications

______ Other

$ ______ Insurance

______ Medical/Dental

______ Burial

______ Car

______ Housing/Rental

______ Other

$ ______ **Automobile**

______ Payments

______ Gas, Oil, Maintenance

______ Other

$ ______ **Recreation**

______ Sports

______ Special Olympics

______ Spectator Sports

______ Vacations

______ TV/VCR

______ Summer Camp

______ Transportation costs

______ Other

$ ______ **Education, Training, Etc.**

______ Transportation

______ Fees

______ Books

______ Other

$ ______ **Employment**

______ Transportation

______ Workshop fees

______ Attendant

______ Training

______ Other

$ ______ **Personal Needs**

______ Haircuts, Beauty Shop

______ Telephone

______ Cigarettes

______ Church/Temple Expenses

______ Hobbies

______ Books, Magazines, Etc.

______ Allowance

______ Other

$ ______ **Special Equipment**

______ Environmental control

______ Elevator

______ Repair of equipment

______ Computer

______ Audio books

______ Ramp

______ Guide dog/other special animals

______ Technical instruction

______ Wheelchair

______ Other

$ ______ **Emergency Reserve**

TOTAL SUPPLEMENTARY EXPENSES $________

After calculating the total costs required for your child, you are ready to decide how much you will need to put in the trust. Remember, you can wait until after both parents die to fund the trust, though you may want to fund it earlier to make sure money is available for your child in the event financial problems develop in the future.

The calculations are complex, and you may need an accountant, a financial planner, or a specialist in estate planning for families that have children with disabilities to assist you. In general, you will need to build in an inflation factor to account for cost increases over time, and a return rate to account for the investment income that the money in the trust will generate. You will then need to account for taxes that the trust will be required to pay and often a fee to compensate the trustee for services.

For example, suppose you have a child who is 35 years old living in a residential facility that is funded by Medicaid. As discussed in Chapter Four, the government will pay for "eats and sheets," so you do not have to worry about items such as room and board. Suppose that after filling out the worksheets provided above you decide that your child will need $150 in supplemental funds each month—$25 for clothes, $5 for laundry, $10 for dental, $5 for medication, $50 for recreation, $40 for transportation, and another $15 for other personal needs.

If we assume an inflation factor of 4 percent, an anticipated after-tax rate of return of 5 percent on money put in your child's trust, and a life expectancy for your child of another 40 years, the amount that you would need to put in a trust to fund your child's supplemental needs over and above what the government provides would be $60,000. If the expenses increase to $400 a month, perhaps to cover advocacy and trustee fees if you do not have friends or family members who live nearby and are willing to help for free, the required amount increases to $160,000.

Of course, this does not mean that you should put exactly $60,000 or $160,000 in your child's trust. You are not likely to die on the date you prepare your estate plan so the trust may not have to fund your child's requirements for 40 years. Moreover, the assumptions about inflation and rate of return may not be accurate. You will also need to consider the possibility that government benefits could be reduced, which would increase your child's need for funds considerably. Finally, you will want to factor in the need to be fair to other children and the presence of other sources of income that may be available to your child such as earnings from employment, Social Security, or Supplemental Security Income.

Obviously, deciding how much to put in your child's trust is not an exact science. However, the calculation described above can help you gain a *reasonable* understanding of what may be required.

Developing Your Financial Plan

Now that you have an idea what you will need to put in your child's trust, what can you do to make sure you will be able to fund it? The key is to develop a comprehensive financial plan that will enable you to leave enough for your child to meet his or her financial needs.

Assistance is available from many sources. In many areas of the country there are private organizations that specialize in estate planning for families with children who have disabilities. Many of these organizations include financial planning as part of a package that includes counselling the family on the development of a life plan for their child and the drafting of wills and trusts. Often the cost is no more than the cost of a will from a typical estate planner.

It is also possible to obtain advice from financial planners. However, you should be sure to choose an advisor who has experience in dealing with families that have members who have disabilities, so that the planner will be familiar with the special problems that such families encounter. You may be able to get some names from local advocacy organizations or from some of the organizations listed in the Directory of Organizations at the end of this book.

Whoever you do select (assuming you select anyone)—some people have faith in their own investment decisions—you should always feel free to question specific financial advice you are given. If you feel uncomfortable with a pending financial decision, talk to specialists in the field before deciding how you wish to proceed. For example, if your advisor suggests that you buy stocks, you might check with several financial planners, comparing their ideas, before accepting any one particular approach. By doing so, you will not only receive a variety of specific financial advice but will also receive general background information likely to help you decide which types of investment are best for you.

Even after hiring an advising firm and learning to work with a particular advisor, you should not lose track of your investments. Watch how each investment opportunity responds to various economic changes. You know your own needs better than any outside advisor and, although you should carefully listen to advice, final decisions about financial matters should always be yours.

One key to a successful financial plan is accurate knowledge of where your money comes from and where it goes. Filling out the forms on the next two pages may help you visualize your current financial status and your future goals. The forms may be reproduced for your convenience.

PERSONAL INCOME STATEMENT

	CURRENT	PROJECTED 1 YEAR	PROJECTED 2 YEAR
ANNUAL INCOME			
Salary & Wages	________	________	________
Interest & Dividends	________	________	________
Capital Gains	________	________	________
Other Income	________	________	________
1. Total Annual Income	________	________	________
EXPENSES			
Housing	________	________	________
Debt Repayment	________	________	________
Insurance	________	________	________
Transportation	________	________	________
Medical	________	________	________
Education/Training	________	________	________
Food	________	________	________
Clothing	________	________	________
Repairs/Utilities	________	________	________
Recreation	________	________	________
Furnishings	________	________	________
Gifts/Contributions	________	________	________
Income Taxes	________	________	________
Property Taxes	________	________	________
Self-Employment Taxes	________	________	________
Social Security Taxes	________	________	________
Other Expenses	________	________	________
2. Total Annual Expense	________	________	________

FAMILY BALANCE SHEET

Assets

Residence $________

Other real estate $________

Bank Accounts $________

Retirement accounts $________

CD's $________

Annuities $________

Stocks, securities $________

Business interests $________

Other assets $________

Liabilities

Mortgage debt $________

Other debt $________

Current Net Worth (current assets less current liabilities) **$** _______

Life Insurance

Death Benefit $________

Premiums $________

Cash Value $__________(can be included in net worth)

Potential Inheritances $ ______

The following are some ideas that may help you build an estate large enough to enable you to meet your family's special needs. You should not assume that any of the approaches is necessarily appropriate for you. Each person's financial situation is unique and necessarily involves an investment strategy consistent with individual circumstances.

Using Insurance to Provide Security

There are two basic risks you will want to protect against: (i) the financial insecurity resulting from your death or the death of your spouse (this is typically covered with life insurance), and (ii) the financial insecurity resulting from injury or illness (this can be covered with disability insurance). While it is typical to buy life insurance, disability insurance tends to be overlooked. This is unfortunate, since at most ages your chance of becoming disabled is greater than your chance of dying.

Insurance decisions are complicated because needs are hard to assess (as you know by now) and because insurance policies (i.e., contracts and their options) are extremely complex. It is therefore important that you shop carefully and find experts who you trust and upon whom you can rely. As you are no doubt aware, several different types of life insurance are available.

Term Insurance

Term insurance offers insurance for a set period of time—one year, five years, or longer. It is the least expensive type of policy, with the cost depending on your current age and health.

Term insurance will pay benefits to the beneficiary only if the insured dies during the term of coverage. What if you become seriously ill just as your coverage expires? You would be unlikely to qualify medically for a new policy. To avoid this problem, you can pay extra to include a guaranteed renewable option.

Term insurance is a good option for young parents in good health. However, as your age increases, each new term becomes more expensive. The cost can become prohibitive for people in their 60's. To avoid this problem, you can purchase convertible term insurance, which gives you the choice of converting to a permanent type of insurance up until a stated age (such as 65), without presenting evidence about your health. Term insurance, unlike whole life or universal insurance, does not build up a cash value.

Universal and Whole Life Insurance

Although more expensive than term insurance, universal life insurance and whole life insurance offer certain advantages. Both universal life insurance and whole life insurance, unlike term insurance, cover the insured for an entire lifetime. Premiums are generally paid at a flat rate annually until the death of the insured, or over a limited period, say 10 or 20 years ("limited payment insurance"). Insurance coverage remains in effect as long as the obligations specified in the insurance contract are satisfied.

Because the premium payments made during the early years of the policy exceed the cost of insurance protection, the policy builds a cash value. In the case of universal life insurance, the rate at which the cash value grows depends on the investment returns earned by the insurance company. In the case of whole life insurance, the rate of growth is stated in the insurance contract and is guaranteed so long as the insurance company remains solvent. This cash value can be used in several ways. You can borrow it from the insurance company, often at very low interest rates, and if you fail to pay back the loan, the insurance company will deduct the outstanding amount (including interest) from the proceeds of the policy. It is also possible to use the cash value to pay premiums or to purchase new policies. Most policies even pay dividends which can also be applied to premiums. One of the unique advantages of the cash value is that it grows tax free. When the insured dies, there is generally no income tax due (on either the cash value or the death benefit). However, the death benefit is calculated in for estate-tax purposes unless the insurance is placed in an irrevocable life insurance trust (see Chapter Nine).

Universal insurance and whole life insurance also assure parents of children who have disabilities that they will always be insured (assuming premiums are paid). Moreover, premiums for such insurance can be set at a flat rate that will not increase as the insured gets older. This is especially important during retirement years, when people are often living on a fixed income.

One method used by some of our clients to pay for a life insurance policy is to set up the premium payments so they will vanish over 8 to 10 years. This type of payment plan is often referred to as a "vanishing premium" plan. Clients who want to pay off their insurance policy before retirement often choose this type of payment plan. This enables Mom and Dad to retire worry free, not always having to worry that every dollar they spend on their retirement will deprive their child of future security.

Some of our clients even place insurance policies into irrevocable special needs trusts for a child with a disability. In essence, the trust is both the owner and the beneficiary of the policy. This enables the parents to guarantee that there will be money in trust for their child, assuming premiums are paid. If Mom or Dad go into a nursing home or get into financial difficulty, the policy is safe from creditors because the trust, and not Mom or Dad, own it. The disadvantage to this approach is that parents lose control over the policy; they can no longer use the cash value or change beneficiaries.

Joint Policies

Another form of life insurance popular among parents who have children with disabilities is commonly referred to as the "second-to-die policy" or a "joint life" policy. This policy pays a death benefit after both of the insureds, usually the mother and father, die. Because this policy pays only after two people die, the premiums are significantly less expensive.

This type of life insurance is used most frequently when there is already enough in the way of assets to provide for the surviving spouse. The joint life policy is generally used to buy less-expensive insurance specifically to provide extra support for the child with a disability. The beneficiary of the policy is frequently a special needs trust created for the child with a disability. (See Chapter Six.)

It is also possible to buy joint "first-to-die policies," which pay at the death of the first of the insureds. Because only one person has to die before the death benefit becomes due, premiums tend to be higher.

A final point. If you do purchase life insurance, you will want to make sure that a child with a disability is not a beneficiary or owner. As you may recall, putting assets in the hands of your child could affect eligibility for Medicaid and SSI and could also result in a state claim for cost-of-care liability. You will also want to make sure that the company issuing the policy is on solid financial footing.

Frequently, you will want to make your spouse the primary beneficiary, with your children who do not have disabilities and a trust for your child who has a disability serving as contingent beneficiaries. That is, your children without disabilities and the trust for your child who has a disability would receive the insurance proceeds if your spouse dies before you. If you use a living trust as part of your estate plan, you will want the trust to serve as beneficiary. Sometimes you will even want your estate to serve as beneficiary. These matters are all discussed in detail in the next three chapters of the book.

Medical Insurance

The cost of medical care can be a major item of expense for your child; therefore, obtaining quality medical insurance can be an important way of providing for your child's supplemental needs. As discussed in the previous chapter, Medicaid and Medicare can help. However, these programs suffer from limitations. Medicare has various copayments and deductibles, and is not helpful for long hospital stays. Medicaid plans differ from state to state; some states are less generous than others. Finally, some physicians do not accept Medicaid patients.

The Association for Retarded Citizens of the United States offers a special "hospital dollars" medical insurance program to its members and their dependents; this can be a good method of supplementing government medical benefits. The program provides up to $200 a day for each day spent in a hospital for a period of up to 365 days. Arc also offers a Medicare group supplement plan to help your child with copayments and deductibles. (If your child receives both Medicaid and Medicare, this help may not be necessary because Medicaid will likely make the copayments.) Medicare supplemental policies are also available from most major insurance carriers.

If your child has a job, medical insurance may be offered as part of the compensation package. During your lifetime, coverage may be provided through your own policy. Many insurance plans cover children who have disabilities even after the children turn 19, so long as the child remains unmarried, lives at home, and is dependent on you, and so long as the insurer is properly notified. However, when your policy lapses (for example, at your death or upon retirement if your insurance is provided through your job), coverage of your child will likely cease as well.

In addition, if you change jobs you will need to make sure your child's disability does not disqualify the child from coverage. Some insurers treat certain types of disabilities as *disqualifying preexisting conditions*. Individual policies differ widely, and you will need to check with your own insurance carrier to determine the extent to which your existing policy covers your child.

It is usually difficult for a person with a disability who is not employed to secure individual coverage. Illinois has championed an innovative medical insurance program for people with disabilities who have been rejected by private companies. The program is called the Comprehensive Health Insurance Plan (CHIPS), and provides coverage, underwritten by major insurance companies, to people with disabilities who have been rejected by private insurance companies. Because of the increased risk of coverage, however, premiums can be expensive. Hopefully this program will be duplicated in other states.

Investments

Choosing a proper investment strategy is important for several reasons. In an inflationary society, the cost of goods increases over time, and an adequate investment return will be necessary to prevent erosion of savings. Moreover, it is often possible to earn investment returns that exceed the rate of inflation. This can result in an increase in your real net worth.

In this section we discuss some of the investment vehicles that are available to you, and we make some general comments to help you choose among them. The section is by no means intended to be a complete guide to investment strategies.

To begin, we limit ourselves to discussing some of the more common types of investments such as stocks, mutual funds, money markets, bonds, treasury bills, and certificates of deposit. We say nothing about more esoteric investments such as real estate, real estate investment trusts, limited partnerships, options, commodities, futures, precious metals, coins, and collectibles. These more esoteric investments tend to be used by experienced investors only, and such investors will have their own financial advisors or will themselves be familiar with these instruments.

Moreover, investment decisions tend to be very personal—what is right for one person is not necessarily right for another. The proper investment strategy for you will depend on such factors as your tolerance for risk, the size of your estate, and your need for liquidity.

Used properly, however, this section can be very useful to you. It can provide you some of the background information you need to talk to your financial advisor and can also give you some of the information you need to develop your own investment strategy.

Much of the information discussed below is very technical, and you may have to read it several times before you understand it. If you do not own a substantial amount of property, much of this will not pertain to your situation and you should feel free to move on to the next chapter.

Stock Investments

Many people associate financial planning primarily with investment in the stock market. This is not the only investment source, but it can be used to advantage if the investor has enough money and time to spend at it. A wise stock investor will *diversify*, spread risk over a variety of stocks. Such a diversified *stock portfolio* lowers the investor's risk because if some stocks decrease in value, others may increase, thereby creating an overall profit, or at least offsetting losses.

A small investor who can buy only a few stocks and who cannot diversify is at a disadvantage. If a particular stock drops in value, the small investor has few other stocks to offset the loss. Small-scale investment in the stock market is rarely profitable enough to justify the long hours that must be spent analyzing stock values.

Mutual Funds

As an alternative to individual stock investments, many firms offer *mutual funds*, which permit people who have similar investment goals to pool their money and, in effect, own shares in a professionally managed, diversified portfolio. The investor purchases shares in the fund (which itself owns shares in other companies) and earns income or incurs losses as the stocks owned by the fund pay dividends or increase or contract in value. Because the funds are managed by professional investors, the fund shareholder receives the benefit of professional investment advice. (The manager is generally compensated by the fund, which reduces the investor's return.)

Shareholders may cash in some or all of their shares at any time. In the case of *closed end funds*, which are actually traded on a stock exchange, such transactions are accomplished on the open market; the seller sells shares of the fund for their market price. In the case of *open end funds*, the fund itself redeems shares for their current *net asset value* (the amount of the original investment plus or minus the amount the shares have earned or lost).

There is a wide variety of mutual funds, and each operates under different investment policies. There are *load funds*, which charge investors a premium to enroll, and *no load funds*, which do not. Although the absence or presence of an enrollment premium is one factor to consider in making your selection, do not automatically assume that no load funds are preferable. Fidelity Magellan, one of the best performers of the 1980's, is a load fund.

When choosing a mutual fund, you should base your selection on the fund's investment policy (what kinds of stocks or other vehicles does it buy and what criteria are used for selecting securities), the experience of the manager, the turnover rate of the portfolio (excessive trading tends to be bad), the expense ratio of the fund, the absence or presence of a *load* or of fees on redemption, and other qualitative factors.

You will also want to make sure that the fund manager's investment strategy is consistent with your own approach. Different funds emphasize different types of investments, and you will want to select a fund or funds that fit your own investment style. Two examples of different types of mutual funds are "growth funds" and "income funds." Investors in a growth fund are generally looking for long-term growth. However, because a growth company's profits will be reinvested to help it expand, the growth fund investor should not expect significant dividends over the short run. On the other hand, investors in income funds seek current income, but generally cannot expect as much long-term increase in their stock prices. In accordance with this goal, managers of income funds buy stocks likely to pay high dividends.

One common mistake is to place undue reliance on short term performance. Several studies have indicated that past success of a fund is not a reliable indicator of future results. Consistently poor results, however, can indicate that a fund is not well managed.

A mutual-fund investor's profit depends on the value of the stock held by the fund and the dividends paid. Although investment managers study both factors to ensure wise investments, they cannot guarantee their management performance. There is always some risk of loss. Government security mutual funds provide an exception to this risk. Those who invest in a mutual fund that holds U.S. government securities take little risk with regard to repayment of principal because the securities held by the fund are backed by the United States government, though the value of the securities will decline if interest rates increase. In such a case you will suffer a loss if you are forced to sell your interest in the fund on the market or have the fund redeem it.

Information about mutual funds is available from many sources. Many discount brokerage firms will provide you with long-term information about funds that they sell. In addition, in the reference section of most libraries you can find a book called *Investment Companies* (Arthur Wiesenberger Services, New York), which will provide you with some basic information on specific funds. It will also give addresses where you may write for more information, including a prospectus. Using a resource like *Morningstar*, which rates various mutual funds, can also be helpful. *Morningstar* can be found in most public libraries.

Bonds

A bond is a certificate of creditorship that is issued to raise capital. The issuer pledges to pay interest on a bond at specified dates and to redeem it at maturity, repaying principal plus interest due. Bonds also may be sold before maturity at their current market value, which is determined by prevailing interest rates and the company's credit worthiness. Corporate bonds are usually issued in increments of $1,000.

With bonds, as with stocks, it is difficult for a small investor to diversify. Diversification is important in reducing overall risk. With bonds backed by the U.S. government, such diversification is not necessary because there is no risk involved, as long as the government remains solvent. However, the higher yielding corporate bonds are only as good as the issuing corporation's ability to repay.

Therefore, for relative safety, a small investor interested in corporate bonds may want to consider a corporate bond mutual fund; like the stock mutual funds discussed above, these permit the investor to participate in diversified bond portfolios. Make sure you pick the right fund—some funds invest in high yielding corporate bonds (so-called junk bonds). While these funds can be profitable, they can also be risky, and you should be careful before investing in them. Some bond funds specialize in municipal obligations, which yield a relatively safe, partially tax-free return (they're not taxed by the federal government, but often are taxed by the states and localities). Again, as with the stock funds above, you may redeem your shares at any time.

Before investing in corporate or municipal bonds, you should consider checking one or more of the rating systems, such as Moodys or Standard & Poors. These firms rate obligations based on the financial wherewithal of the issuer.

Money Market Funds

Just as mutual fund investors jointly invest in stocks or bonds, money market fund investors pool their dollars to invest in money market instruments such as commercial paper, banker's acceptances, and treasury bills. Because these money market instruments are sold at a minimum face value of $10,000, the small investor cannot invest in these instruments except through a money market fund.

Most funds require a $1,000 minimum investment. The shareholder need not wait for individual instruments held by the fund to "mature" before providing investment returns to the fund-holder. Money may be withdrawn at any time. Many funds offer wire redemption services and $500 minimum check writing privileges. When interest rates are high, investment in a money market fund provides high returns. For these reasons, money market instruments can be attractive to investors seeking a reasonable return on liquid investments. When interest rates are low, however, money market funds are less attractive. High bracket investors will want to consider tax-exempt money market funds.

Certificates of Deposit

A certificate of deposit is an interest-bearing bank receipt payable on a specific future date. Certificate of deposit interest rates are set each Tuesday, based on the yield of treasury bills auctioned the day before.

Certificates of deposit that are issued by banks insured by the Federal Deposit Insurance Corporation (FDIC) are insured for up to $100,000 per depositor. However, only the principal is insured, not the interest. The rate of return on a certificate of deposit varies depending on its maturity date, its size, and the creditworthiness of the issuer.

Annuities

Under an annuity plan, an individual contracts to pay the issuer (typically an insurance company) either a lump sum or a series of premium payments in exchange for the company's promise to periodically pay the person a specific amount for life. In most annuity contracts, if the annuitant should die before age 65, the insurance company agrees to pay either the accumulated gross premiums or the cash value of the policy to the annuitant's beneficiary.

A major attraction of annuities is that they grow tax free. The amount invested with the insurance company is not taxed until cash is received by you, and returns can therefore be quite favorable. Annuity contracts are not insured by the government, so you should investigate carefully to make sure that any company you invest with is on solid footing.

The annuity investor or annuitant may choose among several types of contracts, including *fixed-dollar annuities*, variable *annuities*, and *joint* and *last survivor annuities*. Under fixed-dollar annuity contracts, the company periodically pays the annuitant a fixed sum for a definite length of time agreed to in the contract. Under this plan, the annuitant always knows how much money will be received from the insurance company for a particular period.

Under a variable plan, the annuitant receives payments that will vary. The insurance company combines money from numerous premium payments and invests it, often in common stock. The annuitant's income varies with the success of the investment, increasing and decreasing with the value of the stocks. At some investment risk, an investor in a variable plan has the chance of receiving larger annuity payments.

Under joint and last survivorship annuities, payment is made to the first annuitant at regular intervals for life. After the first annuitant dies, the second receives payment. Contracts for this type of annuity are more expensive than those covering only a single life because the insurance company would probably be making payments for a longer period of time than it would if the contract covered only one person. For those eager to provide greater security for family members who survive the family wage earner, joint and last survivorship annuities, though more expensive, should be considered.

Retirement Plans

Tax-deferred retirement plans are excellent vehicles for increasing investment return. These include 401(k) plans, Keoughs, IRAs, profit sharing plans, defined benefit pension plans, and other defined contribution pension plans. You should check with your employer or your tax advisor regarding your ability to participate.

The major benefit of a retirement plan is that earnings are not taxed until cash is actually withdrawn. Under the current rules, you do not have to begin taking distributions until April 1 of the year following the year you reach age seventy and a half. In addition, amounts that you contribute into such plans are generally deductible for income tax purposes. This also has the effect of increasing investment return.

The major disadvantage of a retirement plan is that you can lose liquidity. The plan may not allow you to receive distributions before you terminate employment, and the federal government will generally impose a 10 percent excise tax on distributions which you receive before age 59 and a half, in addition to regular income tax.

Developing an Investment Strategy

No single investment strategy is right for everyone. People differ in earning power, tolerance for risk, and their need for liquidity. All these differences legitimately affect investment decisions.

In deciding how to invest your money, first think about the factors and objectives that affect your finances. Consider your age, present and potential earning power, number and age of dependents, net worth, tax bracket, and other financial data. Think clearly about your family's housing needs, educational goals, and so forth.

Think about your need for liquidity. How often and how urgently would you need to draw on your invested money? A *liquid investment* is one that can be quickly and easily converted to cash. Funds invested in a nonliquid way are inaccessible to the investor for a specified period of time. For example, if you plan to buy a house soon, you should not invest potential down-payment funds in a 30-month savings certificate which cannot, without penalty, be converted to cash for at least 30 months. Instead, you could invest those funds in a highly liquid money market fund, which gives you the option of withdrawing your funds at any time. On the other hand, if you are planning for the future of a child with a disability, you might be willing to tie up your money in a long-term investment if it provides a better return.

Think about risk. How much can you afford to lose? Generally, the higher the potential return, the greater the risk. While everyone desires a large return, clearly not everyone can afford to take large risks. A young couple with a modest income, a mortgage on a new house, and small children should be more cautious with their money than a single person with a higher income and fewer obligations.

To provide some benchmark for what can be expected from various investments, it is helpful to examine historical returns—although, of course, past performance is not a guarantee of future returns. The charts on page 203 and 204 may be helpful. Chart 1 depicts year-by-year returns from 1900 through 1995 of common stocks, taxable investment grade bonds, and U.S. treasury bills. As is apparent, stocks have yielded the best average returns, averaging 11.7 percent annually. This should be compared with a 5.7 percent return for bonds and a 4.1 percent return for treasury bills.

However, stocks have also been riskier. There have been many years in which stocks have gone down in value, sometimes by significant amounts. This suggests that stocks are a good investment for people who can invest their money for long periods of time and can afford to lose money over short-term periods but would not be good as a short-term investment or for people who would have difficulty dealing with losses.

Chart 2 is similar to Chart 1, except that it looks at historical returns over 20-year rolling periods (for example, 1945-1964, 1946-1965, and so on). Chart 2 reveals that over longer periods, there were very few when bonds outpaced stocks. All four 20-year periods where this occurred included part of the Great Depression. If the future resembles the past, most long term investors would do well to keep a sizable portion of their assets in common stocks, assuming they can deal with short term losses.

As a general rule, depending on a client's earning power, assets, and tolerance for risk, we tend to prefer a diversified approach, with a certain percentage of assets invested in stocks (often through mutual funds to diversify within the market), a certain percentage invested in bonds (also through mutual funds), and a certain percentage in money markets, annuities, and certificates of deposit. We advise against trying to "time the market"— that is, guessing when the market is going up or down, due to the difficulty involved. We also discourage excessive trading to cut down on commissions.

The most important investment decision you will make is the fraction of your wealth you allocate to each of these major asset categories. There is no scientific way to determine this fraction, although historical returns can help you understand the trade-offs. A study by a University of Chicago professor some years ago estimated that 80 percent of a portfolio's return owes to the asset allocation of the portfolio; that is, asset diversification is much more important than security selection within an asset class.

One indispensable way to assess asset class risk is to examine historical results. If a planner or advisor suggests allocating, say 40 percent of your assets to stock mutual funds and 60 percent in bond mutual funds, find out how that allocation would have performed over the past twenty years.

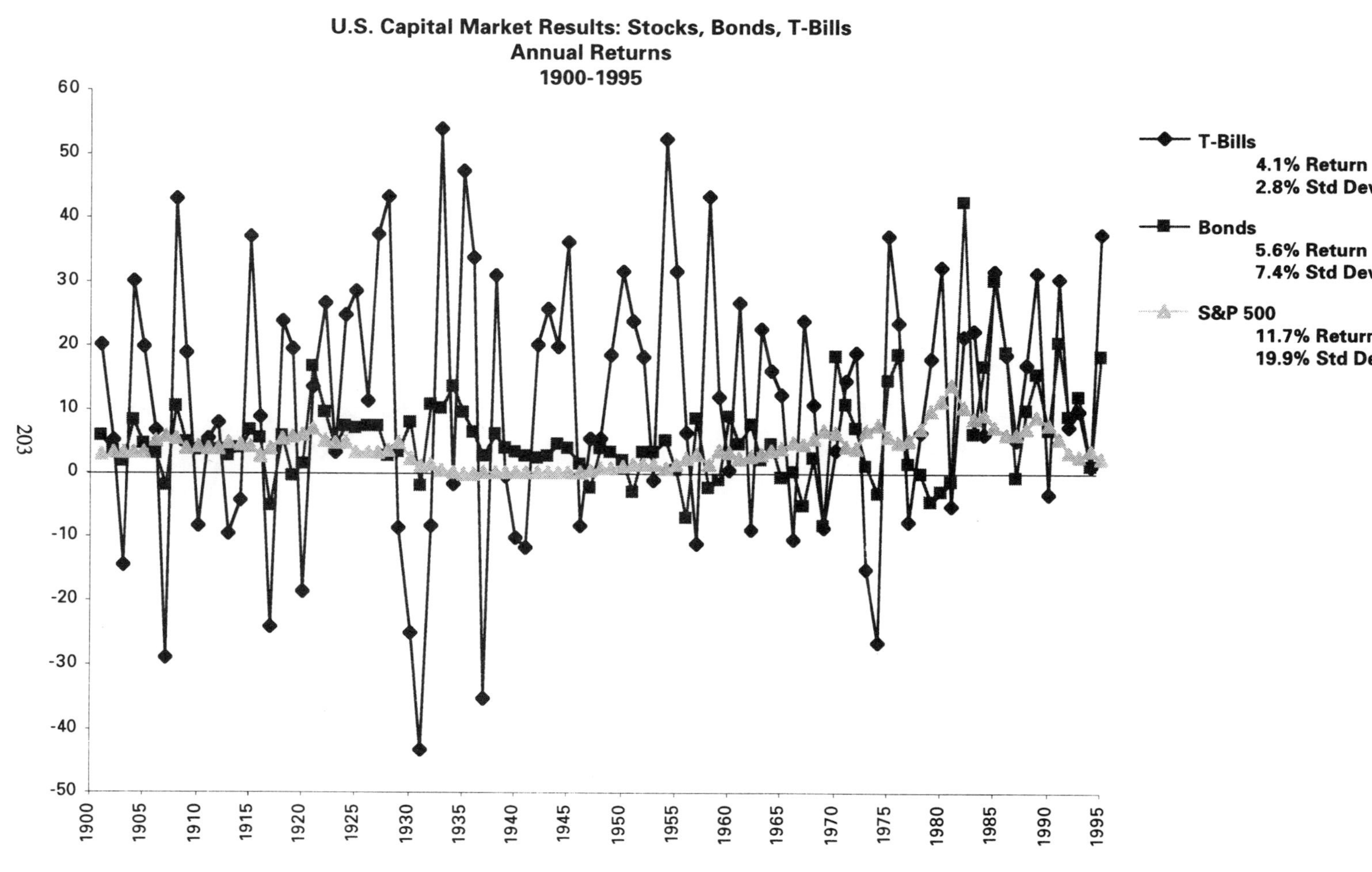

U.S. Capital Market Results: Stocks, Bonds, T-Bills
Annual Returns
1900-1995
T-Bills
4.1% Return
2.8% Std Dev
Bonds
5.6% Return
7.4% Std Dev
S&P 500
11.7% Return
19.9% Std Dev
60
50
40
30
20
10
0
-10
-20
-30
-40
-50
1900
1905
1910
1915
1920
1925
1930
1935
1940
1945
1950
1955
1960
1965
1970
1975
1980
1985
1990
1995

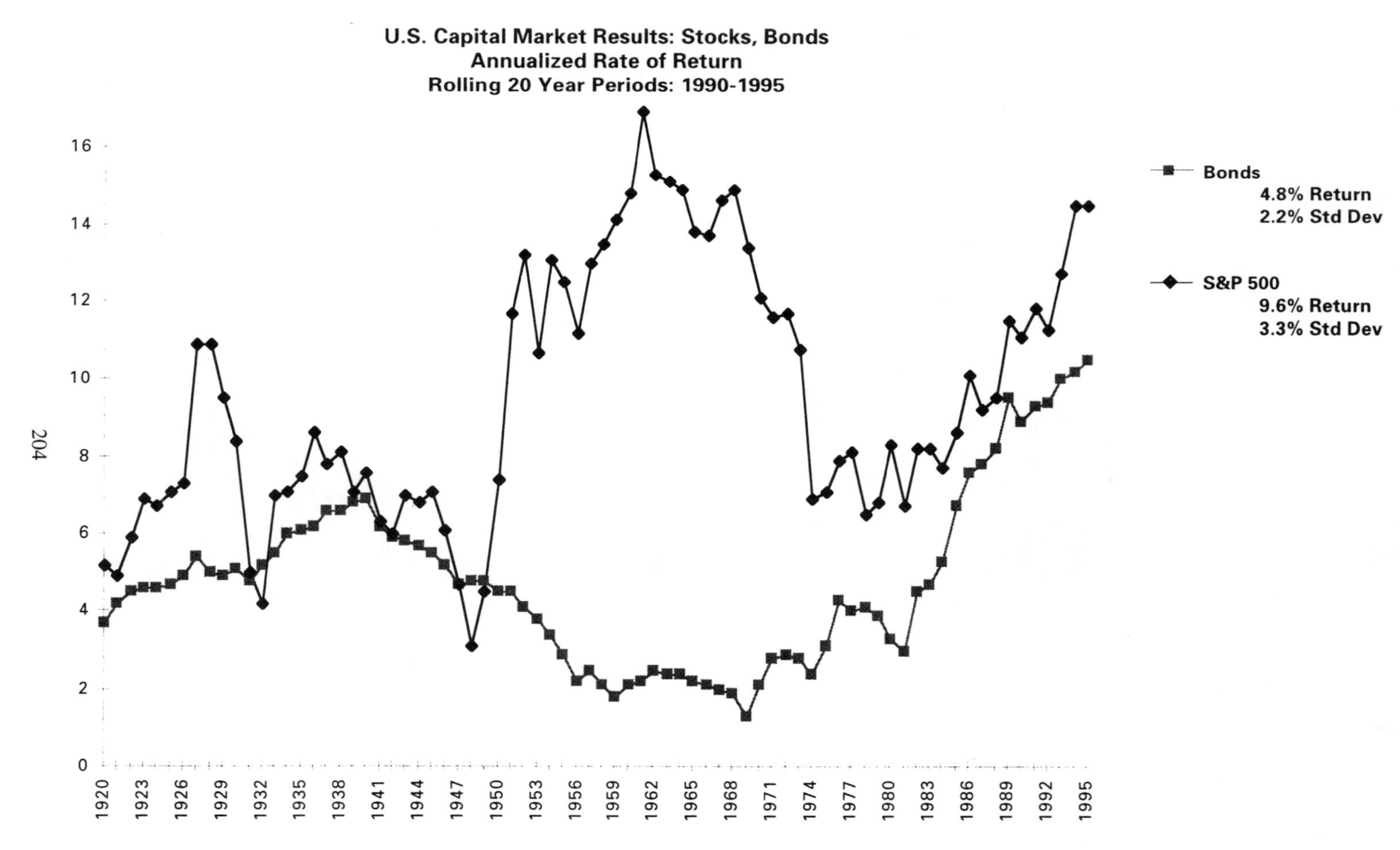

U.S. Capital Market Results: Stocks, Bonds
Annualized Rate of Return
Rolling 20 Year Periods: 1990-1995
Bonds
4.8% Return
2.2% Std Dev
S&P 500
9.6% Return
3.3% Std Dev

Don't rely on unusual performance. If a particular fund did much better than the average fund or the S&P 500 over a period, don't assume the above average performance will continue. Use the average fund or some index to project performance.

Also, you should not rely exclusively on historical performance. Ask your planner or advisor what your worst case scenario is likely to be. The answer to such questions should provide a good idea of the risks the plan carries. Having said that, every plan, even annuities and CD's, carry some risk. Your job, as an investor, is to make sure the risk is reasonable in light of anticipated returns and alternative investment strategies.

CHAPTER 5

CHAPTER 6

THE BASIC ESTATE PLAN:

THE WILL AND THE SPECIAL NEEDS TRUST

REMEMBER WAY BACK IN THE INTRODUCTION OF THIS BOOK, WHEN we told you that estate planning for families with children who have disabilities is different from other types of estate planning? Well, we've completed the first five chapters of this book and have said almost nothing about wills and trusts, which is where estate planning generally begins.

In this chapter we discuss the basic estate plan, consisting of a will, which you can use to control how your property is to be distributed when you die, and a special needs trust, which will generally be used to receive the property you intend to leave for your child.

The Role of a Will in Your Estate Plan

Nobody likes to think about writing a will because it is an acknowledgment of death. But writing a will is essential if your property is to be distributed the way you intend it. If you do not write a will or if you have a legally invalid will, you will lose control over your entire estate plan.

In general, a will serves three vital functions. First, it permits you to name a guardian for your minor children in the event you and your spouse die before your children reach adulthood. As discussed in Chapter Three, you cannot name a guardian for an adult child in your will even if the child has a disability. The law presumes that adults are competent unless they are found to be incompetent in a guardianship hearing. In most states, however, you can nominate a successor guardian for an adult child if you have previously been appointed guardian in a guardianship hearing.

In addition, you can appoint a guardian to act for your minor children, both those who have disabilities and those who do not. The factors to consider in deciding whom to select have been discussed in Chapter Three. Obviously, you will want someone who cares for your children and can be expected to do a good job in raising them. The guardianship is effective until your children become adults; that is, in most states, until they reach age 18.

Second, a will permits you to select the person who will be responsible for doing the administrative tasks that will need to be performed when you die. This person is known as the *executor* of your estate or, in some states, as your *personal representative*. In general, the executor will be responsible for paying your debts (including burial expenses) and for collecting your assets and distributing them in accordance with the provisions contained in your will.

In many cases your executor will be required to submit your will for validation in a court of law in a process known as *probate*, which is the legal process for determining whether your will is valid. The probate system is discussed in the next chapter.

In most cases our clients tend to appoint their spouse as executor, with close relatives such as siblings or adult children acting if the spouse cannot. It is expected that the executor will get aid from an attorney if needed.

Third, a will permits you to decide how your property is to be distributed when you die. In general, you can leave your property to whomever you want, except that most states permit your spouse to insist on a fractional share of your estate (typically one-third) if your spouse does not receive a larger share by will. Your spouse can waive this right in a prenuptial or postnuptial agreement. These rights are also forfeited on divorce or, in some states, if you and your spouse are separated.

Most of our clients tend to leave all their property to their spouse, or to their children (in specified shares) if their spouse dies before them. It is also possible to leave certain pieces of property to a particular individual (perhaps jewelry to your daughter). These are known as specific bequests and are a common way of disposing of personal property. It is best not to go overboard with specific bequests, as things tend to work better if your heirs divide personal property as they choose. However, specific bequests can be a useful way of disposing of property that has sentimental value.

Often our clients write down their wishes about the disposition of their personal property in a separate memorandum, which they keep with their other important papers. Although not legally binding in all states, this permits clients to tell their executor who should get which pieces of property. Because the list is not a part of the will, it can be changed without need of an attorney. Changes to your will typically have to be prepared by your lawyer.

One mistake to avoid: in most cases you will not want to leave money outright to a child who has a disability. It would generally be better to leave money for such a child in trust as described below. This is true for four reasons.

First, leaving money outright to a child who has a disability could result in a loss of eligibility or a reduction in benefits under one or more of the government benefit programs discussed in Chapter Four. These benefits are often relied upon by families to reduce the tremendous costs—often reaching $30,000 annually or more—of providing private care for people with disabilities. As discussed in Chapter Four, some government programs (primarily Medicaid, state "cost-of-care" residential benefit programs, and the Supplemental Security Income program), have eligibility requirements that could be violated if your child owns more than an insignificant amount of property. Leaving money for your child in the type of trust described below generally avoids this problem because, in most states, property held in such trusts is not considered your child's, even though the property will be used for your child's benefit.

Second, also as described in Chapter Four, some states have laws that permit the state to seize property owned by a person who has a disability to pay for current or past services rendered by the state. This type of law is becoming more common among the states as their economic problems increase. The states seek reimbursements from those recipients who can afford to pay, to lessen the burden on other taxpayers. For example, in Illinois the Mental Health Code provides that a person with a disability who is a recipient of state mental health or developmental disability services must pay the state for all current and past services if the person has the resources to do so. As soon as the person with a disability acquires property (by inheritance or otherwise), the state is entitled to seize the property under its reimbursement right.

Trusts frequently avoid this problem because, in most states, money left for a person who has a disability in the type of trust described below is not considered an asset of the person and therefore is not subject to state reimbursement claims.

The third problem associated with receipt of an inheritance by a person who has a disability is that, depending on the nature and severity of the disability, the person may not be able to manage the money effectively. As a consequence, it is frequently necessary to have a guardian of the estate appointed for this purpose. (If you leave money outright to your child and a guardian of the estate is not appointed, no one will have the legal authority to look out for your child's financial interests.)

As we have discussed in more detail in Chapter Three, the appointment of a guardian of the estate may cause many problems: your child may have to be ruled incompetent, there may be fees, the posting of a bond, restrictive investment rules, and complicated approval procedures for expenditures. Trusts avoid this problem because money management responsibilities are left to trustees whom you select.

Fourth, if you leave money outright to your child, your child will have to plan what happens to the money (if any is left) after his or her own death. This may involve writing a will. If your child does not write a will, or if a court determines that the child lacks sufficient mental capacity to write a valid will, the property would be distributed in accordance with the intestacy laws (discussed below) in the state of residence. This may or may not be what you would prefer. Trusts avoid this problem, because a well-drafted trust document will spell out what is to happen to the remaining trust property when the primary beneficiary (your child) dies.

A final point. It is important to understand that not all property passes by will. For example, insurance proceeds pass to the beneficiary designated in the insurance contract. Property that is held in joint tenancy with right of survivorship (often homes and bank accounts) passes to the surviving joint tenant when the first property owner dies. Property in a retirement plan passes under the beneficiary designation contained in the plan.

In preparing your will, it is absolutely critical that you consider what will happen to your property that does not pass by will. Life insurance is an area where mistakes are possible. Parents will frequently take out insurance policies naming their spouse as primary beneficiary and their children as contingent beneficiaries if their spouse does not survive them.

What happens if the insured dies after the spouse? The insurance proceeds go to the children under the terms of the insurance contract; this puts money into the hands of a child who has a disability. As an alternative you should consider naming your children without disabilities and the trust established for your child with a disability as contingent beneficiaries. For example, if you have three children, one with a disability, you will likely want to name your children without disabilities and the trust created for the child with a disability, each in one-third shares, as contingent beneficiaries.

You will also need to think about grandparents, former spouses, and others who might leave property to your child. You should contact them to make sure the property goes to a properly prepared special needs trust.

Guidelines for Creating a Will

It is important that you consult an attorney when you draft a will. Your attorney will know the legal requirements for a valid will in your particular state. Each state has different requirements. For instance, some states require two witnesses, while others require three. Some states permit handwritten wills; others do not. Never attempt to write a will without an attorney.

Without the aid of an attorney, your will might fail to comply with the state's legal requirements, and the probate court might declare your will invalid. If this happens, you lose control over your estate, and the security of your child may be jeopardized.

Another problem with a self-drafted will is that its validity is more likely to be challenged in probate court. If your executor is forced to pay attorney fees to defend your will, the battle could drain much or all of your estate. Again, if your will loses in court, your wishes will be ignored.

Your will can be revoked or changed at any time. As discussed previously, it is a good idea to have your estate plan reviewed periodically, say every five years, or more frequently if there have been major changes in your life, such as the birth or death of a child or a change in your financial situation.

Dying Intestate

What happens if you die without a will? (This is known as dying intestate.)

If you die without a will, the state will write one for you. The state will distribute your property according to its probate laws. These laws are designed for the general public and do not consider the special problems faced by families with children who have disabilities.

In most states, the intestacy laws will distribute your property in accordance with rules that are similar to the rules described below:

- If your spouse is living at the time of your death, one-half of your property goes to your spouse and the remaining half goes to your then-living children, with the descendants of a deceased child taking the share the child would have received had the child survived you.

- If your spouse is not living at the time of your death, your property is divided equally among your children (again, with the descendants of any deceased child taking the deceased child's share).

- If your spouse is not living at the time of your death and if you have no descendant then living, your property is distributed to more distant relatives, such as parents or siblings.

- As is the case when you do have a will, certain types of property will pass outside the probate system in accordance with contractual arrangements that you have entered into during your life. For example, property held in joint tenancy with right of survivorship will be distributed to the surviving joint tenant, and insurance will be distributed to the beneficiary designated in the insurance contract. Other property, such as benefits under retirement plans, may also be distributed outside the probate system.

Obviously, dying without a will is not a preferred choice. Your property may not be distributed in the manner that you would like. Your children with disabilities are likely to receive outright distributions of property, with all the associated problems discussed above. In addition, you will be unable to select your executor or a guardian for your minor children.

Trusts for Beneficiaries with Disabilities

The trust is the most useful estate-planning tool available for providing future financial security for persons with disabilities.

The trust can accomplish many estate-planning goals. For example, a trust can

- Avoid the problems of direct inheritance that may render the person with a disability ineligible for government benefits.
- Avoid the problems of direct inheritance that may expose the assets of a person with a disability to cost-of-care reimbursement claims by governmental authorities.
- Through a trustee, manage the money for a person with a disability by investing it properly, conserving the assets of the trust over the entire lifetime of the person, paying bills, and contracting for care. This money management is one of the most beneficial features of a trust, whether or not the family sets up the trust with government benefits in mind.
- Be used by the parents of the child with a disability to control the distribution of their property not only after their deaths, but also after the death of their child.
- Allow the trust property to bypass probate proceedings, which are often lengthy and costly. (This is discussed in detail in the next chapter.)

What is a trust? In general, a *trust* is a legal relationship under which property is held, managed, and owned by a person or institution (the *trustee*) for the benefit of those persons or organizations for whom the trust was created (the *beneficiary*). The person who places assets into the trust is commonly referred to as the *creator, settlor, grantor*, or *trustor*; this person establishes the trust through a will, or in a legal document known as a *trust agreement* or a *declaration of trust*, which describes the rights and obligations of the trustee.

In effect, the trust is a legal instrument that separates the responsibility of ownership of specific property from the benefit of ownership. The person who has responsibility of ownership, the trustee, manages the assets according to the instructions written in the trust agreement by the creator of the trust for the benefit of the beneficiary. The trustee derives no benefit from the trust property except compensation received for performing his or her duties.

To consider a typical example, Grandfather Jones gives a bank 10,000 shares of Widget Company stock. The bank agrees to hold the stock in trust for the benefit of his son, Mr. Jones, and for Mr. Jones's two children. The trust agreement states that the bank will give Mr. Jones for life all the dividends accrued from the stock (the stock income). After Mr. Jones's death, the stock will be given to his children and the trust will end.

GRANDFATHER JONES
(Creator or Grantor)

TRUSTEE
(Could be an individual instead of a bank)

Trustee owns the stock and can vote the shares (the principal)

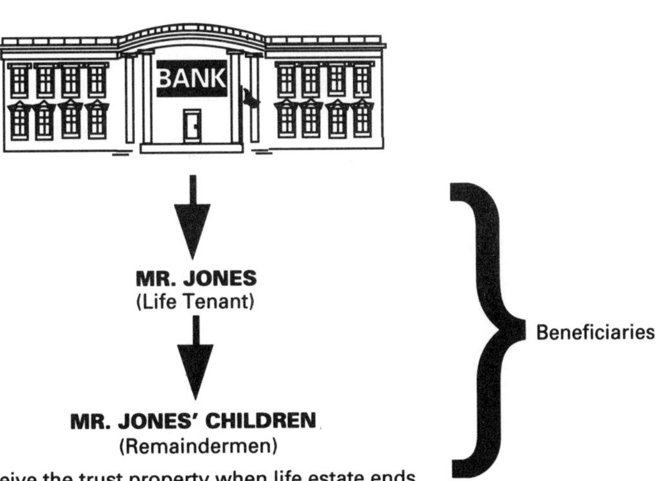

Grandfather Jones is the grantor of the trust—that is, the person who established the trust. The bank is the trustee and has legal ownership of the stock which is the trust principal. However, the bank holds the stock for the benefit of Mr. Jones and his two children, the beneficiaries. The bank, as trustee, has the duty of managing the stock or trust property according to the wishes of the creator, Grandfather Jones, as expressed in the trust agreement.

Obviously, the key to any trust is the instructions given to the trustee. These are contained in the document that creates the trust—either your will, a declaration of trust, or a trust agreement. What instructions are appropriate? The answer depends on the purpose for which the trust has been established.

In the case of trusts involving beneficiaries with disabilities, parents generally have four objectives in mind: (i) they want the trust proceeds to be available to assure a high quality of life for their child; (ii) they do not want the trust to affect their child's eligibility for government benefits; (iii) they want to protect the property in the trust from cost-of-care claims that may be asserted by the government; and (iv) they want the trustee to have sufficient flexibility to use trust funds for their child's primary care if they have difficulty placing their child in government-funded facilities or if such facilities should prove to be inappropriate for their child.

There is more than one way to draft such instructions, and what is appropriate in one state may be inappropriate in another. It is therefore critical that you have your child's trust prepared by an attorney knowledgeable about the laws in your own state relating to trusts for beneficiaries with disabilities. We have discussed how you can locate such attorneys previously in this book.

In many states, a trust will not affect a beneficiary's eligibility for government benefits or be subject to state cost-of-care reimbursement claims so long as the trust is *discretionary*—that is, as long as the trustee has the sole and absolute discretion to determine when and how distributions are to be made. In other words, so long as the trustee has complete control over the amount and frequency of distributions on behalf of the person with a disability, the trust will not affect the beneficiary's eligibility for government benefits. In such states, we generally include a clause that expresses the purpose of the trust so that both the trustee and the government understand that the trust is intended to supplement, and not replace, government benefits. These trusts, because they are intended to meet the beneficiary's *special needs* over and above the needs met through government benefits, are often called *special needs trusts*. For example:

During the lifetime of my son, John Doe (hereinafter referred to as "John") the trust estate shall be held for John and administered for his benefit as follows:

My son, John, has mental retardation and requires special medical care and treatment, and may require custodial services at some point in the future. Because of the constant advances being made in brain research and the development of new therapeutic drugs and procedures, it is my hope that John may someday be able to live an independent, productive, and self-fulfilling life, and the purpose of the trust is to maximize all available resources and apply them so that John will have the best possible chance of becoming self-sufficient. My intent is that trust resources shall be made available to or for John only to provide the "extras" that cannot be obtained from public sources in order to enhance the quality of life for John and provide special medical care and treatment that would not otherwise be available; and I intend the trust to be used only to supplement and never to supplant such public benefits. Without in any way limiting the generality of the foregoing, I intend the trustee to be able to use trust assets for anything consistent with the trust purpose that cannot be provided from public funds at the time of reference, such as special education and therapy; medical care and treatments not otherwise available that the trustee, in consultation with medical personnel, believes may have a chance of aiding recovery; pocket money, special entertainment, clothes, travel, or education to enhance the quality of John's life; vacations with relatives; special job training; vocational education and employment supports to enable John to try to obtain and hold gainful employment; and any other type of supplemental goods or services that the trustee believes to be (a) in John's best interests, and (b) unavailable from public funds at the time of reference.

We then continue with language that expresses the discretionary nature of the trust and gives the trustee guidance about the types of expenditures that are appropriate. The following is typical:

During the life of John, the trustee may pay to, or apply for the benefit of John, such part or all of the income and principal of the trust (even though exhausting the trust) as the trustee, in the trustee's sole and absolute discretion, believes desirable to fulfill the purposes of the trust as specified in the first paragraph above, considering all other income and assets known to the trustee to be available for those purposes from any other source (including public funds) and all other circumstances and factors the trustee considers pertinent. Any undistributed income of the trust shall be accumulated and from time to time added to principal. In no event may income or principal of the trust be paid to or for the benefit of or as a requirement of a governmental agency or department and the trust property shall at all times be free of the claims of such governmental bodies. If a claim is made against the trust property by any such governmental body, or if any such governmental body denies benefits to John as a consequence of the existence of the trust, the trustee may hire legal counsel on behalf of the trust to contest such governmental claim or denial of benefits.

This language is by no means the only way of protecting trust assets from government claims. In states that protect discretionary trusts, all that is typically necessary is that the trustee have absolute discretion over distributions. However, it is generally advisable to state that the purpose of the trust is to supplement government benefits. Some attorneys prefer less specific language, such as the following:

During the life of John, the trustee may distribute for the benefit of John so much or all of the income and principal of the trust as the trustee determines to be in John's welfare and best interests. In making said distributions, the trustee shall be guided by my intent that the trust be used only to supplement, and never to supplant, the government benefits, if any, to which John may be entitled.

A few other provisions will need to be considered:

Spendthrift Clause

We always insert a spendthrift clause in the trust. This clause protects the trust assets from private creditors of the person with a disability. For instance, if someone persuades your child to sign an installment contract to purchase a Rolls Royce automobile, the spendthrift clause will prevent the lender from getting at the trust assets.

Trust Terminations

You can include a trust provision that authorizes the trustee to terminate the trust in the event the government attempts to seize the assets of the trust or if the trust imperils your child's eligibility for government benefits. The intent would be to distribute the trust property to people named in the trust document, presumably people who you believe would spend the money on behalf of your child.

There is not sufficient law to determine whether this provision would be enforceable. However, if enforceable, such a provision could prove useful in two circumstances: (i) in states where the status of special needs trusts is uncertain, the provision could be useful if the state were to suddenly start challenging such trusts; and (ii) in states that are currently favorably disposed toward special needs trusts, a trust-termination provision could prove useful if the law were to change in the future. (Given the budgetary pressures faced by all states, this is always a possibility.)

If you do include such a trust-termination provision, it is a good idea to premise it on an opinion of counsel that the trust cannot be protected from state action (that is, the trust could not be terminated unless a lawyer told the trustee that the trust imperilled your child's government benefits). You will also need to decide whether the assets should be distributed to the same people who will receive the remaining trust property when your child dies.

For example, on the death of a child with a disability, many of our clients will have the property remaining in the trust go to their surviving children, with grandchildren taking the share of any children who have already died. On termination of the trust due to an attempted government seizure of trust property, clients are frequently less comfortable with grandchildren receiving a share. They know their children and are reasonably confident their children will use the property for the person with the disability, but they are less confident about grandchildren who may be very young—or not yet born.

Some clients prefer not to include a trust-termination provision because they do not expect their child to require government benefits. They prefer to make sure the trust remains available for their child, regardless of what the future may bring. This tends to be the exception rather than the rule, as government benefits are very important for most people with disabilities. Parents tend not to include a trust-termination provision where there are no children without disabilities.

Trust Amendment

This clause is similar to the trust-termination provision discussed above. The idea is to permit the trustee to amend the trust if the law changes in such a way that the existence of the trust imperils your child's eligibility for government benefits.

As was the case with the trust-termination provision, it is unclear whether this provision would be enforceable. In addition, its use should be premised on receipt of an opinion by the trustee from a lawyer that amendment of the trust is necessary to protect your child's government benefits.

Trust Remaindermen

In preparing your child's trust, it will also be important to think carefully about who will receive the remaining trust property after your child's death. (These people are known as the *trust remaindermen.*)

In particular, you may need to think about what you want to happen if your child has children. Would you want them to receive the property, or a percentage of it?

For children whose disabilities are very severe, this may not be an issue. For others, it is a possibility that should be considered, and the question becomes more important if you have left a disproportionately large share of your estate to your child's trust.

For example, suppose you have 3 children, one of whom has a disability. You decide to leave 50 percent of your property to that child's trust and 25 percent to each of your other children. If you decide that the remaining trust property is to go to the children of your child with a disability when that child dies, the effect is to give a disproportionate share to those grandchildren. Some of our clients like this, reasoning that those grandchildren will have greater need of the funds. Others prefer to make an equalizing distribution to their other grandchildren.

Often clients provide that a portion of the property remaining in their child's trust go to charity, perhaps to an organization that helped the child during the child's life. Parents are often very grateful to such organizations and want such organizations to be able to provide others with the services that were provided to their own child.

Luxury Trusts

In the few states that are hostile to flexible special needs trusts, great care must be taken if you want to protect your child's eligibility for government benefits. In such states it may be necessary to restrict trust distributions to items that the state does not provide, such as special education and therapy not funded by the state; special entertainment and recreation; vacations; private vocational and employment supports; and medical and dental treatments unavailable from public sources. Providing the trustee with discretion to make distributions for your child's benefit or support may actually jeopardize the trust. These trusts are known as *luxury trusts* because the trustee's discretion is so restricted. In such states, language such as the following may be appropriate:

This trust is established for the benefit of my son, John Doe. The trustee shall distribute the funds of the trust to pay only for luxuries over and above the benefits John otherwise receives as a result of his disability from any local, state, or federal government or from private agencies, any of which provide services or benefits to persons with disabilities, and not for John's primary care. These luxuries include travel expenses to visit friends and relatives, household furniture and appliances, clothing, movies, a record player, and medical care not otherwise available.

Of course, this type of trust is more restrictive than the flexible special needs trusts described previously because the trustee is restricted to distributions for the very narrow purposes listed in the trust document. Thus, for example, trust property would not be available to your child if budgetary pressures were to cause a reduction in state aid. However, in states that count property in a special needs trust as a resource for a beneficiary with a disability, parents may be faced with a choice between an inflexible trust document and the loss of government benefits for their child, or perhaps even a seizure of trust assets by the state as a cost-of-care reimbursement.

In states where the attitude toward special needs trusts is uncertain, parents are again faced with a difficult choice. They can draft a flexible, special needs trust, perhaps relying on a trust termination or amendment clause if the state should later seek reimbursement from the trust. Or they can prepare a restrictive luxury trust, which could limit the trustee's ability to help their child. There is no right or wrong answer to this question, and our sympathy is with parents who must face it.

Fortunately, in most states, properly drafted, flexible special needs trusts do the job. Assets held in such trusts are not considered resources of a beneficiary with a disability for purposes of SSI and Medicaid, and such assets are not subject to state cost-of-care reimbursement claims. In a few states even more restrictive luxury trusts may not be adequate.

Selecting the Trustee

In discussing guardianship and advocacy (Chapter Three), we told you that no matter how carefully thought out the your child's life plan might be, much would depend on the skill and commitment of the advocate you select. The same is true of the trustee. Your child's trust is a vital legal document, but it is, after all, a piece of paper. It is the trustee who will manage the money and decide how it should be spent. The key to the plan is to make sure the right person is selected. Several different possibilities are available:

The Corporate Trustee

A corporate trustee is usually a financial institution such as a bank or a trust company that, as part of its business, serves as trustee of a great many trusts. There are 3 major advantages offered by a corporate trustee:

1. Corporate trustees can be relied on to manage and invest the trust property. Usually, banks acting as trustees have several different investment plans. You should inquire about these, because each plan is designed for a different financial objective and each plan invests differently in terms of risk, income generation, and capital appreciation. Corporate trustees are also experienced in handling the paperwork involved in trust administration, such as the filing of tax returns and the preparation of accountings.

2. Corporate trustees are independent and impartial and will attempt to treat all the trust beneficiaries fairly.

3. Corporate trustees do not die. They will provide continuity of financial management for the entire lifetime of your child.

However, the corporate trustee also has some disadvantages. A major disadvantage is that banks charge an annual fee for their trust services (usually .75 percent to 1.5 percent of the principal per year), often with a minimum fee of $1,500 or more. As a result, it may be uneconomical to use a bank trustee if the trust has less than $100,000. In addition, though the bank's impartiality was cited as an advantage, it may also be a disadvantage if the bank, as trustee, is not interested in being a friend and advocate for your child (particularly after your death).

Occasionally clients will express concern about bank investment strategies, particularly in light of publicity over recent bank failures. Although mismanagement is possible, banks tend to invest trust funds conservatively and reasonably well. Most publicity about risky investments relates to banks' investments of their own funds and not to investments of funds that they hold in trust for others.

The Individual Trustee

An individual trustee is, as you would expect, an individual who manages the money in a trust. Anyone who cares about the person with a disability and can manage the trust property can be an individual trustee. The individual trustee can be someone with a strong, personal concern for the person with a disability; often this trustee is a relative or close friend. There is no minimum trust size, because an individual trustee will manage the trust property regardless of its size. And an individual trustee, especially if a relative, might not charge for services.

Here too, however, there is another side to the coin. The individual trustee may not manage money as skillfully as a bank. Unlike a bank, the individual trustee may die before the beneficiary with a disability. To safeguard against this problem, you should appoint several trustees, to act one after the other as predecessors die. The last surviving trustee can be given the power to appoint his or her successor. In this way, there will always be a trustee of your choice to care for your child.

Another disadvantage of an individual trustee is the potential for conflict of interest. Often siblings without disabilities are the most natural choice for trustee due to their sincere love for their brother or sister and their knowledge of their brother or sister's wants and desires. However, because siblings often also serve as remaindermen (that is, they are to receive the "remaining" property when the person with the disability dies), a potential conflict of interest is created. It is in the financial interest of the sibling to spend less on the person with the disability in order to receive more when the person with the disability dies.

This is not to say that siblings should not be chosen. Often parents are rightfully confident that their children without disabilities will always act in the interest of the person with the disability out of love and concern for their sibling, despite the potential conflict of interest. In fact, it is often the children without disabilities who cause their parents to begin the estate-planning process out of a concern for their sibling's future. However, potential conflict of interest is a factor to be considered in selecting a trustee. It is often a good idea to select cotrustees (discussed below) to reduce the potential impact of the conflict.

Cotrustees

Cotrustees can often solve the problems associated with both the corporate and individual trustee. In fact, it is possible to combine the strengths of both kinds of trustee by naming a bank and an individual as cotrustees. You select the bank trustee to manage and invest the trust property and handle the paperwork, and name an individual trustee to pay for services and goods for the person with a disability. The bank trustee manages money expertly; the individual trustee understands the needs of the beneficiary. The individual trustee can also act as the personal advocate for the person with a disability. It is even possible to give the individual trustee the power to change the cotrustee to another bank. This power gives leverage to the family member if the bank's services are inadequate.

Appointing cotrustees can also guard against conflicts of interest. If your possible trustee candidates are relatives of your child who have a financial conflict of interest, you can appoint two of them as cotrustees with equal power. For example, suppose you have two sons without disabilities and a daughter with a disability. In the trust document the sons will receive the trust property after the death of your daughter. Both sons love their sister, but you are worried that one of them might be tempted to skimp on goods and services for his sister in order to inherit more money after her death. As a safeguard, you can appoint both sons as cotrustees, so that both of them would have to decide to skimp on goods or become dishonest before your daughter could be harmed. As another option, you could appoint one son and an independent third person as cotrustees.

In this way, you can guard against potential conflicts of interest but still have a loving, concerned relative as a trustee for your daughter. However, this arrangement of cotrustees with equal power does carry the possibility of a stalemate if the trustees disagree about a particular course of action.

Although we tend to prefer a cotrustee approach to protect against possible dishonesty and mismanagement, the bottom line is that you need to choose trustees whom you sincerely trust. Clients often ask us who is looking over the trustee's shoulder to insure that the trustee is doing a good job. Our answer is "no one." Unless you have a bank as a trustee, these are private trusts. The only recourse against a trustee who has been negligent, or has even stolen a portion of the trust funds, would be for one of the beneficiaries under the trust (or an agent representing the person with a disability) to sue the trustee in court.

The Pooled-Income Trust

As previously mentioned, a corporate trustee may not be a viable option for trusts that are not large (for example, trusts that have less than $100,000) because it may be difficult to find corporate trustees willing to act and the trustee fees may be too large in relation to the amount in the trust.

To meet these problems, a few areas have developed "pooled-income trusts," which, in essence, are smaller trusts that are pooled together to reduce administrative costs. Trustees are typically private corporations, such as banks or trust companies or nonprofit organizations formed specifically to act as trustee of such trusts.

You can obtain information about pooled-income trusts in your area from local advocacy organizations or from estate planners knowledgeable about the needs of families with children who have disabilities. Some of the larger pooled-income trusts are listed in the Directory of Organizations found in Appendix III.

Making the Choice: Selecting the Trustee

As in the case of your choice of advocate (see Chapter Three), the proper choice of trustee will depend on your own unique family circumstances. You will probably want people who

- Understand the unique needs and abilities of your child.
- Will carry out your wishes after your death.
- Can manage and invest trust property skillfully.
- Most importantly, are people whom you *trust*.

In most cases, we prepare *living trusts* that are effective during the parents' lives; the parents typically act as trustees until they die. These are to be distinguished from *testamentary trusts*, which become effective when the parents die.

It is not strictly necessary to use living trusts if the parents do not fund the trust with significant amounts of property until they die. However, as a general rule we prefer to make the trust effective upon signing. That way the trust can serve as a receptacle in the event someone else wants to leave money to the person with the disability (perhaps a grandparent). Also, the parents' management of the trust can provide a track record that successor trustees can use to determine the types of expenditures that the parents considered appropriate.

In addition, parents sometimes fund the trust during their lives so there will be a guaranteed pool of money available for their child in the event of a family disaster—for example, the entry of a parent into a nursing home. Often this is accomplished by having the special needs trust purchase a life insurance policy. In such cases, it is generally advisable that the trust be irrevocable.

After the parents die, we prefer a cotrustee arrangement—either two individuals, such as a brother and a sister or, depending on the size of the trust, an individual and a bank. Clients will typically give us a list of individuals, to act two at a time (or one at a time with a bank as cotrustee). That way, if the person with the disability outlives the first trustees, a successor is ready to act. If all the people named by the parents die, a bank takes over. Clients also usually give trustees the power to name their successors, in case a change of circumstances justifies a change in plans.

Trusts for Beneficiaries without Disabilities

The plan you develop for your child with a disability will be part of the estate plan you develop for your whole family. This is particularly true if you have children without disabilities who are minors; you will probably want to establish trusts for them as well.

These trusts will generally be similar to trusts for your child with a disability in that distributions will be discretionary in nature. They generally will be a part of your will and not freestanding documents. In essence, the trusts will become effective only if both parents die before your child becomes an adult. Language such as the following is typical:

The trustee may in the trustee's discretion pay to, or use for the benefit of John or any of his descendants such part or all of the income and principal of the trust as the trustee determines to be necessary or desirable for their medical care, support, education (including college and postgraduate), welfare, and best interests.

The trust property would then typically be distributed to John when he reached a specified age—for example, age 23. If the trust was sufficiently large, you could even distribute it in stages—for example, a third at age 25, a third at age 30, and a third at age 35.

Several different methods of structuring these trusts are possible:

1. You could leave your property in one trust for all your children, permitting the trustee to *sprinkle* trust property among your children as needed. The theory behind this *pool approach* is that, if you were living, you would not necessarily spend equal amounts on each of your children because your children may have different needs, and the trustee should have a similar flexibility. (For example, one of your children may become very ill, and the entire trust may be necessary to pay the medical bills.) When the youngest of your children (not counting the child with the disability) reaches a specified age (say age 23), the remaining trust property would be distributed to your children, with the share of the child with a disability remaining in trust for the child's sole benefit.

2. Some parents like the pool approach for their children without disabilities but fear using it for their child with a disability because they want to make sure sufficient funds will be available for that child. In such cases it is possible to carve out the share of the child with the disability, placing it in a separate trust, and to use the pool approach described above for other children.

3. Some parents want to make sure that each child receives an equal share. In such cases, the parents' property can be

divided equally, with a separate trust being held for each child.

What happens if you leave money outright to a minor child—that is, if you do not provide a trust? The property will be your child's, and a guardian of the estate will be required. As discussed in Chapter Three, the guardian will be subject to restrictions relating to investments, the need to obtain court approval for expenditures, and the obligation to file periodic reports.

As an intermediate step between preparing a trust for minor children and leaving property to them outright, it is possible to provide in your will that property left to minors should be transferred to a *custodian* for your child's benefit under your state's Uniform Transfer To Minor's Act. Under the laws in most states, the custodian holds the property for the benefit of your child, using income and principal as needed, until the child reaches age 21 (18 in some states), at which time the remaining property is distributed outright to the child.

Some Sample Estate Plans

Example One

John and Mary have 3 adult children: Bob, Sam, and Julie. Bob and Julie have good jobs and are financially independent. Sam has a schizoid-affective disorder and has limited employment prospects. Bob and Julie each have small children; Sam does not have children at the current time, but it is possible he will have children in the future.

John and Mary have an estate that is worth approximately $250,000 (including insurance and their home). While they would like to treat all their children equally, the whole family (including Bob and Julie) recognizes that Sam has greater needs. John and Mary decide on the following estate plan:

- On the death of the first of them, all property is to be distributed to the survivor.

- On the death of the second, all property is to be held in a special needs trust for Sam (to be combined with other property which John and Mary may have placed in the trust during their lives). Bob and Julie are to serve as cotrustees, and when either of them becomes unable or unwilling to act, a bank is appointed as successor trustee (or sole trustee when both are unable to act). Bob and Julie are each given the power to name successors to act in lieu of the bank (perhaps their children, should they demonstrate sufficient responsibility and concern for Sam when they grow older). The trust also contains a termination provision, with assets to be distributed to Bob and Julie (or the survivor of them if one of them is deceased) should the law change so that the existence of the trust would imperil Sam's eligibility for government benefits. John and Mary believe that government benefits will be very important for Sam, and they are confident that Bob and Julie would use trust assets for Sam should a trust termination occur.

- On the death of Sam, the trust property is to be distributed equally between Sam's children (if any), Bob (or his children if Sam outlives him), Julie (or her children if Sam outlives her), and the local chapter of the National Alliance for the Mentally Ill.

Example Two

The facts are the same as described in Example One, except that John and Mary decide they want to treat all their children equally. John and Mary decide on the following estate plan:

- As in Example One, on the death of John or Mary, all property goes to the survivor.

- On the death of the second of them, their property is divided equally between their children. Bob and Julie receive their shares outright, and Sam's share is held in trust for his life.

The trustee arrangement is identical to the arrangement described in Example One, and the trust contains a trust termination provision that is identical to the provision described in Example One.

- On the death of Sam, the property in his trust is distributed to his then-living descendants, or if there are none, to Bob and Julie, or to their children if Sam outlives them.

Example Three

John and Mary have three young children; Bob, Sam, and Julie. Sam has moderate mental retardation and is expected to move into a group residential facility when he gets older. Bob has just turned 7 and is in the first grade. Julie is age 4 and attends preschool. John and Mary decide on the following estate plan:

- As in Examples One and Two, on the death of John or Mary, all their property goes to the survivor.

- On the death of the second of them, their property is split into two trusts; one-third of their property is held in a special needs trust for Sam to supplement government benefits that are available to him, and two-thirds of their property goes to a separate trust that is held as a single pool for the benefit of Julie and Bob. When Julie reaches age 23, the property in this separate trust is distributed equally between Bob and Julie; Sam's trust remains unchanged. John and Mary had thought about using a single pool for all their children, but they have rejected that approach because they want to make certain that enough is available for Sam. They have also thought about having separate trusts for Bob and Julie, but they have decided against that because they want extra funds available in case Bob or Julie have extraordinary needs.

- John and Mary name John's sister, Margaret, and Mary's brother, Peter, as trustee of all trusts. If one of them cannot act, a bank becomes cotrustee. Margaret and Peter are each given the power to name a successor, and to change banks if the services provided by the selected bank prove to be inadequate. Margaret is also named guardian for Bob, Sam, and Julie during their minority, with the expectation that Margaret will not pursue a court proceeding to continue the guardianship after Sam reaches age 18, unless she finds it necessary.

- John and Mary have included a provision in Sam's trust that would terminate the trust if the law were to change so that the trust imperilled Sam's eligibility for government benefits. They have thought long and hard about this. On a termination, should the assets go to Margaret and Peter, who they believe would use the assets on Sam's behalf? Or should the assets go to Bob and Julie (or their trust if they have not come of age), so the property will remain in the family? Ultimately they decide that the assets should go to Margaret and Peter, with the understanding that they will revisit the issue as Bob and Julie grow older.

- On Sam's death, the property in his trust is to go to Bob and Julie, or their trust if Julie has not yet reached age 23. They consider the possibility of Sam having children sufficiently remote that they do not wish to plan for it.

Trust Distributions

We have told you how a trust can be prepared so that assets held in the trust will not be considered to be owned by your child for purposes of Medicaid, SSI, and state cost-of-care reimbursement programs. We have not told you how trust distributions can be made to avoid the income limitations contained in those programs.

As you may recall from Chapter Four, SSI recipients are entitled to receive $20 of unearned income per month without reduction in SSI benefits. Receipt of unearned income in excess of $20 per month, however, results in a dollar-for-dollar reduction in benefits. Because distributions from trusts are considered unearned income, regular distributions in excess of $20 per month result in a benefit reduction. (SSI also permits your child to receive an additional $20 per month of irregularly or infrequently received unearned income.)

How can this limitation on trust distributions be avoided? Have the trust purchase items for your child and retain ownership, permitting your child to use, but not own, the property.

Under the SSI eligibility rules, trust distributions that do not result in your child receiving food, clothing, or shelter, or anything that can be used to obtain these items, do not count as unearned income. Thus, the trustee can use trust assets to pay for items such as airline tickets, record players, television sets, medical insurance, telephone bills, or furniture without any reduction in benefits.

If, instead, the trustee were to give your child the money to pay for these items, the distribution to your child would count as unearned income, resulting in a possible reduction in benefits. Similarly, if your child were to actually own, rather than merely have the right to use, the item purchased, the receipt of the item would be considered unearned income because the item could be sold and converted to cash.

Trust distributions can also sometimes be structured to maximize SSI benefits if your child lives with someone who provides food and shelter. As you may recall from Chapter Four, under the one-third reduction rule, your child's SSI benefits are reduced by one-third because the Social Security Administration assumes that the value of the "in kind" benefits received by your child (free room and board) equal one-third of the SSI benefits. If, in fact, the child's share of household expenses is less than that amount, the child can pay his or her share out of the trust and receive a smaller reduction.

For example, suppose your child's share of monthly household expenses is $100 and, but for free room and board, the SSI benefit would be $470. If the $100 were to be paid from the trust, it would be treated as unearned income because the $100 will have been used to pay for food and shelter. The result would be a benefit reduction of $80—$100 of unearned income less the $20 allowance.

If, on the other hand, the one-third reduction rule were applied, benefits would be reduced by $157—one-third of $470. Of course, if your child were to pay his or her fair share from the trust, the trust would also be out of pocket for the $100 expense.

Trusts Created With Beneficiary's Own Assets

In most states, a special needs trust that you establish for your child will not affect your child's eligibility for government benefits or be subject to a state cost-of-care reimbursement claim because the trust will be funded with property that belongs to you, and not property that belongs to your child. Often people with disabilities have substantial property of their own, sometimes acquired through work, inheritance or from settlement of a personal injury claim. Special rules apply to trusts created with a beneficiary's own assets, and it is not possible for a person with a disability to remain eligible for government benefits by putting this property in a special needs trust.

However, the assets will not affect eligibility for government benefits or be subject to a state cost-of-care reimbursement claim if they are put in a trust that has the following characteristics. First, the trust must contain assets of a person with a disability who is under the age of sixty-five. Second, the trust must be created by a parent, grandparent or guardian of the person with a disability, or by a court. Note that the trust cannot be created by the person with the disability. Third, the trust must provide that the state is to be reimbursed from the trust at the death of the person with a disability for all amounts expended on behalf of such person under its Medicaid program, assuming there is enough left in the trust when the person with a disability dies. *This requirement that the state be reimbursed from the trust for amounts expended on behalf of the person with a disability when the person with a disability dies does not apply to special needs trusts that you create for your child with your property. It applies only to trusts created with your child's property.*

It is also possible for a person with a disability to transfer assets to a pooled income trust set up by a non-profit association without affecting his or her eligibility for government benefits. The pooled income trust must provide for reimbursement of the state at the death of the person with a disability, unless the funds are retained by the trust for charitable purposes.

Example Four

Mary is receiving SSI and Medicaid. Mary is injured in a car accident and receives a $60,000 settlement. If the $60,000 remains in Mary's name, she will be ineligible for these need-based government benefits until the money is spent down. If instead the money is placed in a trust for Mary's benefit that satisfies the conditions described above, the money will be available for Mary during her life without loss of government benefits. When Mary dies, any remaining property will first be used to reimburse the state for Medicaid expenditures. However, if Mary's parents have also created a special needs trust for her using their own property, the amount required to be paid to the state when Mary dies can be minimized if the trustee uses money from the settlement trust before using money from the special needs trust. This is because money remaining in the special needs trust set up by the parents does not have reimburse the government when Mary dies. Obviously, it is very important that Mary's parents create a separate trust if they intend to leave money for her. If they simply transfer their property to the trust created with Mary's assets, the funds will be available to repay the government when Mary dies.

Chapter 7

Using Living Trusts to Avoid Probate

Thus far we have discussed trusts in two contexts: special needs trusts for children with disabilities, which can be used to provide funds for your child without jeopardizing eligibility under various government benefit programs; and discretionary trusts for children without disabilities, which can be used to provide funds for your other children during the period before they have the judgment and maturity to manage money on their own.

Trusts have a variety of other uses as well, and we will discuss many of these in this and following chapters. For example, in Chapter Nine we will tell you about credit shelter trusts, irrevocable insurance trusts, and generation-skipping trusts, and how these and various other devices can be used to reduce the estate tax owing at your death. (You will not have to worry about estate taxes unless the value of your estate at the time of your death, including proceeds payable under life insurance policies which you may own, exceeds $600,000.)

In this chapter we discuss the living trust, which is a common method of avoiding probate, and the factors you should consider in determining whether a living trust is appropriate for you.

Chapter 7

What Is Probate and Why Should I Attempt to Avoid It?

Probate is the legal process that governs how property that you own at the time of your death is to be passed on to your heirs. The essence of the system is to ensure that the right people receive the correct amount of property from your estate.

While this sounds good in theory, the method the probate system employs to achieve its laudable objective tends to be far more time consuming and expensive than is typically necessary. Although the system differs from state to state, it tends to be similar to the following:

- First, your executor (or more typically, an attorney hired by your executor) files a petition with the probate court to have your will admitted for validation. Notice is sent to interested parties (typically those who would receive your property if your will was considered invalid) to give these people an opportunity to file an objection.

- Your will is then *proved* valid in a court proceeding, typically based on the fact that you signed your will in front of witnesses who signed an *attestation clause* stating that you knew what you were doing when you signed the will.

- Your executor then files a notice to creditors that apprises them that you have died and informs them that they have a specified period of time (usually around 6 months) to assert any claims that they may have against your estate. Notice of your death is also published in newspapers to inform the population in general, in case any of them have any claims against you. Claims that are not asserted within the statutory period generally may not be asserted later against your heirs or your estate.

- Depending on the laws in the state where you reside at the time of your death, your executor may also be responsible for filing an inventory of your assets with the probate court and for reporting to the court on distributions to the beneficiaries of your estate.

- In many states, probate is not required for estates that are sufficiently small (say $30,000 to $60,000). Property can be passed to heirs through a simplified summary procedure.

So what's wrong with the system?

In a word, the system is designed to deal with the most complicated estates, in which a variety of creditors have claims against the deceased person's property, and family members line up to contest the validity of the deceased person's will. By providing a formal system for dealing with the claims of creditors and objections to the will, the system enables property to be passed on free of fraud.

However, few estates require such care. In the normal case, creditors are paid and no one has any objection to the will, and the executor is forced to endure the lengthy and costly probate system for no real reason at all.

And the system can be both lengthy and costly. In general, it takes a minimum of 6 months, and often much longer, to probate a will. A recent study by the American Association for Retired Persons (AARP) put the average time period at over a year.

As for cost, it is impossible to give a figure with any degree of certainty, because cost will vary depending on the state where you reside and the attorney your executor employs. In some states the fee is based on a percentage of the gross value of the deceased person's property. (The percentage may be set by law or custom, with additional charges permitted if the estate is unusually complicated.) In other states the attorney is entitled to *reasonable compensation*, which is based on the amount of time the attorney spends, the size of the estate involved, and the difficulty of the attorney's job (for example, whether the administration of the estate was unusual in any way).

A 1988 telephone survey of probate practitioners by the California Law Revision Commission Staff indicated the following were typical charges for probate in their home states:

State	Fee for Estate of Indicated Value		
	$100,000	**$300,000**	**$600,000**
California	$3,150	$7,150	$13,150
Florida	2,000	7,500	18,000
Georgia	2,500	7,500	12,000
Illinois	5,000	10,000	16,000
Michigan	3,000	7,000	10,000
New York	5,000	13,000	22,000
Ohio	3,000	6,000	10,000
Pennsylvania	5,000	13,000	22,000
Texas	3,000	7,000	9,000
Virginia	3,000	7,000	9,000

The figures assume a relatively uncomplicated estate, and the costs would be greater if complications arise. In addition, as mentioned above, the figures are based on a survey of probate practitioners. Such practitioners may have an incentive to underestimate the actual costs involved, since many of them make their livings through the probate system. Other writers have put the cost at a higher figure, estimating the average probate cost at anywhere from 4 to 11 percent of the value of the deceased person's property.

In truth, there is probably no reliable data regarding average probate costs. One thing, however, is painfully clear. The system is far more costly and time consuming than is typically necessary to distribute a deceased person's property. The usual result is that the deceased person's loved ones endure a lengthy and costly process that saps them of patience and unnecessarily depletes the deceased person's estate.

Perhaps the AARP study cited above put it best, concluding that the system is "costly, slow, and outmoded...[a] sad state of affairs."

Avoiding Probate with a Living Trust

So now you know a little bit about the probate system and why you will probably want to avoid it. The key to doing so is to remember that probate is required only if you *own* a significant amount of property at the time of your death. Although the amount varies by state, probate will typically not be required if you own less than $30,000.

A *living trust* operates under the legal fiction that property that is placed in trust is *owned* by the trust and not by the beneficiaries of the trust. How do you make use of this fiction to avoid the probate system?

You create a trust, naming yourself as beneficiary and trustee, retaining the power to distribute property to whomever you would like and to amend the trust whenever and however you would like. You then transfer your property into the trust during your life. Because the property is owned by the trust and not by you, you own nothing at the time of your death, and probate is therefore avoided.

It sounds complicated, but we assure you that it is not. The existence of the trust will make little, if any, difference during your life. You will be sole trustee and will be able to spend money that you place in the trust however you would like. The only difference is that the name on your bank accounts, your stocks and securities, and your house will read "John Doe, trustee" and not "John Doe."

In the eyes of all but the probate court, you will own your property as completely as you do currently. There is no obligation that your trust be registered with anyone, or that it file a tax return while you live and are acting as trustee. You simply go to a lawyer, prepare a declaration of trust naming yourself as trustee, and transfer your property to the trust (for example, by signing papers at your bank changing the name on your accounts, contacting financial advisors to make sure the name on your stocks is changed to the trust, and having your attorney prepare a new deed for your home). You then conduct your financial affairs exactly as you do now. Income earned by the trust is reported on your personal tax return with no mention of the trust at all.

When you die, however, the existence of the trust becomes very important.

- Because your property is owned by your trust at the time of your death, and not by you, there is no need to go through probate. Instead, a successor trustee, whom you select when you prepare your trust document, distributes your property in accordance with the instructions that you have written in the trust document.

- As a result, the cost and delay of the probate system is completely avoided. Your successor trustee can begin distributing property shortly after your death. (Delay will be unavoidable, however, if you have a taxable estate. Your successor trustee will be unable to make distributions until the estate-tax audit is complete. We discuss estate tax in Chapter Nine.)

- Although there will be costs in setting up the trust, the expense is much less than that involved in probating a will. You need only refer to the chart of typical probate charges a few pages back for comparison.

Sample Estate Plans Using Living Trusts

Example One

John and Mary have three adult children: Bob, Sam, and Julie. Bob and Julie have good jobs and are financially independent. Sam has mild mental retardation and works as an orderly at the local hospital. John and Mary are proud of Sam's work, but they realize he could lose his job and require government benefits in the future. Bob and Julie each have small children. While Sam does not have children at the current time, it is possible he will have children in the future.

John and Mary have an estate that is worth approximately $250,000 (including insurance and their home). While they would like to treat all their children equally, the whole family (including Bob and Julie) recognizes that Sam has greater needs. John and Mary decide on the following estate plan:

- John and Mary create a living trust, naming themselves as trustees, and transfer all their property to the trust (that is, the trust becomes owner of their home and other property and is named as beneficiary of their insurance). The trust can be amended or revoked at any time, and the trust instrument permits either of them to use trust property for any purpose. On the death of the first of them, the survivor becomes sole trustee and retains the ability to amend or revoke the trust and to use trust property for any purpose. If the survivor feels he or she needs help managing money, Bob or Julie could even be named as cotrustee.

- On the death of the second, the property remains in trust for Sam. The trust provides that distributions are to be made to meet Sam's supplemental needs over and above government benefits. That is, the trust converts into a special needs trust that is prepared in accordance with the provisions found in Chapter Six, so Sam will be eligible for government benefits if needed in the future, and is combined with other property that John and Mary may have placed in trust for Sam during their lives. Bob and Julie are to serve as cotrustees. When either of them becomes unable or unwilling to act, a bank is appointed as successor trustee (or sole trustee when both Bob and Julie are unable to act). Bob and Julie are each given the power to name successors to act in lieu of the bank (perhaps their children, should they demonstrate sufficient responsibility and concern for Sam when they grow older). The trust also contains a termination provision, with assets to be distributed to Bob and Julie (or the survivor of them if one of them is deceased) should the law change in such a way that the existence of the trust imperils Sam's eligibility for government benefits. John and Mary believe that government benefits could be very important for Sam, and they are confident that Bob and Julie would use trust assets for Sam should a trust termination occur.

- On the death of Sam, the trust property is to be distributed equally between Sam's children (if any), Bob (or his children if Sam outlives him), Julie (or her children if Sam outlives her), and the local chapter of The Association for Retarded Citizens of the United States.

Example Two

The facts are the same as described in Example One, except that John and Mary decide they want to treat all their children equally. John and Mary decide on the following estate plan:

- As in Example One, John and Mary create a living trust, naming themselves as trustees, and transfer all their property to the trust. The provisions of the trust are the same as in Example One: either of them can amend or revoke the trust at any time or use trust property for any purpose. On the death of the first of them, the survivor becomes sole trustee and retains the ability to amend or revoke the trust and to use trust property for any purpose.

- On the death of the second, the trust property is divided into equal parts—one for each of Bob, Julie, and Sam. Bob and Julie receive their shares outright. Sam's share remains in trust for his life. As in Example One, the trust is prepared so Sam remains eligible for government benefits. Bob and Julie are named as trustees, and the trust contains a trust termination provision identical to the provision in Example One.

- On the death of Sam, the remaining trust property is to be distributed to Sam's children (if any), or if there are none, in equal shares to Bob (or his children if Sam outlives him) and Julie (or her children if Sam outlives her).

Example Three

John and Mary have three young children: Bob, Sam, and Julie. Sam has Down syndrome and is expected to move into a group home when he gets older. Bob has just turned 7 and is in the first grade. Julie is age 4 and attends preschool. John and Mary decide on the following estate plan:

- As in Examples One and Two, John and Mary create a living trust, naming themselves as trustees, and transfer all their property to the trust. The provisions of the trust are the same as in Examples One and Two: either of them can amend or revoke the trust at any time or use trust property for any purpose. On the death of the first of them, the survivor becomes sole trustee and retains the ability to amend or revoke the trust and to use trust property for any purpose.

- On the death of the second of them, the trust is split into two parts. One-third of the property is held in a special needs trust for Sam to supplement government benefits that are available to him. Two-thirds of the property is held as a single pool for the benefit of Julie and Bob. When Julie reaches age 23, the remaining property in this separate pool is distributed equally between Bob and Julie. Sam's trust remains unchanged.

- John and Mary name John's sister, Margaret, and Mary's brother, Peter, as successor trustees after their deaths. If one of them cannot act, a bank becomes cotrustee. Margaret and Peter are each given the power to name a successor. Margaret is also named guardian for Bob, Sam, and Julie during their minority, with the expectation that Margaret will not pursue a court proceeding to continue the guardianship after Sam reaches age 18, unless she finds it necessary.

- On Sam's death, the property in his trust is to go to Bob and Julie, or their trust if Julie has not yet reached age 23.

As is apparent, a living trust can be drawn as flexibly as you would like. In fact, as you may have noticed, the examples discussed in this chapter are similar to the examples discussed in Chapter Six. This was done intentionally, to prove a point, that whatever you do with a will, you can do with a living trust as well. The only difference between the approaches is that a living trust avoids probate and therefore saves both cost and time.

A living trust can have other advantages as well. For example:

- A living trust can protect the privacy of your estate. As discussed above, if you rely on a will to dispose of your property, an inventory of your assets will generally need to be filed with the probate court, and the identity of the recipients of those assets will typically be disclosed. A living trust is a private document. There is no need for anyone to disclose its contents publicly.

- A living trust will also be useful to you during your own life if you become disabled. It is possible to define disability in the trust document so that a court determination is unnecessary, and a successor trustee (who you will have named in the trust) will step in to manage your affairs, invest your money, and pay your bills. This is far more convenient than a guardianship proceeding which would be required to give someone else the authority to protect your property. Although it is possible to take other steps to guard against disability (see discussion of durable powers of attorney in Chapter Eight), these other methods tend to be less effective.

Other Probate-Avoidance Techniques

In Chapter Six we told you of certain types of property that pass outside your will. Included were property held in joint tenancy with right of survivorship (often a home or bank account) which passes to the surviving joint tenant by operation of law; and property that passes under a contractual arrangement, such as the proceeds under a life insurance contract or a retirement plan, which pass to the beneficiary designated under the insurance policy or retirement plan.

Because such property does not pass by will, it is not subject to probate. Some estate planners use joint tenancy and beneficiary designations as tools for avoiding the probate system. Unfortunately, while this technique works reasonably well for a married couple to pass property to the surviving spouse, it tends not to work as well for passing property to the next generation. As a result, the surviving spouse generally needs a living trust if probate is to be avoided at his or her death.

Example Four

John and Mary have three children: Bob, Sam, and Julie. Bob and Julie have good jobs and are financially independent. Sam had a serious automobile accident which resulted in severe physical impairments. The value of John and Mary's estate is approximately $450,000, consisting of the following:

- A home that has a value (net of their mortgage) of $100,000
- Stocks with a value of $30,000
- Certificates of deposit with a value of $10,000

- A bank account with a value of $10,000
- John's retirement account with a value of $50,000
- Mary's retirement account with a value of $50,000
- Insurance on John's life with a death benefit of $100,000
- Insurance on Mary's life with a death benefit of $100,000

John and Mary can easily use joint ownership and beneficiary designations to avoid probate on the first of their deaths. All that is necessary is that they hold title to their home, stocks, certificates of deposit, and bank account as joint tenants with right of survivorship and name each other as beneficiaries on their retirement plans and life insurance policies.

If John were to die first, Mary would acquire ownership of the home, stocks, certificates of deposit, and bank account by operation of law without need of probate, because she is the surviving joint tenant. Similarly, she would receive the proceeds from John's retirement account and his life insurance, because she is designated as beneficiary.

However, now Mary would need to create an estate plan that would enable her to pass her property to Bob, Sam, and Julie when she dies. What options would she have?

The same options already discussed in this and the previous chapter. She could:

- Create a will and a special needs trust. This is the basic estate plan discussed in Chapter Six. The will would divide Mary's property among her children. The special needs trust would serve as a receptacle for Sam's share of Mary's estate, so that Sam could remain eligible for badly needed government benefits and avoid government claims for cost-of-care reimbursement. For example, Mary's will could leave her property equally between Bob, Julie, and Sam's trust. Mary could also name Bob, Julie, and Sam's trust as beneficiaries of her retirement plan and life insurance policy.

Unfortunately, while this approach would enable Mary to divide her property among her children in the manner that she would like and also make sure that Sam remains eligible for government benefits, it would not avoid probate at Mary's death. Alternatively, Mary could:

- Create a living trust (as previously described in this chapter). Mary would transfer all her property to the trust and name the trust as beneficiary under her retirement plan and life insurance policy. During her life, she would be sole trustee and would be entitled to use trust property however she would like. On her death, if Mary wanted to treat her children equally, Bob and Julie would each receive one-third of Mary's property, and Sam's share would remain in trust. This would permit Mary to avoid probate and would also permit Sam to remain eligible for government benefits and avoid cost-of-care reimbursement claims.

If avoiding probate is one of John and Mary's objectives, a living trust will be required. Joint tenancy and beneficiary designations can be used to avoid probate at the first of their deaths, but if they are to avoid probate at the death of the survivor, a living trust is necessary.

As long as a living trust will be needed, it makes sense for it to be created while John and Mary are both still living, so that both of them will have input into how their property will be divided. Moreover, if they decided to rely on joint tenancy and beneficiary designations while they were both living with the intention of having the survivor create a living trust after the death of the first of them, they would not avoid probate if they were to die simultaneously.

Why can't John and Mary avoid probate simply by having the survivor create a joint tenancy with his or her children? The answer is that they can, but there are severe drawbacks to doing so.

Example Five

The facts are the same as in Example Four, except that John has died and Mary has received property from John as a joint tenant and as beneficiary under John's retirement plan and life insurance policy. Mary now owns the following:

- A home that has a value (net of their mortgage) of $100,000, which she owned as joint tenant with John and inherited by virtue of being the surviving joint tenant
- Stocks with a value of $30,000, also received as surviving joint tenant
- Certificates of deposit with a value of $10,000, also received as surviving joint tenant
- A bank account with a value of $10,000, also received as surviving joint tenant
- Cash of $150,000, received as beneficiary under John's retirement plan and life insurance policy
- Her own retirement account with a value of $50,000
- Her own insurance with a death benefit of $100,000

Because Mary inherited property from John only as a surviving joint tenant and a beneficiary under John's retirement plan and life insurance policy, probate was not required at John's death. Mary seeks to avoid probate at her death without creating a living trust so she does the following:

- Places her cash, home, stocks, and certificates of deposit in joint tenancy naming Bob, Julie, and Sam's special needs trust as joint tenants.

- Names Bob, Julie, and Sam's trust as beneficiaries under her retirement plan and life insurance policy.

Like a living trust, this approach has the benefit of avoiding probate at Mary's death and permitting Sam to remain eligible for government benefits. However, the approach also suffers from severe limitations.

First, because Bob and Julie will be joint tenants, they will have ownership rights to Mary's property even while Mary is still living. The law permits a joint tenant to sell his or her interest in the property and to retain a proportionate share of the proceeds. Thus, if Mary and her children were to have a serious disagreement—and this can and does happen—Mary's ability to enjoy her property could be severely restricted.

Mary could guard against this possibility by placing her cash and certificates of deposit in an informal bank-trust account, also known as a "Totten Trust." Under such an arrangement, Bob, Julie, and Sam's trust would receive the cash at Mary's death only and would have no rights to the property during Mary's life.

However, these informal bank-trust accounts generally cannot be used for other types of assets, such as stocks, bonds, mutual funds, or real estate. Accordingly, if Mary owns assets of these types and wishes to avoid probate at her death, she must place them in joint tenancy and risk losing control of her property during her life. (A few states have special trusts for real estate, known as "land trusts," which operate much like the Totten trusts described above.)

Second, because Bob and Julie will be joint tenants, any creditors that they may have will have rights against their interests in Mary's property. Thus, if Bob or Julie were to incur significant debts, a creditor could seize their interests in the property, making things extremely uncomfortable for Mary. For example, the creditor could occupy a portion of Mary's house and perhaps even force her to sell it, keeping a pro rata portion of the proceeds.

Finally, a joint tenancy between Mary and her children would restrict Mary's flexibility in deciding how to distribute her property among her children. For example, if Mary were to name Bob, Julie, and Sam's trust as joint tenants, each of them would be entitled to one-third of the joint tenancy property at Mary's death. It would not be possible to give Sam's trust a larger share of the property, say 50 percent, because joint tenancy does not work that way. Each joint tenant receives an equal share by operation of law.

Clearly, a living trust provides far more safety and flexibility than does joint tenancy. As trustee of her own trust, Mary has the absolute right to do whatever she wants with her property and has no need to worry about disputes with family or the possible appearance of her childrens' creditors. She can leave the property to her children in whatever proportions she wants and can freely change her mind whenever she wants.

Moreover, as previously mentioned, a living trust permits Mary to plan for her own disability by giving her the power to name successor trustees. There is no need to endure a demeaning guardianship proceeding or to rely on a power of attorney that may or may not be accepted by third parties.

Conclusion

Like many of the common-law rules in our country, the probate system owes its beginnings to English law as it existed at the time our country was founded. This is hardly surprising, given that our most influential citizens at the time were fresh from England. How else to model the system they created, but from the laws and procedures they knew so well?

Unfortunately, even at that time the probate system was woefully out of date. The system began in the feudal era, when wealth and power meant ownership of land. The king had a direct interest in knowing how land passed when the owner died, and the probate system became the king's way of supervising the laws of descent.

Land passed only through costly and complicated probate proceedings, which took place in common-law courts known as the king's courts. Other property escaped such close supervision, with stocks, bonds, and personal property passing under less-formalized methods. In our own beginnings, we adopted the probate system for personal property as well as land.

Will the system ever be reformed?

The British have largely abolished it. In England, the deceased person's executor merely files an accounting of the decedent's property with the revenue department so the government can determine whether any tax is due. The property is then distributed to the decedent's creditors and heirs. Court supervision is required only if a will is contested or additional debts are claimed.

The system in many Western European countries is even simpler. The deceased person's representative simply distributes the decedent's property in accordance with the instructions contained in the will, without any governmental supervision at all. Disputes regarding the validity of a will are handled like other legal issues: the party claiming to be aggrieved files suit in court.

In our own country, however, the probate system remains largely intact. Reform efforts have been made. The American Bar Association, together with the National Conference of Commissioners on Uniform State Laws, has proposed a Uniform Probate Code that would simplify the probate system. Unfortunately, states have been slow to adopt the suggested changes, and progress has been spotty and generally inadequate.

The living trust represents a private-market response to the inadequacies of the probate system. Seeing the frustration generated by unnecessary cost and delay, enterprising individuals reasoned that probate is required only if an individual owned legal title to property at the time of death. They developed the living trust as a method of permitting an individual to forfeit legal title to property—and thereby avoid the probate system—while still retaining the right to use the property however he or she saw fit.

Is a living trust appropriate for everyone?

Despite our general enthusiasm for the approach, the answer is "not always."

If you are young and healthy, it may be advisable to forego the trust approach. While it is true that the living trust will save money at your death, it does cost more to prepare than a simple will. If you are young and healthy, you will likely live a very long time. As time passes you will want to revise your estate plan in any case, and you can always prepare a living trust at a later date.

Moreover, in certain very special cases, avoiding the probate system may not be the best thing to do. Remember, the probate system is designed to pass the decedent's property on to heirs free of the claims of creditors or other family members. Notice is given of the decedent's death to creditors and other interested parties, and they are given a certain period of time (typically about 6 months) to assert any claims against the decedent's estate. Claims that are not asserted within the statutory period are forever lost, and the decedent's heirs will not be forced to give back property that they have received.

Trusts do not afford the same certainty. Because there is no formal system for adjudicating the legitimacy of creditors' claims, creditors have a longer period of time to assert them. Although, as discussed earlier, this benefit of the probate system is usually not worth the time and cost that it engenders, people with complicated debt situations may feel differently.

Estate planning is not formulaic. What is right for one person is not necessarily right for another. The proper estate plan for a given individual depends on that individual's own particular needs and desires.

For many people, however, the living trust will be an important part of their estate plan. Placing your property in a properly drawn trust will have no effect on your ability to use your property however you would like. A living trust is as flexible as a will. You can change it whenever you like and leave your property to whomever you wish. (For example, some of your property can be distributed to children without disabilities, while other property remains in trust for a child with a disability.) The considerable time and expense of the probate system can be avoided.

However, there is one very important fact to keep in mind. If you are to avoid the probate system, you must transfer your property into the trust *during your lifetime*. Most estate plans that make use of living trusts also include documents known as *pour-over wills*, which transfer property that you own at your death into your trust.

These pour-over wills are not substitutes for lifetime transfers. They are backstops only, designed to make sure your property gets into the trust if you have mistakenly neglected to carry through with property transfers during your life. If your executor is required to use the pour-over will to transfer property into your trust, probate will be necessary as well, and the primary reason for using a living trust will not have been realized.

CHAPTER 7

Chapter 8

The Living Will and the Durable Power of Attorney

While few people would seriously question the benefits of the tremendous advances in medical technology over the last half of the twentieth century, it is an unfortunate fact that these advances have had a "dark side" as well. With the rise in medical malpractice suits and the "save life at all costs" approach inculcated by medical schools, doctors have spent a great deal of time in efforts to extend life. Until very recently, however, little time has been spent in determining whether the condition of the patient warrants such heroic measures. Advances in medical technology have not been matched by advances in medical ethics.

Fortunately, documents such as the living will and the durable power of attorney have been developed to enable people to retain some measure of control over the type of medical treatment given to them in the event of catastrophic illness or injury. What can happen if such a document is not prepared for you?

The well-known case of Karen Ann Quinlan, which received a great deal of media attention, represents an obvious case in point.

Karen Ann Quinlan was 21 when she lapsed into a coma, apparently after ingesting a mixture of alcohol and barbiturates at a party. She was placed on a respirator and remained in a chronic, persistent vegetative state.

After discussing the matter with his priest, Karen's father requested that the respirator be removed. Viewing this as a violation of medical ethics, the attending physician refused. The local prosecutor and the state attorney general threatened criminal proceedings. A court battle ensued, and Karen remained on a respirator for 2 years, more dead than alive, until the New Jersey Supreme Court finally granted her father's request that the respirator be removed. Amazingly, Karen lived for another 9 years, no longer hooked to a respirator, but fed through means of other "marvels" of modern medicine.

Another notable case, which was featured on the television program "20/20" in 1985, involved a fireman and emergency medical technician by the name of Paul Brophy.

Mr. Brophy was 45 when an artery burst in his brain. He never regained consciousness and was fed through a tube that was surgically implanted in his stomach. Mr. Brophy had never executed a durable power of attorney or a living will, but he had discussed the Quinlan case with family members, stating that he would never want to live on life-support systems. In fact, after rescuing a man from a burning truck who lingered for some time with severe burns before dying, Mr. Brophy expressed regret for the rescue and explicitly stated that the "plug should be pulled" if he were in a similar state.

Two years after her husband lapsed into a coma, Mrs. Brophy consulted with the family priest. She eventually contacted the church's ethicist in Washington, D.C., who advised her that it would be appropriate to request that the feeding tubes be removed.

Mrs. Brophy made the request, but the hospital refused. A lawsuit was filed. The trial judge refused to order removal of the feeding tube, reasoning that Mr. Brophy was not terminally ill because the feeding tube could be expected to keep him alive for the foreseeable future.

Mrs. Brophy appealed and eventually won in the Massachusetts Supreme Court. The feeding tube was removed and Mr.

Brophy died 8 days later, more than 3 years after he became comatose and more than a year after Mrs. Brophy requested that the artificial feeding tube be removed.

Perhaps the most famous case concerning the right to die was that of Nancy Cruzan, whose fate was ultimately decided by the United States Supreme Court in 1990.

On January 11, 1983, Nancy Cruzan, then 26, skidded while driving home. Her car overturned and she was thrown more than 20 feet and knocked unconscious. Paramedics arrived approximately 20 minutes later and began resuscitative efforts. On February 3, 1983, with the consent of her (then) husband, a feeding tube was inserted. Ms. Cruzan remained in a persistent vegetative state, and doctors indicated there was no realistic chance of recovery.

Nancy's parents requested that the tube be removed in the fall of 1986, approximately three and a half years after the accident. The hospital refused, perhaps fearing potential liability under Missouri state law, and a lawsuit was filed. Eventually an order to discontinue feedings was issued, but the State of Missouri appealed.

Like many people, Nancy Cruzan had taken no *formal* steps to indicate the type of medical treatment she would consider appropriate in the event of a tragic accident or incurable illness. Apparently, however, she had told a friend that she would never want to live in an irreversible coma, because she did not consider life worth living under such circumstances.

The Missouri Supreme Court refused to order the hospital to remove the feeding tube, finding Nancy's conversation with her friend to be insufficient proof that she would have wanted the feedings stopped. The United States Supreme Court upheld the decision, finding that the State of Missouri was within its rights to refuse to withhold feedings from a comatose patient who had not clearly expressed her intention. Fortunately, however, a new case was brought and "new evidence" was presented to indicate Nancy's intent. The tube was removed and Nancy died 12 days later, the day after Christmas, 1990, almost 8 years after the accident.

The cases of Nancy Cruzan, Paul Brophy, and Karen Ann Quinlan are not the only times where it was necessary for family members to go to court to force doctors and hospitals to stop artificial, life-sustaining treatments and permit loved ones, who were for all intents and purposes already dead, to die with dignity.

The cases are many and varied, and it is unwise to generalize too much. However, one point does stand out: if you do suffer a tragic accident and are unable to make medical decisions on your own, it is quite possible that doctors and hospitals will employ the entire array of medical techniques available to keep you alive indefinitely in circumstances in which death might be preferable. It might be possible for family members to bring a court case to force well-meaning health professionals to end their heroic efforts, but the emotional and financial cost involved cannot be overestimated.

Fortunately, however, techniques are available to insure that you will not suffer the fate endured by Nancy Cruzan, Paul Brophy, Karen Ann Quinlan, and many others. Many states have enacted living will or durable power of attorney statutes. These permit you to make your feelings known to doctors in a form that will be respected; they also allow you to appoint surrogates to make decisions on your behalf if you are not in condition to do so. Some states even permit family members to make decisions for relatives when a living will or durable power of attorney has not been prepared.

In most cases, we provide each of our clients with durable powers of attorney for health care and property to provide protection in circumstances of serious illness or injury.

The Power of Attorney for Health Care

The primary purpose of the power of attorney for health care is to enable you to appoint an agent to make medical decisions for you if you are unable to do so. The document would typically be prepared for you, though one can be prepared for a person with a disability as well if the person is able to understand the nature and purpose of the document.

Most people appoint a family member or a close friend as their agent. The document is fully revocable and can be revised at any time. Although the prescribed form varies somewhat by state, the following (which is for use in the State of Illinois) is typical.

ILLINOIS STATUTORY SHORT FORM POWER OF ATTORNEY FOR HEALTH CARE

(Notice: the purpose of this power of attorney is to give the person you designate [your "agent"] broad powers to make health care decisions for you, including power to require, consent to or withdraw any type of personal care or medical treatment for any physical or mental condition and to admit you to or discharge you from any hospital, home, or other institution. This form does not impose a duty on your agent to exercise granted powers; but when powers are exercised, your agent will have to use due care to act for your benefit and in accordance with this form and keep a record of receipts, disbursements, and significant actions taken as agent. A court can take away the powers of your agent if it finds the agent is not acting properly. You may name successor agents under this form but not co-agents, and no health care provider may be named. Unless you expressly limit the duration of this power in the manner provided below, until you revoke this power or a court acting on your behalf terminates it, your agent may exercise the powers given here throughout your lifetime, even after you become disabled. The powers you give your agent, your right to revoke those powers, and the penalties for violating the law are explained more fully in sections 4-5, 4-6, 4-9 and 4-10(b) of the Illinois "Powers of Attorney for Health Care Law" of which this form is a part. That law expressly permits the use of any different form of power of attorney you may desire. If there is anything about this form that you do not understand, you should ask a lawyer to explain it to you.)

POWER OF ATTORNEY made this __________ day of ____________, 19______.
(month) (year)

1. I, ____
(insert name and address of principal)

hereby appoint ______________________________________
(insert name and address of agent)

as my attorney-in-fact (my "agent") to act for me and in my name (in any way I could act in person) to make any and all decisions for me concerning my personal care, medical treatment, hospitalization, and health care and to require, withhold, or withdraw any type of medical treatment or procedure, even though my death may ensue. My agent shall have the same access to my medical records that I have, including the right to disclose the contents to others. My agent shall also have full power to make a disposition of any part or all of my body for medical purposes, authorize an autopsy, and direct the disposition of my remains.

(The above grant of power is intended to be as broad as possible so that your agent will have authority to make any decision you could make to obtain or terminate any type of health care, including withdrawal of food and water and other life-sustaining measures, if your agent believes such action would be consistent with your intent and desires. If you wish to limit the scope of your agent's powers or prescribe special rules or limit the power to make an anatomical gift, authorize autopsy, or dispose of remains, you may do so in the following paragraphs.)

2. The powers granted above shall not include the following powers or shall be subject to the following rules or limitations (here you may include any specific limitations you deem appropriate, such as: your own definition of when life-sustaining

measures should be withheld; a direction to continue food and fluids or life-sustaining treatment in all events; or instructions to refuse any specific types of treatment that are inconsistent with your religious beliefs or unacceptable to you for any other reason, such as blood transfusion, electro-convulsive therapy, amputation, psycho-surgery, voluntary admission to a mental institution, etc.):

____

____

____

____

(The subject of life-sustaining treatment is of particular importance. For your convenience in dealing with that subject, some general statements concerning the withholding or removal of life-sustaining treatment are set forth below. If you agree with one of these statements, you may initial that statement; but do not initial more than one):

______ I do not want my life to be prolonged nor do I want life-sustaining treatment to be provided or continued if my agent believes the burdens of the treatment outweigh the expected benefits. I want my agent to consider the relief of suffering, the expense involved, and the quality as well as the possible extension of my life in making decisions concerning life-sustaining treatment.

______ I want my life to be prolonged and I want life-sustaining treatment to be provided or continued unless I am in a coma which my attending physician believes to be irreversible, in accordance with reasonable medical standards at the time of reference. If and when I have suffered irreversible coma, I want life-sustaining treatment to be withheld or discontinued.

______ I want my life to be prolonged to the greatest extent possible without regard to my condition, the chances I have for recovery, or the cost of the procedures.

(This power of attorney may be amended or revoked by you in the manner provided in section 4-6 of the Illinois "Powers of Attorney for Health Care Law." Absent amendment or revocation, the authority granted in this power of attorney will become effective at the time this power is signed and will continue until your death, and beyond if anatomical gift, autopsy, or disposition of remains is authorized, unless a limitation on the beginning date or duration is made by initialing and completing either or both of the following:)

3. ( ) This power of attorney shall become effective on ___

____

(insert a future date or event during your lifetime, such as a court determination of your disability, when you want this power to first take effect)

4. ( ) This power of attorney shall terminate on _________

____

(insert a future date or event, such as a court determination of your disability, when you want this power to terminate prior to your death)

(If you wish to name successor agents, insert the names and addresses of such successors in the following paragraph.)

5. If any agent named by me shall die, become incompetent, resign, refuse to accept the office of agent or be unavailable, I name the following (each to act alone and successively, in the order named) as successors to such agent:

____

____

____

____

For purposes of this paragraph 5, a person shall be considered to be incompetent if and while the person is a minor or an adjudicated incompetent or disabled person or the person is unable to give prompt and intelligent consideration to health care matters, as certified by a licensed physician.

(If you wish to name your agent as guardian of your person, in the event a court decides that one should be appointed, you may, but are not required to, do so by retaining the following paragraph. The court will appoint your agent if the court finds that such appointment will serve your best interests and welfare. Strike out paragraph 6 if you do not want your agent to act as guardian.)

6. If a guardian of my person is to be appointed, I nominate the agent acting under this power of attorney as such guardian, to serve without bond or security.

7. I am fully informed as to all the contents of this form and understand the full import of this grant of powers to my agent.

Signed ____________________________________
(principal)

The principal has had an opportunity to read the above form and has signed the form or acknowledged his or her signature or mark on the form in my presence.

____________________ Residing at ____________________
(witness)

(You may, but are not required to, request your agent and successor agents to provide specimen signatures below. If you include specimen signatures in this power of attorney, you must complete the certification opposite the signatures of the agents.)

Specimen signatures of agent (and successors).	I certify that the signatures of my agent (and successors) are correct.
____________________ (agent)	____________________ (principal)
____________________ (successor agent)	____________________ (principal)
____________________ (successor agent)	____________________ (principal)

As is apparent, you appoint your agent by filling in item 1. Item 2 permits you to place certain limits on your agent's powers. Our clients usually do not fill this in because they are appointing someone whom they trust, and they do not want to restrict their agent's ability to act. Item 2 also permits you to give generalized instructions to your agent by placing your initials by one of three choices. Most people select the top choice, which gives their agent the broadest discretion; some feel more comfortable with the middle choice.

Items 3 and 4 permit you to state a period during which the document is effective. We usually leave these blank, which makes the power effective from the date the document is signed until the date of revocation (that is, the date you rip it up).

Item 5 is very important; it permits you to name successor agents in case the person you name in item 1 is unable to act. Remember, there is no guarantee that you won't outlive the person whom you select initially, and it is generally a good idea to have a couple of people named in reserve.

Finally, it is a good idea to talk about your feelings respecting appropriate medical care with the person you select as agent. Remember, this person will be attempting to act as you would yourself. There is no better way for them to determine what you would want, than to hear it straight from you.

The Living Will

A living will differs from the health-care power of attorney in that, where a durable power of attorney for health care enables you to appoint and instruct an agent, the living will addresses your doctor directly. In recent years the power of attorney has become the preferred means of protecting a person's right to control medical decisions, and living wills have declined in usage. This is true primarily for three reasons.

First, a living will is less flexible than a power of attorney for health care, because the doctor is necessarily confined to the four corners of the document. The doctor can interpret what is said in the document but lacks the flexibility to respond to events that you may not have anticipated when you wrote it. The power of attorney for health care appoints a trusted individual to act for you, and that person will presumably be able to respond to changed circumstances.

Second, a power of attorney for health care permits you to appoint someone you trust to oversee your medical care. While a living will tells your doctor what you want, there is no guarantee your wishes will be carried out. Remember, the doctor whom you know and trust may not be your doctor when an emergency ultimately arises; he or she may die before you.

Finally, a living will is restricted to instructions about life-sustaining treatments. A power of attorney for health care allows your agent to give permission for various types of treatment, as well as to withhold consent for procedures designed merely to artificially extend your life.

Notwithstanding the above, however, some people like to have a living will in addition to a power of attorney for health care. If you fit into this category, you will need to make sure your living will is consistent with the power of attorney for health care. The following is the form of living will prescribed by the state of Illinois.

ILLINOIS STATUTORY FORM OF LIVING WILL

This declaration is made this ____day of ______________

____________________(month, year).

I,____being of sound mind, willfully and voluntarily make known my desires that my moment of death shall not be artificially postponed.

If at any time I should have an incurable and irreversible injury, disease, or illness judged to be a terminal condition by my attending physician who has personally examined me and has determined that my death is imminent except for death-delaying procedures, I direct that such procedures which would only prolong the dying process be withheld or withdrawn, and that I be permitted to die naturally with only the administration of medication, sustenance, or the performance of any medical procedure deemed necessary by my attending physician to provide me with comfort care.

In the absence of my ability to give directions regarding the use of such death-delaying procedures, it is my intention that this declaration shall be honored by my family and physician as the final expression of my legal right to refuse medical or surgical treatment and accept the consequences from such refusal.

Signed ______________________________________

City, County and State of Residence ________________

The declarant is personally known to me and I believe him or her to be of sound mind. I saw the declarant sign the declaration in my presence, or the declarant acknowledged in my presence that he or she had signed the declaration, and I signed the declaration as a witness in the presence of the declarant. I did not sign the declarant's signature above for or at the direction of the declarant. At the date of this instrument, I am not entitled to any portion of the estate of the declarant according to the laws of intestate succession or to the best of my knowledge and belief, under any will of declarant or other instrument taking effect at declarant's death or directly financially responsible for declarant's medical care.

Witness ______________________________________

Witness ______________________________________

The Power of Attorney for Property

The power of attorney for property is designed to give someone the power to manage your property if you are unable to do so. As you may recall from Chapter Three, if you do become disabled, a guardian of your estate can be appointed to protect your financial interests. However, this entails a court proceeding which can be costly, time consuming, and demeaning. The power of attorney for property is an alternative to guardianship and is designed to protect your financial interests without need of a guardianship proceeding.

For most clients, we recommend that a power of attorney for property be prepared. Clients who prepare living trusts may not need the document because such clients presumably will have transferred their property to their living trusts, which provide for successor trustees in the event of disability (see Chapter Seven). However, the property power of attorney will be useful for property that may, either intentionally or inadvertently, have been left out of the trust. For example, certain assets, such as retirement accounts, cannot be transferred to a living trust, and your spouse may need to be able to make decisions about investments or distributions if you become disabled.

The statutory form of property power of attorney for use in the state of Illinois is shown below.

ILLINOIS STATUTORY SHORT FORM POWER OF ATTORNEY FOR PROPERTY

(Notice: The purpose of this power of attorney is to give the person you designate (your "agent") broad powers to handle your property which may include powers to pledge, sell, or otherwise dispose of any real or personal property without advance notice to you or approval by you. This form does not impose a duty on your agent to exercise granted powers; but when powers are exercised, your agent will have to use due care to act for your benefit and in accordance with this form and keep a record of receipts, disbursements, and significant actions taken as agent. A court can take away the powers of your agent if it finds the agent is not acting properly. You may name successor agents under this form but not co-agents. Unless you expressly limit the duration of this power in the manner provided below, until you revoke this power or a court acting on your behalf terminates it, your agent may exercise the powers given here throughout your lifetime, even after you become disabled. The powers you give your agent are explained more fully in Section 3-4 of the Illinois "Statutory Short Form Power of Attorney for Property Law" of which this form is a part. That law expressly permits the use of any different form of power of attorney you may desire. If there is anything about this form that you do not understand, you should ask a lawyer to explain it to you.)

POWER OF ATTORNEY made this _____ day of

______________, _______.
(month) (year)

1. I, ____
(insert name and address of principal)

hereby appoint: ______________________________________
(insert name and address of agent)

as my attorney-in-fact (my "agent") to act for me and in my name (in any way I could act in person) with respect to the following powers, as defined in Section 3-4 of the "Statutory Short Form Power of Attorney for Property Law" (including all amendments), but subject to any limitations on or additions to the specified powers inserted in paragraph 2 or 3 below:

(YOU MUST STRIKE OUT ANY ONE OR MORE OF THE FOLLOWING CATEGORIES OF POWERS YOU DO NOT WANT YOUR AGENT TO HAVE. FAILURE TO STRIKE THE TITLE OF ANY CATEGORY WILL CAUSE THE POWERS DESCRIBED IN THAT CATEGORY TO BE GRANTED TO THE AGENT. TO STRIKE OUT A CATEGORY YOU MUST DRAW A LINE THROUGH THE TITLE OF THAT CATEGORY.)

(a) Real estate transactions.
(b) Financial institution transactions.
(c) Stock and bond transactions.
(d) Tangible personal property transactions.
(e) Safe deposit box transactions.
(f) Insurance and annuity transactions.
(g) Retirement plan transactions.

(h) Social Security, employment, and military service benefits.
(i) Tax matters.
(j) Claims and litigation.
(k) Commodity and options transactions.
(l) Business operations.
(m) Borrowing transactions.
(n) Estate transactions.
(o) All other property powers and transactions.

(LIMITATIONS ON AND ADDITIONS TO THE AGENT'S POWERS MAY BE INCLUDED IN THIS POWER OF ATTORNEY IF THEY ARE SPECIFICALLY DESCRIBED BELOW.)

2. The powers granted above shall not include the following powers or shall be modified or limited in the following particulars (here you may include any specific limitations you deem appropriate, such as a prohibition or conditions on the sale of particular stock or real estate or special rules on borrowing by the agent):

____

____

____

____

3. In addition to the powers granted above, I grant my agent the following powers (here you may add any other delegable powers including, without limitation, power to make gifts, exercise

powers of appointment, name or change beneficiaries or joint tenants, or revoke or amend any trust specifically referred to below):

____

____

____

____

(YOUR AGENT WILL HAVE AUTHORITY TO EMPLOY OTHER PERSONS AS NECESSARY TO ENABLE THE AGENT TO PROPERLY EXERCISE THE POWERS GRANTED IN THIS FORM, BUT YOUR AGENT WILL HAVE TO MAKE ALL DISCRETIONARY DECISIONS. IF YOU WANT TO GIVE YOUR AGENT THE RIGHT TO DELEGATE DISCRETIONARY DECISION-MAKING POWERS TO OTHERS, YOU SHOULD KEEP THE NEXT SENTENCE, OTHERWISE IT SHOULD BE STRUCK OUT.)

4. My agent shall have the right by written instrument to delegate any or all of the foregoing powers involving discretionary decision-making to any person or persons whom my agent may select, but such delegation may be amended or revoked by any agent (including any successor) named by me who is acting under this power of attorney at the time of reference.

(YOUR AGENT WILL BE ENTITLED TO REIMBURSEMENT FOR ALL REASONABLE EXPENSES INCURRED IN ACTING UNDER THIS POWER OF ATTORNEY. STRIKE OUT THE NEXT SENTENCE IF YOU DO NOT WANT YOUR AGENT TO ALSO BE ENTITLED TO REASONABLE COMPENSATION FOR SERVICES AS AGENT.)

5. My agent shall be entitled to reasonable compensation for services rendered as agent under this power of attorney.

(THIS POWER OF ATTORNEY MAY BE AMENDED OR REVOKED BY YOU AT ANY TIME AND IN ANY MANNER. ABSENT AMENDMENT OR REVOCATION, THE AUTHORITY GRANTED IN THIS POWER OF ATTORNEY WILL BECOME EFFECTIVE AT THE TIME THIS POWER IS SIGNED AND WILL CONTINUE UNTIL YOUR DEATH UNLESS A LIMITATION ON THE BEGINNING DATE OR DURATION IS MADE BY INITIALING AND COMPLETING EITHER (OR BOTH) OF THE FOLLOWING:)

6. ( ) This power of attorney shall become effective on

____

____

(insert a future date or event during your lifetime, such as court determination of your disability when you want this power to first take effect)

7. ( ) This power of attorney shall terminate on_________

____

(Insert a future date or event, such as court determination of your disability, when you want this power to terminate prior to your death)

(IF YOU WISH TO NAME SUCCESSOR AGENTS, INSERT THE NAME(S) AND ADDRESS(ES) OF SUCH SUCCESSOR(S) IN THE FOLLOWING PARAGRAPH.)

8. If any agent named by me shall die, become incompetent, resign or refuse to accept the office of agent, I name the following (each to act alone and successively, in the order named) as successor(s) to such agent:

____

____

For purposes of this paragraph 8, a person shall be considered to be incompetent if and while the person is a minor or an adjudicated incompetent or disabled person or the person is unable to give prompt and intelligent consideration to business matters, as certified by a licensed physician.

(IF YOU WISH TO NAME YOUR AGENT AS GUARDIAN OF YOUR ESTATE, IN THE EVENT A COURT DECIDES THAT ONE SHOULD BE APPOINTED, YOU MAY, BUT ARE NOT REQUIRED TO, DO SO BY RETAINING THE FOLLOWING PARAGRAPH. THE COURT WILL APPOINT YOUR AGENT IF THE COURT FINDS THAT SUCH APPOINTMENT WILL SERVE YOUR BEST INTERESTS AND WELFARE. STRIKE OUT PARAGRAPH 9 IF YOU DO NOT WANT YOUR AGENT TO ACT AS GUARDIAN.)

9. If a guardian of my estate (my property) is to be appointed, I nominate the agent acting under this power of attorney as such guardian, to serve without bond or security.

10. I am fully informed as to all the contents of this form and understand the full import of this grant of powers to my agent.

Signed ____

(principal)

(YOU MAY, BUT ARE NOT REQUIRED TO, REQUEST YOUR AGENT AND SUCCESSOR AGENTS TO PROVIDE SPECIMEN SIGNATURES BELOW. IF YOU INCLUDE SPECIMEN SIGNATURES IN THE POWER OF ATTORNEY, YOU MUST COMPLETE THE CERTIFICATION OPPOSITE THE SIGNATURES OF THE AGENTS.)

Specimen signatures of agent (and successors).	I certify that the signatures of my agent (and successors) are correct.
____________________ (agent)	____________________ (principal)
____________________ (successor agent)	____________________ (principal)
____________________ (successor agent)	____________________ (principal)

(THIS POWER OF ATTORNEY WILL NOT BE EFFECTIVE UNLESS IT IS NOTARIZED, USING THE FORM BELOW.)

State of ____________________________)

County of ___________________________)

The undersigned, a notary public in and for the above county and state, certifies that ______________________________ known to me to be the same person whose name is subscribed as principal to the foregoing power of attorney, appeared before me in person and acknowledged signing and delivering the instrument as the free and voluntary act of the principal, for the uses and purposes therein set forth, and certified to the correctness of the signature(s) of the agent(s).

Dated: ________________________________

(SEAL)________________________________

Notary Public

My commission expires: ___________

(THE NAME AND ADDRESS OF THE PERSON PREPARING THIS FORM SHOULD BE INSERTED IF THE AGENT WILL HAVE POWER TO CONVEY ANY INTEREST IN REAL ESTATE.)

This document was prepared by:

____

The agent is appointed by filling in item 1. Item 2 permits the person preparing the power to place certain restrictions on their agent's ability to act. Although there are exceptions, our clients usually do not add restrictions. If you want to restrict your agent, you probably should not be preparing the power.

We also tend not to fill in items 6 or 7, which permit you to state when the power becomes effective. It is difficult to know what to say that would be helpful. For example, if you said the power was to be effective upon a court's determination that you were disabled, your agent would need to go to court in order to use the power. But going to court to establish disability is precisely what the power of attorney is designed to avoid. Your loved ones can do that anyway—without the power—to have themselves named as your guardian.

Alternatively, the power could be triggered by some future event, such as a doctor's determination of disability. However, it is questionable how helpful the power would be in this case; people with whom your agent might want to deal might be hesitant to rely on the power.

As a result, we tend to make the power effective upon signing. It then becomes vitally important that steps be taken to make sure it is not misused. Remember, the power gives your agent the right to do virtually anything you could do with your property. You need to make sure that you trust absolutely the person you select as agent. In many cases we hold the document for our clients, with the understanding that we will give it to their agent only after we determine that the client is disabled. Obviously, you must also be able to trust the person you ask to hold the power.

Conclusion

The power of attorney for health care offers you the power to appoint an agent to make health-care decisions for you if you are unable to do so. Virtually all of our clients have such documents prepared for them, though some prefer to leave the decision in the hands of their doctor.

The living will gives you the power to give instructions to your doctor. For the reasons discussed earlier, it is less flexible than the power of attorney and is therefore less commonly used.

The power of attorney for property gives you the opportunity to name someone to protect your property in the event you become disabled. Most of our clients have such documents prepared for them, though some do not, preferring the court supervision inherent in a guardianship proceeding.

If you do have such a document prepared for you, you need to decide whether you want it to become effective immediately, or when triggered by some future event, such as a doctor's determination that you are disabled. For the reasons discussed above, we typically recommend that the document be effective upon signing. Some clients prefer that it not be effective until a doctor's determination of disability, despite the risk that such a provision may make the document less useful in actual practice. It is vitally important that you take steps to make sure the power is not misused—by naming as agent someone whom you trust absolutely and perhaps by asking someone other than the agent to hold the power, with instructions that it not be given to the agent unless you become disabled.

All of these documents—the power of attorney for health care, the living will, and the power of attorney for property—can be amended or revoked at any time.

Chapter 8

CHAPTER 9

REDUCING THE ESTATE TAX OWING AT YOUR DEATH

IN GENERAL, THE FEDERAL GOVERNMENT PERMITS YOU TO LEAVE ANY amount of property to your spouse free of federal estate tax (assuming your spouse is a U.S. citizen), and up to $600,000 to any other person free of such tax. Thus, if the value of the property that you own at the time of your death is less than $600,000, no federal estate tax will be owing, and the planning ideas discussed in the remainder of this chapter (which are designed to reduce the tax owing at your death) will not be relevant to you. There is no need to plan to reduce estate tax if the law already provides that no estate tax is owing.

In determining whether the value of your estate reaches this $600,000 threshold figure, however, there are a few things you should keep in mind:

- First, property that you place in a revocable living trust will be considered your property for purposes of the computation. This may be a little confusing. In Chapter Seven we told you that placing property in a living trust avoids probate because the property is not considered yours by state probate courts. But here we're dealing with the Internal Revenue Service and not the states, and the Internal Revenue Service applies a different set of rules.

- Second, the proceeds of any life insurance policies payable on account of your death will be considered part of your estate if you have any ownership rights under the policies (for example, the right to change beneficiaries). For example, if you have a term insurance policy with a death benefit of $500,000, the Internal Revenue Service will count the $500,000 as part of your estate, even though you never "owned" any of the money during your life. (Life insurance proceeds are generally exempt from income tax, but estate tax is different.)

- Third, if you are married, you need to think about your spouse's assets as well as your own. Remember, estate tax generally will not be owing until the death of the second of you, and you need to consider property that you will receive from your spouse (assuming your spouse dies before you) as well as property you own currently. For example, if you and your spouse own a house with a value (net of debt) of $100,000, stocks and securities worth $50,000, and you each have life insurance of $250,000, your estate is worth $650,000.

If you do have a taxable estate, the tax is figured at a graduated rate; the greater the value of your estate, the higher the rate. The tax begins at 37 percent on estates worth more than $600,000 and increases gradually on larger estates up to a maximum of 55 percent for estates with a value in excess of $3 million.

Example One

John and Mary have an estate with a value of approximately $1 million: a home with a value (net of mortgage) of $200,000; stocks with a value of $100,000; John's retirement account with a value of $150,000; Mary's retirement account with a value of

$150,000; insurance on John's life, naming Mary as beneficiary, with a death benefit of $200,000; and life insurance on Mary, also with a death benefit of $200,000, naming John as beneficiary.

Assuming John dies first and leaves all his property to Mary, no tax is owing on John's death because federal estate tax does not apply to property left to a surviving spouse, no matter how great the amount. Estate tax will be owing when Mary dies if the value of her property exceeds $600,000. Assuming Mary has an estate worth $1 million the tax will be $153,000. No estate tax will be owing on the first $600,000 of value, but the tax on the remaining $400,000 will be computed at a "blended rate" of 38.25 percent.

The result is unchanged if John and Mary put their property in a living trust to avoid probate, as described in Chapter Seven. Fortunately, however, there are steps John and Mary can take to reduce or completely eliminate the tax.

Using the Credit-Shelter Trust to Reduce Estate Tax

The *credit-shelter trust*, also known as the *marital-bypass trust*, is perhaps the best estate-tax planning device available to upper middle-class couples. The trust is used to permit each member of the couple to use their $600,000 exemption.

In Example One above, John and Mary had an estate that was worth $1 million. Because their estate plan was designed to leave all their property to the survivor on the death of the first of them, the survivor was left with $1 million. That resulted in the survivor having a taxable estate (that is, an estate in excess of $600,000).

In effect, John wasted his $600,000 exemption. Had John left his $500,000 share of their net worth to someone other than Mary (perhaps to his children), no tax would have been owing at his death: the law permits him to leave up to $600,000 free of tax to people other than Mary. Similarly, no tax would have been owing at Mary's death because she would have had less than $600,000. It was only because John left his $500,000 to Mary that a taxable estate was created; otherwise Mary would have had less than the $600,000 threshold amount.

But John did not want to leave his property to anyone other than Mary. He wanted her to have the use and benefit of the $500,000.

The credit-shelter trust would have offered John a way out of his dilemma. The law permits John to create a trust for Mary, entitling her to the use and benefit of his property. If the trust is properly drawn, the property will not be considered Mary's for purposes of computing the estate tax owing at Mary's death.

In order for this to work, the law requires that certain limitations be placed on Mary's use of the trust property. However, in actual practice, these limitations are more theoretical than real.

For example, Mary can be named sole trustee of the trust after John's death and can be given the right to all the income of the trust, and principal to the extent required for her maintenance in health and reasonable comfort. Technically, Mary is not able to use the trust money for whatever purpose she wants because her ability to use trust principal is limited to use for her maintenance in health and *reasonable* comfort. However, since reasonable is interpreted taking into account Mary's prior standard of living, Mary can use the trust principal to continue in her accustomed lifestyle.

Moreover, in the interest of flexibility, Mary will typically be given the ability to direct that the remainder of the trust be distributed among one or more of a selected group of recipients at her death (for example, among such of John and Mary's descendants as are selected by Mary.) This ability of Mary's to appoint the remaining trust property away from undeserving children is likely to ensure that Mary's wishes will be respected.

Example Two

John and Mary have three young children: Bob, Sam, and Julie. Sam has epilepsy and retardation and is expected to move into a group home when he gets older. Bob has just turned 7 and is in the first grade. Julie is age 4 and attends preschool.

John and Mary have an estate with a value of approximately $1 million: a home with a value (net of mortgage) of $200,000; stocks with a value of $200,000; John's retirement account with a value of $100,000; Mary's retirement account with a value of $100,000; insurance on John's life, naming Mary as beneficiary, with a death benefit of $200,000; and life insurance on Mary, also with a death benefit of $200,000, naming John as beneficiary.

This information is summarized below:

Doe Family Balance Sheet

Asset	**John**	**Mary**	**Joint**
Home			$200,000
Stocks			$200,000
Retirement Plan	$100,000	$100,000	
Insurance	$200,000	$200,000	
	$300,000	$300,000	$400,000

John and Mary would like all their property to be available for the survivor of them. At the death of the survivor, they want to divide the property equally between their children. They expect that Sam will require group housing and they want to keep their options open by making sure Sam remains eligible for government benefits. They are also fearful of providing too much money for Bob and Julie at too early an age. They want to make sure Bob and Julie will have the maturity and experience to manage their money properly, and they believe it unhealthy for young adults to inherit significant amounts of money. They don't want to stifle Bob and Julie's initiative.

John and Mary have read Example One and studied it carefully. They realize that if they prepare simple estate plans, leaving all their property to the survivor of them, estate tax will be owing at the death of the second of them. Assuming the survivor dies with an estate of $1 million (including insurance), the tax will be $153,000.

John and Mary decide on the following estate plan:

- John and Mary each create credit-shelter trusts, naming themselves as trustee. That is, John is named trustee of his trust, Mary is named trustee of her trust, and each of them is entitled to use the property in his or her trust however he or she would like. On the death of the first of them, the survivor becomes trustee of the decedent's trust as well, and is entitled to all of the income of the trust and all principal to the extent required for the survivor's maintenance in health and reasonable comfort.

- John and Mary then divide their property between their respective trusts. Each of their trusts receives a one-half interest as tenant in common in their home; each trust receives $100,000 in stock; John's trust is named beneficiary of the insurance on his life; and Mary's trust is named beneficiary of the insurance on her life. John names Mary, or if she predeceases him, his trust, as beneficiary of his retirement plan. Mary names John, or if he dies before her, her trust, as beneficiary under her retirement plan. The new ownership arrangement is summarized below:

Revised Balance Sheet

Asset	John	Mary	Joint
Home	$100,000	$100,000	
Stocks	$100,000	$100,000	
Insurance	$200,000	$200,000	
Retirement Plan	$100,000	$100,000	
	$500,000	$500,000	$0

Now see what happens on the death of John or Mary. If John dies first, $400,000 (the $100,000 value of John's one-half interest in the home, $100,000 in stock, and $200,000 of insurance on John's life) remains in a credit-shelter trust for Mary. Mary has assets with a value of $600,000 ($100,000 from John's retirement plan, the $100,000 value of her interest in the home, $100,000 from her own retirement plan, $100,000 in stock, and $200,0000 in insurance on her life). Mary has the use and benefit of the entire $1 million and, assuming Mary has less than $600,000 at the time of her death, no estate tax will be owing. That is, John has achieved his objective of making sure that Mary receives all their property at his death. He has also saved $153,000 in estate tax that would have been owing at Mary's death had he not made use of the credit-shelter trust.

Similarly, if Mary dies first, $400,000 (the $100,000 value of Mary's one-half interest in the home, $100,000 in stock, and $200,000 in insurance on Mary's life) remains in a credit-shelter trust for John. John has assets with a value of $600,000 ($100,000 from Mary's retirement plan, the $100,000 value of his interest in the home, $100,000 from his own retirement plan, $100,000 in stock, and $200,0000 in insurance on his life).

John and Mary have also retained maximum flexibility to decide how their property is to be distributed among their children at the death of the survivor of them. One approach would be to provide that their trusts are split into three shares, one for each of their children. Sam's share would remain in a special needs trust (drafted in accordance with the provisions in Chapter Six), so Sam would remain eligible for government benefits in the future.

Bob and Julie's shares would be distributed among them in stages: a third at age 25, a third at age 30, and a third at age 35. In the meantime, the successor trustee would be directed to use Bob and Julie's shares for their health, education, and general welfare. This would permit John and Mary to make sure the money is available to Bob and Julie but would also restrict their access so that Bob and Julie would not have too much money at too early an age.

John and Mary would also typically retain the flexibility to make needed revisions in case a change in circumstances required a change in plans.

As is apparent, John and Mary have made use of the credit-shelter trust to generate substantial estate-tax savings (more than

$150,000) and have retained maximum flexibility in their estate plan. The key to the estate-tax savings was John and Mary's ability to divide their property between them so that the survivor would have less than $600,000 in assets at his or her death. This is accomplished by having them divide their property between their credit-shelter trusts and naming the trusts as beneficiaries under their life insurance policies.

As a general rule, our clients do not name the trusts as *primary* beneficiary of retirement plans. This is because there are income-tax advantages in naming the surviving spouse as beneficiary, although sometimes the trust must be named to gain maximum estate-tax savings. We typically name the surviving spouse as primary beneficiary and the trust as secondary beneficiary. Thus, John would name Mary as primary beneficiary. John's trust would be beneficiary if Mary died before him. Similarly, Mary would name John as primary beneficiary under her retirement plan. Mary's trust would be beneficiary if John died before her.

In John and Mary's case the property division was very easy. Each of them put $200,000 in life insurance, $100,000 in stocks, and their interest in their home (also valued at $100,000) in their credit-shelter trust. This left the survivor with $600,000 (as well as access to the funds in the credit-shelter trust).

Sometimes the property division is not so smooth. For example, in some cases one spouse may own most of the property and may not feel comfortable transferring ownership of significant amounts of property to the other. This is very common in the case of a second marriage or in a first marriage when the couple has not been married for a very long time.

Is a credit-shelter trust helpful when property cannot be divided among spouses? The answer is "maybe," depending on which of the spouses dies first.

Example Three

John and Mary are in their early sixties and have been married for a long time. John has two children from a previous marriage: Bob, who has a bipolar disorder (also known as manic depression), and Julie, who is married and has a family of her own. Mary's child, Sam, is also married and is a successful businessman.

John has worked for many years and has a sizable estate: a home with a value (net of mortgage) of $350,000; stocks and securities with a value of $150,000; life insurance with a death benefit of $200,000; and a retirement account with a value of $400,000. Mary spent most of her life making a home for her family and used what savings she did have to put Sam through school.

John and Mary would like most of their property to be available for the survivor of them, though John does want $100,000 to be set aside for Bob, "just in case something should happen." At the death of the survivor, they want to divide the property equally among all of their children. John has read Example Two and understands the value of the credit-shelter trust. However, he does not feel comfortable putting his property in Mary's name. He trusts her implicitly but does not think it appropriate for her to have the ability to disinherit Bob or Julie.

John and Mary decide on the following estate plan:

- John creates a living trust, naming himself as trustee. He transfers ownership of the house and his stock and securities to the trust, and names the trust as beneficiary of his retirement plan. At his death, the trust divides into three parts: $100,000 goes into a special needs trust for Bob; $500,000 goes into a credit-shelter trust so John and Mary can realize the estate tax savings described in Example 2; and the remaining $500,000 goes into a special trust, known as a QTIP trust, to be held for Mary. This trust is prepared in accordance with special provisions contained in the Internal Revenue Code that permit John to restrict Mary's use of the money while counting the money as Mary's for estate tax purposes.

- John wants Mary to have the use and benefit of the $1 million placed in the QTIP and credit-shelter trusts, but he wants some restriction on her ability to use the money so something will be left for Bob and Julie. John names Mary as trustee and beneficiary of the trusts, but he names a bank, or perhaps Julie, as cotrustee.

- On the death of Mary, the property is divided equally between Bob, Sam, and Julie, except that an equalizing distribution is made to Sam and Julie to account for the fact that Bob received $100,000 when John died. Bob's share remains in a special needs trust, so he remains eligible for government benefits.

Now let's examine the estate-tax consequences of the plan, keeping in mind the general rule that an individual can leave any amount of property to his or her spouse free of tax, and up to $600,000 to any other persons free of tax.

If John dies first, $100,000 goes into a special needs trust for Bob, $500,000 is held in the credit-shelter trust for Mary, and $500,000 is held in the QTIP trust. Because the money in the QTIP is considered Mary's for estate-tax purposes, John is treated as if he gave $500,000 to Mary and $600,000 to persons other than Mary ($100,000 to Bob's trust and $500,000 to the credit-shelter trust). No tax is owing. Similarly, when Mary dies, no estate tax will be owing because she will have less than $600,000; only the $500,000 in the QTIP trust will be considered hers.

So far so good. The problem arises if Mary dies first. Because John did not make transfers of property to Mary during his life, he is left with more than $600,000. He owns $1.1 million, and an estate tax of approximately $195,000 will have to be paid (assuming John still has $1.1 million when he dies).

This is not to say that John should make the transfers in his lifetime; he has very good reasons for not doing so. However, John's failure to make property transfers will cause an increase in estate tax if he dies after Mary.

Reducing Estate Tax with the Irrevocable Insurance Trust

The credit-shelter trust can be used by a married couple to protect up to $1.2 million from estate tax. The *irrevocable insurance trust* can be used to save estate tax by couples who have more than $1.2 million, and by individuals who have more than $600,000.

Properly drafted, the trust permits life-insurance proceeds to escape estate tax altogether. The idea is for the trust to be both owner and beneficiary under the insurance policy. Because the insured has no ownership rights under the policy (for example, the insured is not allowed to change the beneficiary or to borrow against the policy) none of the proceeds are includable for estate-tax purposes.

In order for the plan to succeed, ownership of policies must be transferred to the trust at least 3 years before the insured dies (assuming the insured had ownership rights before the transfer). It is necessary that the trust be irrevocable, and that the insured give up *all* ownership rights under the policy. For example, the insured cannot retain the right to change beneficiaries or have access to any cash value in the policies or be named trustee of the insurance trust. Thus, the trust is less flexible than the credit-shelter trust, which can be amended or revoked at any time.

Notwithstanding this reduced degree of flexibility, however, the estate-tax savings resulting from the irrevocable insurance trust can be enormous. The trust can therefore be a valuable estate-planning tool for wealthy and upper middle-class individuals and couples. In addition, though the irrevocable insurance trust may not be as flexible as the credit-shelter trust, it remains possible for the insured to retain a considerable degree of flexibility.

For example, the trust can be funded with term insurance. If circumstances change and the insured no longer finds the terms of the trust to be appropriate, the insured can "revoke" the trust by failing to pay premiums on the policy. Assuming the person remains insurable, a new policy can be issued, perhaps to a new irrevocable insurance trust that is more appropriate to the insured's changed circumstances. Similarly, if the insured is married, the spouse can be given a limited power to alter the disposition of the trust.

Example Four

John and Mary have three young children: Bob, Sam (who has autism), and Julie. Bob has just turned 7 and is in the first grade. Julie is age 4 and attends preschool.

John and Mary have an estate with a value of approximately $1.5 million: a home with a value (net of mortgage) of $200,000; stocks with a value of $200,000; John's retirement account with a value of $100,000; Mary's retirement account with a value of $100,000; insurance on John's life, naming Mary as beneficiary, with a death benefit of $700,000; and life insurance on Mary with a death benefit of $200,000, naming John as beneficiary.

This information is summarized below:

Doe Family Balance Sheet

Asset	John	Mary	Joint
Home			$200,000
Stocks			$200,000
Retirement Plan	$100,000	$100,000	
Insurance	$700,000	$200,000	
	$800,000	$300,000	$400,000

John and Mary are aware that they can shelter up to $1.2 million from estate tax by dividing their assets and using the credit-shelter trust as described in Example Two. However, because the value of their estate exceeds $1.2 million, this will not be enough to completely eliminate the tax. Assuming the value of their estate remains constant at $1.5 million, $300,000 will be subject to tax at the death of the second of them, and the tax will be approximately $110,000.

John and Mary decide on the following estate plan:

- First, they each create credit-shelter trusts, naming themselves as trustee. That is, John is named trustee of his trust, Mary is named trustee of her trust, and each of them is entitled to use the property in his or her trust however he or she would like. On the death of the first of them, the survivor becomes trustee of the decedent's trust as well, and is entitled to all of the income of the trust and all principal to the extent required for the survivor's maintenance in health and reasonable comfort.

- Second, John creates an irrevocable insurance trust to serve as owner and beneficiary of the insurance on his life, naming Mary as trustee. The terms of the trust are substantially similar to the terms of John's credit-shelter trust. Mary is entitled to all the income of the trust and principal to the extent required for her maintenance in health and reasonable comfort. It would also be possible for Mary to create an irrevocable insurance trust naming John as trustee, but the size of their estate does not justify such a step.

- Third, they divide their property between their credit-shelter trusts to make use of their $600,000 exemptions. One approach would be for them to transfer a one-half interest in their home and $100,000 in stock to each of their trusts. Mary's trust would be named beneficiary of the insurance on her life. John would name Mary, or if she predeceases him, his trust, as beneficiary of his retirement plan. Mary would name John, or if he dies before her, her trust, as beneficiary under her retirement plan. The new ownership arrangement is summarized below:

Revised Balance Sheet

Asset	John	Mary	Insurance Trust
Home	$100,000	$100,000	
Stocks	$100,000	$100,000	
Insurance	0	$200,000	$700,000
Retirement Plan	$100,000	$100,000	
	$300,000	$500,000	$700,000

Now see what happens on the death of John or Mary. If John dies first, $200,000 (the $100,000 value of John's one-half interest in the home and $100,000 in stock) remains in a credit-shelter trust for Mary, and $700,000 is paid to the irrevocable insurance trust. In addition, Mary has assets with a value of $600,000 ($100,000 from John's retirement plan, the $100,000 value of her interest in the home, $100,000 from her own retirement plan, $100,000 in stock, and $200,0000 in insurance on her life). Mary has the use and benefit of all the family's property and, assuming Mary has less than $600,000 in her name or the name of her trust at the time of her death, no estate tax will be owing.

Similarly, if Mary dies first, $400,000 (the $100,000 value of Mary's one-half interest in the home, $100,000 in stock, and $200,000 in insurance on Mary's life) remains in a credit-shelter trust for John. John has assets with a value of $400,000 ($100,000 from Mary's retirement plan, the $100,000 value of his interest in the home, $100,000 from his own retirement plan, and $100,000 in stock). The insurance trust continues to own the $700,000 in insurance on John's life, and a new trustee is chosen.

John and Mary have also retained maximum flexibility to decide how their property is to be distributed among their children at the death of the survivor of them. One approach would be to provide that their trusts are split into three shares, one for each of their children. Sam's share would remain in a special needs trust (drafted in accordance with the provisions in Chapter Six), so Sam would remain eligible for government benefits in the future.

Bob and Julie's shares would be distributed among them in stages: a third at age 25, a third at age 30, and a third at age 35. In the meantime, the successor trustee would be directed to use Bob and Julie's shares for their health, education, and general welfare. This would permit John and Mary to make sure the money is available to Bob and Julie but would also restrict their access so Bob and Julie would not have too much money at too early an age.

John and Mary would also typically retain the flexibility to make needed revisions in case a change in circumstances required a change in plans.

As is apparent, John and Mary have used the irrevocable insurance trust to augment the power of the credit-shelter trust without changing their basic estate plan, to make all their property available to the survivor and then to place it in carefully tailored trusts for their children. The only real difference is that the irrevocable trust permits them to shelter a larger share of their property from estate tax.

The irrevocable insurance trust can also be used to save estate tax for those for whom a credit-shelter trust would typically be inappropriate (for example, people who are not married).

Example Five

Mary is a widow with two children: Bob, who is happily married with 3 children of his own, and Julie, who has schizophrenia and is unable to hold a job. Mary has $800,000 in assets: a home with a value of $250,000, insurance with a death benefit of $250,000, and stocks and securities with a market value of $300,000.

Because Mary has more than $600,000 in property, without advance planning, estate tax will be owing at Mary's death. Assuming the value of Mary's estate remains constant, the tax will be approximately $75,000. Because Mary is unmarried, a credit-shelter trust will not be helpful.

Accordingly, Mary decides on the following estate plan:

- First, Mary creates a living trust as described in Chapter Seven, and makes the trust the owner of her home, her stocks, and securities. This will not help with estate tax, but it will enable Mary to avoid probate.

- Second, Mary creates an irrevocable insurance trust, and she names the trust owner and beneficiary under the policy. Because the value of Mary's estate is now reduced to $550,000, estate tax will not be owing at her death (assuming her estate does not grow by more than $50,000).

- Third, Mary has the trusts prepared so that, at her death, half the trust property is distributed to Bob, and the remaining half is held in a special needs trust for Julie.

Another use of an irrevocable insurance trust is to reduce estate tax that will be owing if couples who do not want to shift ownership of their assets do not die "in the right order."

Example Six

The facts are the same as in Example Three. John has an estate with a value of $1.1 million: a home with a value (net of mortgage) of $350,000, stocks and securities with a value of $150,000, life insurance with a death benefit of $200,000, and a retirement account with a value of $400,000. He is unwilling (perhaps for very good reasons) to transfer ownership of any of his property to his wife, Mary.

As illustrated in Example Three, John can use a credit-shelter trust to eliminate estate tax if he dies before Mary; $600,000 could go into the credit-shelter trust and the remaining $500,000 could be held in a special QTIP trust for Mary. Because the money in the QTIP is considered Mary's even though her ability to use it is restricted, no tax is owing on John's death. The law permits him to leave any amount of property to Mary and up to $600,000 to persons other than Mary free of tax and that is precisely what John has done. He has left $500,000 to Mary (because the money in the

QTIP trust is considered hers) and $600,000 to persons other than Mary. Similarly, on Mary's death, no tax is owing because she has less than $600,000.

However, if Mary dies first, John will be left with the entire $1.1 million, and estate tax will be owing. John can reduce the tax by transferring his $200,000 insurance policy to the irrevocable insurance trust. This reduces his estate to $900,000 and thereby reduces the tax.

John can, of course, wait to see if Mary dies first and transfer the policy into trust at that time. This would eliminate a trust-preparation fee that would prove unnecessary if John were to die first. However, as stated above, the irrevocable insurance trust works for existing policies owned by the insured only if the policies are transferred to the trust at least three years before the insured dies. Waiting to see who dies first increases the risk that John will run afoul of this three-year rule.

In preparing an irrevocable insurance trust, special care has to be taken to reduce any gift tax consequences resulting from payment of premiums or the transfer of policies that have a cash value into the trust. Your attorney will be able to help you with this.

Reducing Estate Tax Through Gifting Programs

Lifetime property transfers, or gifts, represent a common method of reducing estate tax for families that are unable to eliminate the tax through use of the credit-shelter trust and the irrevocable insurance trust. Before making a gift, however, you should make sure you will not need the property that you give away, recognizing that your financial requirements may increase as time goes on. Gifts are, by their very nature, irrevocable, and it is important that you do not risk your own lifetime security in order to reduce the amount of estate tax that will be owing at your death.

Having said that, however, lifetime gifts can be a very valuable estate-planning device for the affluent. Although the law imposes a *gift tax* to limit their tax-reducing potential, lifetime gifts remain a useful device for reducing transfer taxes applicable to the wealthy.

The Gift Tax and the Annual Exclusion Gift

Stripped to its barest essentials, the gift tax serves as a "backstop" to the tax on transfers at death. Without a tax on lifetime transfers, the estate tax would be easy to defeat indeed. A person could simply make lifetime transfers of the bulk of his or her property to family members, perhaps even making such transfers while at death's door.

The gift tax defeats this strategy by imposing a tax on lifetime transfers. In general, the tax works hand in hand with the tax on transfers at death. Lifetime gifts reduce the $600,000 estate-tax exemption on a dollar for dollar basis and are subject to tax to the extent that they exceed $600,000.

Under an important exception to this rule, however, a person is entitled to give away up to $10,000 *per donee per year* without causing a reduction in the $600,000 exclusion or the imposition of any gift tax. This is known as the *annual exclusion gift* and is the most common method of using gifts to reduce transfer taxes. Assuming enough donees and enough years, the amount of estate tax saved can be staggering.

Example Seven

John and Mary have an estate worth approximately $10 million. They have little need for so much money and are interested in making annual exclusion gifts to reduce the tax owing when they die. They have 3 daughters, each of whom is married with 3 children of her own.

Assuming John and Mary make annual exclusion gifts to each of their daughters, sons-in-law and grandchildren, they can make a total of $300,000 in gifts each year ($10,000 from each of them to each of nine grandchildren, three daughters, and three sons-in-law) without any reduction in their $600,000 exclusions or the imposition of any gift tax. Because John and Mary are in the 55 percent gift and estate tax bracket, each year's gifts save a *minimum* of $165,000 in taxes.

In fact, the tax savings attributable to each year's gifts are significantly greater. The property given away will grow through investments, but since John and Mary have given the property away, the appreciation will not be included in their estate. Assuming the property could have been invested at a 7 percent annual return, the $300,000 given away each year will double in value every 10 years, which means the estate-tax savings attributable to each year's gifts doubles in value as well.

If John and Mary are nervous about the effect that such large gifts might have on family members, the gifts could be made in trust. This would be the typical approach for gifts to young children or grandchildren. The trusts would need to be specially drawn so the gifts would qualify for the annual exclusion. Gifts to children with disabilities would typically be made through special needs trusts.

Gifts Exceeding the Annual Exclusion

A common belief of people who regularly make annual exclusion gifts is that it is unwise to increase such gifts above the annual exclusion amount. This belief could not be further from the truth.

It is true that gifts in excess of the annual exclusion reduce the donor's $600,000 estate-tax exclusion and result in gift tax after the exclusion is reduced to zero. However, such excess gifts almost always result in a net transfer-tax savings. This is true for two reasons.

First, the value of the estate of a wealthy individual tends to increase as time passes because the individual's earnings (including investment earnings) will usually exceed living expenses. By making large gifts, the donor removes both the gifted property and the earnings that the property generates from his or her estate. In effect, then, by using up the $600,000 exemption during his or her life, an individual increases the value of that exemption. This principle is demonstrated in Example Eight below.

Second, although the statement seems paradoxical, paying gift tax actually reduces total transfer taxes. This is because the money used to pay the gift tax is generally not part of the donor's estate. Importantly, however, the gift tax is brought back into the donor's estate if the donor dies within three years of making the gift. This will be illustrated in Example Nine.

Example Eight

John and Mary have a very large estate. In addition to making annual exclusion gifts as described in Example Seven, they each give $600,000 to their children. As described above, this gift reduces each of their $600,000 estate-tax exclusions to zero. However, by accelerating use of the exemption, they have significantly increased its value.

To illustrate, suppose John and Mary had retained the $1.2 million, invested it at 7 percent, and died twenty years later. The $1.2 million would have been worth $4.8 million when they died (it would have doubled in value every 10 years), and $3.6 million would have been subject to tax. By accelerating use of their $600,000 lifetime exemptions, John and Mary have increased the value of their aggregate exemptions from $1.2 million to $4.8 million.

Example Nine

John and Mary have a very large estate. In addition to making annual exclusion gifts as described in Example Seven and using up their estate-tax exemptions as described in Example Eight, they make additional gifts giving rise to gift tax of $500,000. Assuming John and Mary live for at least three years after the date of the gift, the gift tax will not be included in their estates and John and Mary will have saved $275,000 in taxes (because if they did not pay the gift tax and instead kept the $500,000, it would have been taxed at a 55 percent rate). The tax savings potential of the gift will be even greater when we take account of the fact that John and Mary will not be subject to estate tax on the earnings generated by the gifted property.

A final caveat. In making gifts of property other than cash, you will need to give some thought to the income tax that will be owing when the property is ultimately sold. In general, such tax will be based on the gain *realized* when the property is sold. This, in turn, will be measured by the difference between the *sales price* and the property's *tax basis*.

Although tax basis is generally measured by cost, property that is inherited at the owner's death takes a *stepped-up basis* equal to the property's fair market value at the date of death (or sometimes on an alternate valuation date). Because property that is given away during the donor's life retains its cost basis, giving away property that has appreciated in value, or is likely to appreciate in value, will frequently result in increased income tax when the property is eventually sold.

Example Ten

John owns 100 shares of IBM stock, which he bought for $5,000. He gives the stock to Steve, who sells it at John's death when the value of the stock is $15,000. John's gain is $10,000, and the tax will be approximately $3,000. Had Steve received the stock as a result of John's death, the stock would have received a stepped-up basis to $15,000 and the tax would have been eliminated.

Of course, by making the gift, John has reduced the value of his estate by $15,000, which could result in a reduction in estate tax of more than $3,000 ($7,500, assuming a 50 percent effective tax rate). In addition, if Steve dies while still owning the stock, it will receive a stepped-up basis at that time.

The loss of a stepped-up basis does not mean gifts of appreciated property should not be made. However, the loss should be considered before any gifting program is begun.

Generation-Skipping Transfers

Thus far we have talked about methods of reducing the amount of estate tax that will be owing at your death. Estate planning can also involve planning to permit the passage of wealth through multiple generations.

To consider an obvious example, suppose you have a taxable estate (that is, an estate with a value in excess of $600,000) and you expect your children to have taxable estates as well. If you leave your property to your children, the property will be subject to estate tax at your death, and also when your children die.

Example Eleven

John and Mary have an estate with a value of $3 million. Their children have good jobs and are expected to amass substantial estates of their own.

Assuming John and Mary make maximum use of the credit-shelter trust, and assuming the irrevocable insurance trust is not helpful to them (perhaps because they have no life insurance), $1.8 million of their property will be subject to tax when they die, and the tax will be approximately $800,000. Thus, John and Mary's children will receive $2.2 million ($3 million less $800,000 of tax) at the death of John and Mary.

Assuming the $2.2 million does not increase in value, and assuming John and Mary's children are in the 55 percent estate tax bracket, this $2.2 million will then be subject to a tax of approximately $1.2 million when it is passed on to John and Mary's grandchildren. Thus, John and Mary's grandchildren will receive approximately $1 million ($2.2 million less $1.2 million of tax).

Of course, John and Mary can eliminate the tax at the death of their children by giving the money directly to their grandchildren. (Actually they can give their grandchildren only $2 million of the $2.2 million, or they will be subject to a special generation-skipping tax.)

However, it is unlikely that they would wish to do so. In most cases, John and Mary will want to leave their money to their children; they want their children to be comfortable, and it may be detrimental to the development of their grandchildren to have access to such a large amount of money.

The *generation-skipping trust*, also known as the *dynasty trust* or *mega-trust*, would enable John and Mary to meet their objective. In general, John and Mary can leave their property in trust for their children, enabling them to have access to trust property if needed. But the trust can be prepared so that the property will not be taxed when John and Mary's children die.

Example Twelve

John and Mary have an estate with a value of $3 million. Their children have good jobs and are expected to amass substantial estates of their own.

As in Example Eleven, assuming John and Mary make maximum use of the credit-shelter trust and divide their property equally between them, $1.8 million of John and Mary's property will be subject to tax when they die, and the tax will be approximately $800,000. However, instead of leaving the remaining $2.2 million (after estate tax is paid) directly to their children, suppose John and Mary place $2 million in generation-skipping trusts and leave just $200,000 directly to their children.

Under the terms of the generation-skipping trusts, John and Mary's children would be entitled to income and principal from the trusts as needed, and the trusts would go to John and Mary's grandchildren on the death of John and Mary's children. John and Mary's children could even be given the power to appoint the trusts away from undeserving grandchildren.

Now look what happens on the death of John and Mary's children. In Example Eleven John and Mary's children received $2.2 million, and the tax when they died was $1.2 million, leaving $1 million for the grandchildren. Here, however, John and Mary's children have received only $200,000, though they have access to the entire $2.2 million. The estate tax on the death of John and Mary's children has been reduced to approximately $100,000. Thus, John and Mary's grandchildren end up with $2.1 million ($2.2 million less $100,000). This is $1.1 million more than if a generation skipping trust is not used.

The benefit of the generation-skipping trust appears even greater when we consider the earnings the money could generate. If we assume the $2.2 million has grown to $5 million by the time John and Mary's children die, and this takes just seventeen years assuming an after tax return of 5 percent, the tax if a generation-skipping trust is not used is $2.75 million (55 percent of $5 million). If a generation-skipping trust is used, the tax is approximately $250,000 (because only the $200,000 left to John and Mary's children and the appreciation attributable to that $200,000 is subject to tax). Thus, the tax savings increases to $2.5 million.

In fact, the savings can be greater yet, because the trust can be prepared so that the money is not distributed until the death of John and Mary's grandchildren. This means that another generation of tax will be avoided and even more savings will result as a consequence of the accrual of earnings.

Little wonder, then, that the trust is sometimes referred to as a *dynasty* or *mega* trust. (A complicated law known as the *rule against perpetuities* keeps the trust from remaining in existence in perpetuity.)

Conclusion

Planning to reduce the amount of tax owing at your death is complicated, and this chapter is not intended to be a "do it yourself guide" to estate-tax planning. Rather, our intention is to describe some of the more common techniques that are available, to make you aware of the magnitude of savings that is possible, and to enable you to discuss your options intelligently with estate-planning professionals.

If the value of your estate is less than $600,000, no estate tax will be owing at your death, and estate-tax planning will not be necessary. If your estate exceeds $600,000 and you are married, a credit-shelter trust should be considered. If your estate exceeds $600,000 and you are unmarried, or if you are married and the savings generated through use of a credit-shelter trust will not eliminate the estate tax owing at your death, you should think about establishing an irrevocable insurance trust. If your estate is sufficiently large, some type of gifting program and generation-skipping strategy should be considered. In fact, a generation-skipping trust can be beneficial even if you are not "rich," if your children are wealthy.

Some of the more esoteric estate-tax planning strategies have not been discussed, because they are useful only to the very wealthy and only in very limited circumstances. For example, it is possible to make use of *grantor-retained income trusts* (GRITs), *grantor-retained annuity trusts* (GRATs), or *grantor retained unitrusts* (GRUTs) to increase the estate-tax savings potential of your gifts without actually increasing their size.

For those who are charitably inclined, gifts to charities are generally deductible for both income and transfer-tax purposes. It is possible to make such gifts through charitable remainder trusts, so that you will continue to have access to the income generated by the gifted property during your life. Because such trusts are exempt from capital gains tax, they can also be used by those who wish to convert assets that do not produce current income (such as growth stocks or real estate) to income producing property.

If it all sounds complicated, that's because it is. If you have a sizable estate, it is very important that you receive assistance from estate planners who are familiar with all the various tax-saving techniques that are potentially available to you. You should be aware that not all estate planners are familiar with the various possibilities. You should shop carefully for someone who has the requisite tax expertise.

CHAPTER 9

CHAPTER 10

PROTECTING YOUR PROPERTY FROM NURSING-HOME EXPENSES

PLANNING YOUR ESTATE TO ENSURE YOUR CHILD'S FINANCIAL future will do little good if the bulk of your property is "used up" to pay nursing-home expenses in your final years. The statistics are frightening.

Americans are growing older, and the need for nursing-home assistance is increasing. According to the best available evidence, over 65 million Americans are age 65 or older, and approximately half of them can be expected to require nursing-home care at some time during their lives, most for between 1 and 5 years or longer. In 40 years, 1 in 5 Americans is projected to fit in the "senior citizen" category, and the numbers will continue to grow.

With improvements in health care and increased attention to diet and exercise, life expectancy can only increase. The "old-timer" at the turn of the century was under 50 years of age; average life expectancy in the United States was just 47 years. A person born today can expect to live until the age of 75; many live much longer.

How great can the expense of nursing-home care be?

The price is soaring and is already beyond the means of all but the wealthy. The average cost of nursing-home care is estimated at $24,000 per year nationally and can run as high as $60,000 annually in the Northeast. In 30 years, average annual costs are expected to increase from $24,000 to $55,000.

And don't be fooled into believing that you're "protected" because you have Medicare or private medical insurance. Neither Medicare nor private medical insurance pay for nursing-home care.

Medicare can provide some help if you're moved to a *skilled nursing facility* for *medically necessary care* directly after a hospital stay. Assuming the bed assigned to you is Medicare-certified, Medicare will pay for the first 20 days of care, and for up to 80 additional days after you pay the first $92 each day during the extended 80-day period (based on 1996 benefit levels).

However, most nursing homes are not skilled nursing facilities, and nursing-home care tends to be *custodial* and not *medical*. Most residents are elderly, suffering from senility, or Alzheimer's or Parkinson's disease, or the effects a stroke. Many need help eating, bathing, dressing, and taking medication, but not the care of physicians, nurses, or other medical professionals, and medicare is completely unavailable to them.

Even in those few cases when Medicare is available (because the care is medically necessary, comes immediately after a hospital stay of at least three consecutive days, is provided at a Medicare-approved skilled nursing facility, and can only be provided at such a facility), the benefit levels are woefully inadequate. Remember, benefits run out after 100 days, and most nursing-home stays are far greater in duration.

As for standard private medical insurance, forget it. Standard private medical insurance policies, including most Medicare supplement policies, pay for *medical* care, not *custodial* care. As stated above, most nursing-home care does not qualify. The following example is all too typical.

Example One

John and Mary have been married for many years. They have 3 children: Sam, who has an obsessive compulsive disorder, and Jane and Julie, who have good jobs and families of their own.

John and Mary have worked hard their entire lives and have saved a substantial sum of money that they intend to leave to Sam to make his life easier after they are gone. They have read Chapters One through Nine of this book and have prepared Letters of Intent and trusts for Sam, choosing trustees and advocates carefully, and are reasonably confident that Sam's future is assured.

Unfortunately, John becomes very ill, and a substantial portion of their property is used to pay medical and related bills. Mary becomes worn down caring for John and enters a nursing home shortly after John's death. The money that she had intended for Sam is consumed by her nursing-home expenses.

Fortunately, there are steps John and Mary could take to protect Sam's future. One possibility has already been discussed. John and Mary could fund Sam's special needs trust during their lives, perhaps with a life insurance policy. Other approaches are discussed in the remainder of this chapter.

Using Medicaid to Pay Nursing-Home Expenses

Although Medicare will not pay the cost of long-term nursing-home care, funds are available if you qualify under the strict guidelines for eligibility under the joint federal and state Medicaid program. Unfortunately, as you probably recall from Chapter Four, Medicaid is for the very poor, and people with income or assets above a very low minimum amount are not eligible.

Medicaid Eligibility—The Basics

Medicaid is jointly funded and administered by the federal government and the states. The federal government provides funds for state-operated Medicaid programs but requires the states to follow its rules and regulations. Some of these rules are very specific, but others afford a fair degree of flexibility. Accordingly, the rules in your state may differ somewhat from the rules discussed in this chapter, and it will be necessary for you to consult with a lawyer in your own state to gain a thorough understanding of the rules that apply to you.

To briefly summarize the basic eligibility requirements (you may want to review the relevant sections of Chapter Four to refresh your memory), Medicaid will not be available to you if your *countable* assets exceed $2,000 ($3,000 in some states). In making this determination, however, certain assets are excluded. The following are some of the more important:

- Household goods and personal effects (some states limit the value that may be protected).

- A car of any value. In some states the car is protected only if its value does not exceed $4,500, though even in these states the entire value will typically be excluded if the car is necessary for employment or medical treatment, or if it is modified for a person with a disability.

- Cash value of life insurance policies provided the death benefit does not exceed $1,500, burial policies, burial plots, segregated burial accounts of up to $2,500, and term insurance policies, regardless of the death benefit.

- One wedding ring and one engagement ring.

- Up to $6,000 in equity value of income-producing property essential to self-support (such as machinery used in a small business). Some states provide greater protection.

In addition, all states provide some measure of protection for your home, although the degree varies depending upon where you live. In most states your home will be protected as long as you intend to return there after your nursing-home stay, or as long as your spouse, a minor child, or a child with a disability lives there.

However, it may not remain exempt. For example, if your spouse has died and you go into a nursing home, your home could be seized by Medicaid authorities at your death (or when it becomes apparent that you will not return there), assuming a minor child or a child with a disability does not live there. If such a child does live there, the home will likely be seized when the child moves out.

Medicaid also provides income limitations, although these tend to be less important than the asset limits discussed above. In most states the rules are rather simple: Medicaid will not pay if your monthly income exceeds your nursing-home expense. If your monthly income is less than your nursing home bills, Medicaid makes up the difference.

Some states, however (so-called "income cap states"), have stricter limits and will not permit you to receive benefits under the Medicaid program if your income exceeds a statutorily determined amount. The amount varies from state to state and is revised periodically. In 1996, most of these "income cap states" denied Medicaid to applicants whose income exceeded $1,410 per month. This can cause severe hardship. While income that is slightly above $1,410 per month is enough to cause income cap states to deny Medicaid coverage, it is not sufficient to cover nursing home expenses. Fortunately, the law generally permits residents of income cap states to qualify for Medicaid by creating trusts to receive income in excess of the income cap (for 1996, $1,410 per month). The trusts must satisfy requirements set forth in the Medicaid statutes.

States generally allow nursing-home residents to keep a monthly allowance for personal needs (typically $30, though the amount is slightly higher in some states), a monthly premium to pay for medical insurance (including Medicare), and a home-maintenance allowance (if the resident is expected to go home after the nursing home stay).

Special Rules for Married Couples—Asset Protection

In 1988 Congress enacted a new law known as the Spousal Impoverishment Act, which was designed to provide some measure of protection for spouses of people who were about to enter nursing homes. The law was intended to deal with situations like the following.

Example Two

John and Mary have been married for many years and have lived thriftily, saving a substantial sum for their "golden years." Their house is completely paid for, and they have accumulated an additional $100,000 in investment assets. As with most married couples, their assets are owned jointly.

In the absence of special rules for married couples, if either John or Mary were to fall ill and require nursing-home care, they would have to *spend down* virtually all their *nonexempt* assets before government aid for nursing-home expenses would be available. In effect, the "well spouse" would be left with a house (because it is an exempt asset) and $2,000, turning the "golden years" to lead.

The Spousal Impoverishment Act attempts to rectify the problem by allowing the stay-at-home spouse to keep a larger percentage of the couple's property, although the amount still remains smaller than it should. The calculation is relatively simple.

On the day John or Mary enters the nursing home, most states require that the couple total all their nonexempt assets, regardless of whose name they are in. The stay-at-home spouse is then allowed to keep one-half of the total assets up to a maximum of $76,740, but not less than $15,348. The numbers are based on the rules in effect in 1996 and will increase each year to account for inflation. States can elect to raise the $15,348 minimum, and several states have chosen to do so.

In order to gain the benefit of the spousal-asset allowance, it is typically necessary that assets equal in amount to the allowance be transferred to the stay-at-home spouse.

Example Three

John and Mary have been married for many years. John enters a nursing home owning nonexempt assets totaling $30,000. Mary has nonexempt assets worth $40,000, and their jointly owned nonexempt assets have a value of $50,000.

Mary is allowed to keep assets with a value of $60,000, calculated as follows: on the day John enters the nursing home John and Mary have nonexempt assets with a value of $120,000. That amount is divided by 2, yielding a result of $60,000. Since $60,000 is more than $15,348 and less than $76,740, that is what Mary is allowed to keep.

If John and Mary had nonexempt assets worth $200,000, Mary would keep $76,740 (since $76,740 is less than one-half of $200,000). Similarly, if John and Mary had nonexempt assets worth $25,000, Mary would have been allowed to keep $15,348 (since $15,348 is more than one half of $25,000). If John and Mary lived in a state that has raised the minimum spousal-asset allowance to $76,740 (and several states have elected to do so), that is the amount Mary would be allowed to keep, regardless of the value of John and Mary's nonexempt assets (assuming, of course, that John and Mary had at least $76,740 of nonexempt assets).

To get the benefit of the spousal-asset allowance, it is usually necessary for Mary to have nonexempt assets in her name with a value equal to the spousal-asset allowance. Mary will also want to change her will so that the property will not be distributed to John in the event she dies before him. Otherwise, the property could be seized by the government under a cost-of-care claim or cause John to lose his Medicaid eligibility.

Mary could leave the property to her children. Alternatively, if Mary is concerned about what might happen to John if she dies before him, she may fear that he may need "a little extra" because Medicaid may not provide adequate resources to enable John to have the kind of life that Mary would like, she can create a special needs trust for John in her will. The trust would be similar to the special needs trust described in Chapter Six and would provide for John's requirements over and above those supplied by the government. The trust would need to be created in Mary's will, and not by living trust, as special rules would treat the property as John's for Medicaid eligibility purposes if it were created other than by will.

Special Rules for Married Couples—Income Protection

Medicaid also provides special rules that permit the stay-at-home spouse to keep a portion of the couple's joint income. In general the stay-at-home spouse is entitled to keep all of his or her income, plus a share of the nursing-home resident's income to the extent required to increase the stay-at-home spouse's share to a minimum amount. The amount is determined by a complicated formula and varies by state, but it is typically between $1,254 and $1,918. (The numbers are based on the rules in effect for 1996 and will increase each year to account for inflation.)

States that provide the minimum basic allowance of $1,254 are also required to provide an "excess shelter allowance" for stay-at-home spouses who have high housing expenses. The calculations are complicated, and the Medicaid authorities in your state will be able to help you with them, but the total amount will not exceed the maximum allowance ($1,918 for 1996).

Example Four

John goes into a nursing home after having been married to Mary for many years. They have total income of approximately $2,100 per month: John's $900 monthly Social Security payment, Mary's $450 Social Security check, and John's $750 monthly pension benefit.

Assuming John and Mary live in a state that permits Mary to keep the minimum $1,254 spousal allowance, Mary will be allowed to keep $804 out of John's $1,650 monthly income in addition to her own $450 Social Security payment (that gets her to the $1,254 minimum). If John and Mary live in a state that permits Mary to keep the $1,918 maximum, she will be able to keep $1,468 (in addition to her own Social Security benefits).

These calculations are designed to determine what portion of the nursing-home spouse's monthly income the stay-at-home spouse is allowed to keep. The stay-at-home spouse is always entitled to keep all of his or her own income. This differs from the rules relating to assets, which can often require the stay-at-home spouse to spend down his or her own assets before the nursing-home spouse qualifies for Medicaid benefits.

Example Five

Mary goes into a nursing home after having been married to John for many years. They have total income of approximately $3,000 per month: John's $900 monthly Social Security payment, Mary's $450 Social Security check, and John's $1,650 monthly pension benefit.

John will be entitled to keep his entire $2,550 monthly income, even though it exceeds the state's monthly spousal-income allowance because Medicaid does not require the stay-at-home spouse to spend his or her own income to pay a spouse's nursing home costs.

Medicaid Planning: Qualifying for Aid While Protecting Your Estate

The goal of Medicaid planning is to permit people who are entering nursing homes to qualify for Medicaid while retaining as much of their property as possible for family members and other loved ones. This frequently involves making large gifts of property either before or shortly after entry into a nursing home. Before making such gifts, however, it is important that you weigh the potential disadvantages, and compare them to the benefits of Medicaid eligibility.

First, nursing homes on average collect about 20 percent less from Medicaid than from private-pay patients. As a result, not all nursing homes accept Medicaid residents, and some that do reportedly put them in less-desirable rooms, despite federal law that prohibits discrimination against Medicaid recipients. Therefore, before you begin transferring assets, you need to make sure an acceptable placement will be available to you.

Second, if you do transfer a large portion of your property and never enter a nursing home, or if you go into a nursing home and later recover, the transferred assets may not be available to you. It is therefore vitally important that you transfer assets only to someone you can trust absolutely.

For people whose assets are relatively modest, however, Medicaid planning can make a great deal of sense. Such individuals will not want to leave spouses or children with disabilities destitute, and a great deal can be done to help them.

Medicaid Planning—Basic Rules on Asset Transfers

Planning to qualify under the Medicaid program would be a simple matter if the law pertaining to Medicaid eligibility did not contain rules restricting asset transfers. All you would need to do is transfer your property to your children before entering a nursing home, and qualification would be instantaneous.

Unfortunately, things are not that simple. Medicaid will generally not be available to you if you transfer assets for less than fair market value within 36 months of your Medicaid application. The ineligibility period begins on the date of the asset transfer and ends on the date determined by dividing the value of the transferred property by the average cost of nursing-home care in the state of your residence. In the case of certain transfers from trusts, asset transfers within 60 months of your Medicaid application can be problematic. As a result, if you establish a living trust (see Chapter Seven) and you wish to make a gift, you should transfer the property that you intend to give away into your own name before making the gift. That way, if you enter a nursing home, the gift will affect your eligibility for Medicaid only if it is made within 36 months of your Medicaid application, as opposed to 60 months if the gift is made directly from your living trust.

Medicaid will still be available if denial of benefits results in undue hardship, though application of this exception is generally uncertain, and it is not advisable to rely on it. In addition, Medicaid will be available if all assets which you transfer for less than fair market value are returned to you. The Medicaid transfer rules can also result in ineligibility for certain in-home services if assets are transferred within 36 months of your Medicaid application (or 60 months if the transfer is directly from a trust) .

Example Six

One year before John enters a nursing home he gives $45,000 to his children. The average monthly cost of nursing-home care in the state where John resides is $3,000.

Under the Medicaid transfer rules John is ineligible for Medicaid coverage for a period of 15 months (45,000 divided by 3,000), beginning on the date of the transfer. Because the transfer took place a year before John entered the nursing home, he will be eligible for Medicaid in three months.

Medicaid does permit certain asset transfers within the 36-month period. You can:

- Transfer your home to your spouse; a child who is under age 21, blind, or permanently and totally disabled; a child who provided care to you and resided in your home for at least 2 years immediately prior to the date you entered the nursing home; or a sibling who has an ownership interest in the home and who resided there for at least 1 year immediately before the date you entered the nursing home.

- Transfer any property to your spouse or to another person for the sole benefit of your spouse; or a child who is under age 21, blind, or permanently and totally disabled or to a trust established solely for the benefit of such a child.

- Transfer exempt assets, other than your home, to anyone.

- Transfer any property to anyone if you can prove you intended to transfer the property for its fair market value, or that you transferred it for a purpose other than to qualify for Medicaid.

Now that you know the rules, it is time to see how you can use them to your benefit. Keep in mind that the rules relating to Medicaid eligibility are complex, and there is a great deal of variation among the states. Before you try any of the techniques discussed below, it is absolutely vital that you consult an attorney familiar with the laws governing Medicaid eligibility in the state where you reside.

Transferring Assets to Your Spouse

As described above, on the day a person enters a nursing home, a "snapshot" is taken of the assets owned by the person and his or her spouse. Medicaid then permits the spouse to keep one-half of the assets, with a minimum spousal share of $15,348 and a maximum of $76,740. This suggests that little is to be accomplished through spousal-asset transfers. Why transfer assets to your spouse if the property is included in the "snapshot"?

Example Seven

John and Mary have been married for many years. When John enters a nursing home, they own a house with a value of $150,000 and nonexempt assets with a value of $100,000. If John later applies for Medicaid, Mary will be allowed to keep the house as long as she lives there and one-half of the nonexempt assets (or $50,000), though Mary will likely need to have $50,000 in her name to get the benefit of the spousal-asset allowance.

There is, however, an important benefit to spousal-asset transfers. Think about what happens if Mary dies before John. Assuming one-half of the nonexempt assets are held in Mary's name, $50,000 would pass under the terms of her will, which presumably had been changed so the $50,000 would not be left directly to John (otherwise John would be ineligible for Medicaid). The remaining property would be in John's name alone and would have to be spent before John would be eligible for Medicaid, though the home would remain an exempt asset until John dies or it becomes apparent that John would be unable to live there. At that time it would probably be seized by Medicaid authorities.

Suppose instead that all the assets are transferred to Mary. In some states, when Mary dies she can transfer whatever remains at her death to her children or to a special needs trust for John. That may exceed $50,000 if John's nursing-home bill has not yet reached that amount, and nothing is left for Medicaid. (Special rules prohibit Mary from making lifetime transfers.)

An important note. Some states would consider a transfer to Mary to be *nonexempt* to the extent that nonexempt assets transferred to her exceed the spousal-asset allowance (in Example Seven, $50,000). Even in many of these states, however, significant benefits can be gained by making sure the house (which is exempt) and property with a value equal to the spousal-asset allowance are in Mary's name alone. Mary would then be able to leave this property to her children when she dies, or to a special needs trust for John in the event Mary dies before him.

Transfers to Children or Other Trusted Relatives

As described above, the Medicaid transfer rules are designed to disqualify you from Medicaid if you transfer assets within 36 months of your Medicaid application. This means that asset transfers that take place more than 36 months before the application will not count against you. An obvious strategy for making yourself eligible for Medicaid, then, is to transfer assets more than 36 months before Medicaid will be requested.

Example Eight

John is a widower with incipient Alzheimer's. He has a very close, loving relationship with his children, and he trusts them absolutely. John realizes his condition is deteriorating, and he expects to enter a nursing home at some point in the future, though the exact date remains unknown. John has approximately $70,000 in nonexempt assets.

John transfers the nonexempt assets to his children, with the informal understanding that they will use them for John's benefit. John's children could even transfer the property to a trust established for John's benefit, though it is best that they not do so immediately after they receive the property from John. Assuming John does not enter a nursing home for at least 36 months after he transfers his property to his children, he will be immediately eligible for Medicaid upon entry.

Of course, in most cases people will not want to transfer their property to their children, particularly if it is uncertain whether or when nursing home assistance would be required. Are asset transfers still helpful when nursing home assistance is more imminent? The answer requires a thorough understanding of the rules relating to the Medicaid ineligibility period.

As you no doubt recall, asset transfers can make you ineligible for Medicaid if they occur within 36 months of your Medicaid application. The ineligibility period is determined by dividing the amount transferred by the average cost of nursing-home care in the state in which you reside. These rules permit you to transfer significant assets, while retaining enough to permit you to meet your needs during the Medicaid ineligibility period.

Example Nine

John is about to enter a nursing home that has a monthly cost for private pay patients equal to $3,000, which is also the average monthly cost of nursing-home care in the state where John resides. John has approximately $120,000 in nonexempt assets.

If John were to transfer his nonexempt assets to his children, the ineligibility period would be 40 months. This is determined by dividing the value of the nonexempt assets ($120,000) by the average monthly nursing home charge in the state of John's residence ($3,000).

Suppose instead that John were to transfer only $60,000 to his children. John would be ineligible for Medicaid for 20 months ($60,000 divided by $3,000), but he would have $60,000 to pay the first 20 month's expenses. This is known by attorneys who practice in elder law as the "half-a-loaf" method, because it permits Medicaid applicants to retain one-half of their nonexempt assets. John could even consider retaining an additional amount to serve as a "cushion" in the event that costs increase within the 20-month period.

The Medicaid Trust

For many years, the Medicaid Trust was used to place assets beyond the reach of Medicaid authorities without actually transferring ownership of the assets to another person. The concept first gained popularity in the 1970s.

The Medicaid applicant would transfer ownership of property to an irrevocable trust, naming a child or another loved one as trustee, and would give the trustee the discretion to distribute income and principal to the applicant as the trustee saw fit. Because the applicant would not have legal control over the trust property—the applicant could not force the trustee to make distributions—the property in the trust was not considered the applicant's for Medicaid qualification purposes. In reality, however, because the applicant would choose trustees carefully, the trust property would be readily available. Legislation enacted by Congress in 1986 and strengthened in 1993 restricted use of this planning device. It remains possible to transfer property to a trust and retain rights to income only. However, very few people wish to give up the right to principal so the approach tends not to be useful. In addition, the "look back" period for such transfers is 60 months.

Gifts to Children with Disabilities

As you may recall, transfers to children with disabilities or to trusts established solely for the benefit of such children are generally exempt from the Medicaid transfer rules. This means you can transfer property to a child with a disability or to a trust established solely for the benefit of such a child shortly before applying for Medicaid without having to worry about the 36-month rule.

As you know from prior chapters in this book, it is rarely a good idea to transfer assets directly to a person with a disability. However, although the law is not entirely clear, it seems that a transfer to a special needs trust created for a child with a disability should qualify as an exempt transfer because such a trust should be considered to have been established solely for the benefit of a child with a disability. Depending on the terms of the trust, however, it may be possible for the state to take the position that the trust has not been established for the *sole* benefit of the child with a disability.

Example Ten

John is about to enter a nursing home. He has three children: Fred, who has mild retardation and a bipolar brain disorder, and Bob and Julie, who have good jobs of their own. John owns a home, and he has approximately $50,000 in stocks and bonds.

Shortly before entering the nursing home (the transfer could actually take place at any time, though it is generally best to do it before John applies for Medicaid), John transfers his property to a special needs trust for the benefit of Fred. The trust is prepared in accordance with the principles outlined in Chapter Six. Distributions are to be made for Fred's benefit during his life, and any property remaining when Fred dies is to be distributed to Bob and Julie, or their children if Fred outlives them.

The issue that arises is whether the trust has been created *solely* for Fred's benefit. Although Fred is the only beneficiary during his life, any remaining property goes to Bob and Julie (or their children) after Fred dies, so Bob and Julie and their children may be considered beneficiaries as well.

If John lives in a state that considers such a trust to be for Fred's sole benefit, the transfer does not affect John's ability to receive Medicaid. Similarly, as discussed in Chapter Six, in most states it will not affect Fred's ability to receive government benefits either.

What if John does not live in a state that considers the trust to be for Fred's sole benefit? A slightly modified approach can be employed.

Example Eleven

John is about to enter a nursing home. He has three children: Fred, who has mild retardation and a bipolar brain disorder, and Bob and Julie, who have good jobs of their own. John owns a home, and he has approximately $50,000 in stocks and bonds.

Shortly before entering the nursing home, John transfers his property to a special needs trust for the benefit of Fred. The trust is identical to the trust outlined in Example Ten except that, before distributing the property remaining at Fred's death to Bob and Julie, the trustee is first to reimburse the state for any government benefits provided to Fred during his life.

This trust will be considered to be for Fred's *sole* benefit under the Medicaid rules, and John can transfer his property to the trust without affecting his eligibility for government benefits. However, the trust may not serve John's purposes as well as the trust described in Example Ten because it will not permit John to get as much property to Bob and Julie when Fred dies. John can, however, combine gifts to Fred's trust with other techniques discussed elsewhere in this chapter that are designed to get property in Bob and Julie's hands.

What if John lives in a state that has not determined whether a trust like the trust in Example Ten will be considered to be for Fred's sole benefit? Although the answer depends on John's willingness to take risks, the authors feel strongly that John should use a trust like the trust described in Example Eleven. The reason is that if John transfers his property to a trust that the state claims is not for Fred's sole benefit, John will have lost control of his property and may not be eligible for the aid he needs to pay for nursing home assistance.

Hiding Property in Exempt Assets

As mentioned above, certain assets are not *countable* for Medicaid purposes. These *noncountable* assets can be owned by you without jeopardizing your Medicaid eligibility, and a common strategy is to convert countable assets into noncountables. This *conversion* is accomplished by spending countable assets to acquire or improve noncountable assets.

Although many different types of assets are considered noncountable under the Medicaid rules (lists are provided at the beginning of this chapter and in Chapter Four), the most mileage can be achieved with your house. You can convert countable assets to noncountables by paying down a mortgage or by paying for needed repairs. If you do not own a house, you might consider buying one, assuming you intend to live in it. Other possibilities include purchasing an automobile, buying a burial plot, or buying an interest in a child's home.

Example Twelve

John and Mary have a home worth about $200,000, with a $40,000 mortgage, and nonexempt assets of approximately $130,000. The home needs approximately $30,000 in repairs. John is ill and is likely to enter a nursing home within the next several months. John and Mary live in a state that provides for a minimum spousal-asset allowance of $76,740.

John and Mary use $40,000 from their nonexempt assets to pay off their mortgage and $30,000 to effect needed repairs. John is now eligible for Medicaid. Mary will not be required to spend any of the remaining $60,000 of nonexempt assets, because $60,000 is less than the minimum spousal-asset allowance in John and Mary's home state. For the reasons discussed above (see "Transferring Assets To Your Spouse"), it would probably be advisable for John and Mary to transfer the home to Mary before John applies for Medicaid.

Example Thirteen

John and Mary have a home worth about $200,000, with a $40,000 mortgage, and nonexempt assets of approximately $130,000. The home needs approximately $30,000 in repairs. John is ill and is likely to enter a nursing home within the next several months. Unlike Example Twelve, John and Mary do not live in a state that has raised the minimum spousal asset allowance.

John and Mary will want to take the same steps as in Example Twelve, but they will want to wait until after John enters the nursing home. If they spend the $70,000 before John enters the nursing home, they will have $60,000 of nonexempt assets and Mary's spousal share will be $30,000 (one half of $60,000). If they wait until John enters the nursing home, Mary's spousal share will be $65,000 (one half of $130,000) because the determination is made when John enters the nursing home. They can then use John's $65,000 to pay for the home repairs and to pay off the mortgage. The net result is that significantly more money is available for Mary.

Example Fourteen

John and Mary have about $200,000 of nonexempt assets and live in a rental apartment. John is ill and is likely to enter a nursing home within the next several months. John and Mary live in a state that provides for a minimum spousal-asset allowance of $76,740.

Before John enters a nursing home, he and Mary purchase a condo, which is intended to be Mary's residence, for $135,000. John is now eligible for Medicaid. Mary will not be required to spend any of the remaining $65,000 of nonexempt assets because $65,000 is less than the minimum spousal-asset allowance in John and Mary's home state. It would be advisable for John and Mary to make sure the condo is in Mary's name alone.

If John and Mary do not live in a state that has raised the minimum asset allowance above $65,000, they will want to wait to purchase the condo until after John enters the nursing home for the reasons illustrated in Example Thirteen.

Example Fifteen

John has $60,000 in nonexempt assets and is about to enter a nursing home. His attorney has an appraisal of John's daughter's home prepared and informs John that he can purchase a life estate in his daughter's home for $60,000. This life estate gives John the right to live in his daughter's home, though John does not plan to do so. John purchases the life estate and is instantly eligible for Medicaid.

Purchasing an Annuity

The annuity strategy is similar to the conversion of exempt assets into nonexempt assets. The idea is to use nonexempt assets to purchase an irrevocable, nontransferable annuity. Because such an annuity provides only a right to income, it is not considered an asset for Medicaid purposes and is therefore not subject to the Medicaid spend-down requirements. In addition, because the annuity is purchased at fair market value, the 30-month waiting period is inapplicable.

This technique is controversial and has not been accepted by all states.

Example Sixteen

John and Mary have $100,000 of nonexempt assets. John has become ill and is about to enter a nursing home.

John and Mary use the $100,000 to purchase an annuity that gives Mary the right to receive $1,000 a month during her life. The $100,000 has "disappeared," and John is immediately eligible for Medicaid. Mary is not required to spend any of the income on John because the income is hers and, as discussed previously, the Medicaid rules permit Mary to keep all of her income, even while John receives Medicaid.

Paying Children for Their Help

Entering a nursing home is generally a last resort. Before doing so, it is not unusual for elderly people to try and make it on their own with help from children and other relatives. This help typically will involve aid with meals, financial matters, and assorted errands.

In almost all cases, these services are performed without any expectation of payment, out of love for the parent, or in recognition of what the parent has previously done for the child. This is right, and as it should be.

However, when a parent is about to enter a nursing home, paying for these services is a method of transferring property out of the parent's name. Because these payments are not "gifts," they can be made within 36 months of applying for Medicaid without triggering any ineligibility period.

Of course, the payments must be reasonable in amount. You cannot pay your child $50,000 for doing your laundry once a week. But you can pay your child what it would cost you to get a stranger to perform similar services.

Special Considerations Relating to Your Home

The home is a very special asset. In many cases it is the single most valuable piece of property that a family will have. For this reason, and for emotional reasons as well, protecting the home often becomes the single driving force behind Medicaid planning in the minds of those expecting to need nursing-home care.

Many of the planning methods for protecting your home have already been discussed. However, the topic is so paramount in the minds of so many of our clients that we risk being repetitive for the sake of completeness.

- In most states, your home will be protected from Medicaid authorities as long as it is reasonable to expect you to return there, or as long as your spouse or a minor child or a child with a disability lives there. However, it may not remain exempt. For example, if your spouse has died and you go into a nursing home, your home could be seized by Medicaid authorities at your death (or when it becomes apparent that you will not return there), assuming a minor child or a child with a disability does not live there. If such a child does live there, the home will likely be seized when they move out.

- You can transfer your home to anyone without affecting your ability to receive Medicaid, as long as the transfer occurs more than 36 months before your Medicaid application. Of course, many people are reluctant to do so, because they do not want to lose control over their homes before the need for nursing-home care is imminent.

- You can transfer your home to your spouse at any time without affecting your eligibility for Medicaid. As described in Example Seven, this will generally enable you to protect your home for your children unless, of course, your spouse also enters a nursing home in the future. In order for this technique to work, your spouse's will may need to be changed. In addition, in many states it will be advisable to make the transfer before you apply for Medicaid.

- In some states you can transfer your home to a trust established for a child with a disability without affecting your eligibility for Medicaid (even if the transfer is made within the 36-month period). You can also transfer your home to a child who provided care to you and resided in your home for at least 2 years prior to the date you entered the nursing home, or to a sibling who has an ownership interest in the home and who resided there for at least 1 year before the date you entered the nursing home. Again, it is generally advisable to make the transfer before you submit your Medicaid application.

There are two additional methods of protecting your home that we have not discussed. First, in some states transferring your home to a revocable living trust will protect against Medicaid liens. Because the trust is revocable, the transfer into trust typically will not be considered a transfer for Medicaid purposes, and Medicaid will not impose a waiting period.

Second, you can transfer your home to your children while retaining the right to live there (in legal terms, a life estate). This technique is very complicated and has many implications, which should be explored fully with your attorney.

Nursing Home Insurance

Although neither private medical insurance policies or Medicare supplement policies typically cover nursing home costs, some companies offer long-term care insurance policies that are specifically designed to cover the cost of long-term custodial care. These policies vary widely in coverage and cost, and the old adage "let the buyer beware" is particularly appropriate.

That is not to say that long-term care policies are never helpful, but simply that you should shop carefully, with the aid of a trusted financial advisor or an attorney who practices in the elder law area, so you can be sure you are getting the type of policy that is most useful.

In general:

1. You will want to make sure the policy covers the expenses you are most likely to incur. You will not want a policy restricted to nurses and doctors. Private medical insurance policies and Medicare often cover those. Rather, you will want to make sure *custodial* care is covered. Many policies cover both custodial and medically necessary care, often providing reimbursement for expenses that you may incur in your home—for example, the cost of a home companion.

2. You will want to make sure you understand what conditions are covered. Often policies exclude coverage for conditions such as mental illness, mental retardation, Alzheimer's disease, Parkinson's disease, and senility. Policies also typically exclude coverage for *preexisting conditions*, illnesses that you may have at the time of your insurance application.

3. You will want to make sure the policy covers the "proper" period. As you no doubt recall, you can give away any amount of property and still receive Medicaid so long as you wait at least 36 months after you make your gift. Coverage for more than 36 months, or perhaps 42 months to be safe, tends not to be important, and you should not pay too much for the extended coverage. Assuming you retain your competence or have properly prepared a power of attorney, you can buy coverage for 36 months, give away your property, and rely on Medicaid when your coverage runs out. However, you will want to investigate whether such a policy will restrict your admittance into the nursing home of your choice.

You should also be aware that a policy may impose a waiting period. You may not be eligible until you have been in a nursing home for a minimum period of time (say 20 to 100 days). You will need to make sure you will be able to afford care on your own for that minimum period if you select a policy with such a restriction. Remember, Medicare is not likely to cover you during the waiting period.

4. You will want to make sure the policy is affordable. Can premiums be increased so that you will not be able to afford it as you grow older? Can you be cancelled after reaching a certain age? Will premiums be waived when you begin receiving benefits? Remember, after you enter a nursing home, you will be unlikely to be able to afford further premiums.

5. You will want to make sure the benefit levels are sufficiently high. The cost of nursing-home care when you need it may be much higher than it is today, and you should consider getting a policy that adjusts benefit levels for inflation. Some policies limit coverage to 80 percent of nursing home costs. Before getting such a policy, you will want to make sure you can afford the remaining 20 percent.

6. You will want to make sure the policy does not impose overly restrictive conditions. Some policies provide no coverage unless you spend a couple of days in a hospital before beginning nursing-home care.

7. Finally, you will want to make sure the insurer is reputable. Avoid "fly by nights" that are not likely to be around when coverage is needed. You should consider checking Consumer Reports so you will know how the companies you are considering have been rated.

Conclusion

Planning to avoid the potentially catastrophic costs of nursing-home care is not easy. As you have seen, a wide variety of alternatives is available, each with its own particular benefits and detriments. It is often difficult to choose among them.

You should not believe that reading this chapter has made you an expert in the field. Several entire books have been written on the subject, and some of them are cited in the bibliography found in Appendix II at the end of this book.

The chapter will, however, give you a sense of the alternatives available to you and hopefully convince you to consult an expert in the field before it becomes necessary for you or a loved one to receive nursing-home care.

Although the plan that is most appropriate for you will depend on your own unique circumstances—such as the amount of income or property that you have, the type of facility in which you wish to reside, and your own particular family situation—as a general rule we do not do very much in the way of nursing-home planning until the need for nursing-home care becomes imminent. The reason should be fairly obvious.

The most effective plan is to transfer your property more than 36 months before entering a nursing home, either to a trusted friend or relative. Qualification for Medicaid would then be instantaneous.

It seems rather drastic, however, for healthy people to give control of their property to others, simply because nursing-home care may prove necessary at some point in the future. Asset transfers are necessarily irrevocable. Once you give your property to a friend or relative, you cannot get it back unless they choose to return it, and it is always possible that the law will change in the future. Planning too far in advance, then, could result in losing control of your property without gaining any advantage in terms of paying for long-term nursing-home care because the law may change in such a way that your asset transfers become irrelevant.

Typically, then, we like to work within the 36-month period, advising clients to transfer the optimal amount of property after nursing-home care becomes imminent and to rely on retained property or insurance during the ineligibility period. Depending on the facts of a particular case, some of the other methods described above can prove invaluable: such as transfers between spouses, transfers to trusts for beneficiaries with disabilities, purchasing annuities, or using cash to improve or purchase a home.

However, don't wait too long. A person with a mental disability may not be able to make legally valid asset transfers, so you will want to make sure you take the needed steps before it is too late. One possibility is to have a Durable Power of Attorney for Property to provide protection against the all too human tendency to wait until the last moment before taking steps that can be unpleasant, but at the same time also very important.

CHAPTER 11

INCOME TAXES

ALTHOUGH A DISCUSSION OF INCOME TAX PLANNING MAY NOT strictly belong in a book that is primarily about estate and life planning, our clients frequently have questions about income taxes, and we therefore feel this information may be useful to you. The chapter discusses only the specific deductions and credits that apply to taxpayers with dependents who have disabilities and not the various business tax incentives that promote their employment.

The tax laws are tedious, and it is not necessary that you master everything on the first reading. It will be sufficient if you gain a general understanding of the rules relating to the relevant deductions and credits and then use the chapter as a resource if specific questions arise in the future.

The major points are these:

- If you provide more than one-half of your child's support, you will probably be able to claim your child as a personal exemption. If your child is over 18 (24 if a student), you will not be entitled to the deduction if your child's adjusted gross income exceeds a minimum amount (for 1996, $2,550). Other requirements and special rules for divorced parents are discussed below.

- If you provide more than one-half of your child's support, you will probably be able to deduct medical expenses that you incur on your child's behalf if your total medical expenses for the year exceed 7.5 percent of your adjusted gross income. Medical expenses are defined broadly to include many types of expenditures that are not typically considered "medical." A listing of these expenses and a discussion of other general rules and limitations can be found below.

- If you incur child-care expenses to enable you to work, you will probably be entitled to take the dependent care credit. The credit is discussed in detail below.

Exemptions for Dependents

You can take an exemption for yourself, and for each person who is your dependent. The exemption amount increases each year to account for inflation. For 1996, the exemption amount was $2,550. Thus, for example, if you had two dependents and you and your spouse file a joint tax return, you would be entitled to a deduction from your taxable income of $10,200. The deduction is reduced by 2 percent for each $2,500 by which a taxpayer's adjusted gross income exceeds a threshold amount (in 1996, $176,950 for married taxpayers filing joint returns and surviving spouses, and $147,450 for heads of households).

Determining dependents is relatively easy. The following five tests must be met for a person to qualify as your dependent:

1. Support Test
2. Member of Household or Relationship Test
3. Citizenship Test
4. Joint Return Test
5. Gross Income Test

Support Test

You must provide more than half the dependent's total support during the calendar year. You determine whether you have provided more than half the dependent's support by comparing the amount you contributed to the dependent's support to the entire amount of support received from all sources, including the dependent's own funds and government funds.

Total support includes amounts spent to provide food, shelter, clothing, education, medical and dental care, recreation, allowance, gifts, vacations, and the like. Support is not limited to necessities.

Medical insurance premiums, including premiums you pay for supplementary Medicare coverage, are included in the total support you provide for the dependent. Medical insurance benefits, including basic and supplementary Medicare benefits, are not part of support.

If a dependent receives Social Security benefits and uses them toward his or her own support, the payments are considered as provided by the dependent. State benefit payments based on need are considered as support provided by the state and not the parent, unless it is shown otherwise. For example, Aid to Families with Dependent Children (AFDC) payments are not considered support provided by the parent. They are support provided by the state.

Scholarships received by your dependent, if your dependent is a full-time student, are not included in total support. This includes the value of education, room, and board provided for your dependent. This also applies to scholarships for room, board, and tuition provided for a child with a disability attending a special school. It similarly would apply to a scholarship for a child with mental retardation to attend an educational institution if the institution certifies that it is making an effort to educate or train the child, even if the payments are made by the state. For example, the state pays $30,000 for your daughter's room, board and tuition at a residential facility that qualifies as an educational organization. In the same year you provide $5,000 as her only other support. You may take her as a dependent because the scholarship is not included. As described below, the $5,000 that you pay may be a deductible medical expense.

Member of household or relationship test

To meet this test, a member of your household must live with you for the entire year (except for temporary absences such as for vacation or school) *or* be related to you. Thus, a child will satisfy this test, even if that child does not live with you.

Citizenship test

Your dependent must be a U.S. citizen, either resident or national, or a resident of Canada or Mexico for some part of the calendar year in which your tax year begins.

Joint return test

You are generally not allowed an exemption for your dependent if the dependent files a joint income tax return. For example, you supported your daughter for the entire year while her husband was in the armed forces. The couple files a joint return. Even though all the other tests are met, you may not take your daughter as a dependent.

Gross income test

Generally, you may take an exemption for a dependent only if that person's gross income was less than the *exemption amount* for the year ($2,550 for 1996). The gross income test does not apply if your child was under 19 years of age at the end of the year or was a student and was under the age of 24. To qualify as a student your child must have been, during some part of each of 5 months of the calendar year (not necessarily consecutive), a full-time student at a school that has a regular teaching staff, course of study, and regular enrolled student body.

Multiple-Support Agreement

In some situations, more than one person will be supporting an individual with a disability. As indicated above, a taxpayer must furnish more than half of the total support of a person during the calendar year to claim the person as a dependent. A *Multiple-Support Agreement* is used to claim a dependent when two or more people provide more than half a dependent's support, but no one alone provides more than half. In this situation, you may agree that one of you who individually provides more than 10 percent of the dependent's support may claim the exemption for the dependent. *Only one of the supporters can do this.* Each of the others must file a written statement agreeing not to claim the person as a dependent. This form must be filed with the income tax return of the person who claims the exemption.

Form 2120
Department of the Treasury-
Internal Revenue Service OMB No.

MULTIPLE SUPPORT DECLARATION

During the calendar year 19__, I paid over 10% of the support of ______________________________

(name of person)

I could have claimed this person as a dependent except that I did not pay more than 50% of his or her support. I understand that this person is being claimed as a dependent on the income tax return of ______________________________

(name)

____

(address)

I agree not to claim an exemption for this person on my Federal income tax return for any tax year that began in this calendar year.

____

(Your signature) (Your social security No.)

____

(date) (Address)

For example, you, your brother, and your two aunts provide the entire support for your sister during the year. You provide 45 percent, your brother 35 percent, and your two aunts provide 10 percent each. Either you or your brother may claim an exemption for your sister. If you claim your sister as a dependent, your brother, since he provided more than 10 percent of the support, must file a written statement on Form 2120. He thereby agrees not to claim your sister as a dependent or to receive the exemption. Neither of the aunts has to file Form 2120 because neither provides over 10 percent of the dependent's support.

Divorced or Separated Parents

The parent who has custody of the child for the greater part of the year is generally considered the parent who provides more than half of the child's support. Parents can, however, arrange for the non-custodial parent to be treated as satisfying the test either in their divorce decree or by having the custodial parent file Form 8332. If either parent can claim a child as a dependent, each parent can include the medical expenses he or she pays for the child (see discussion of Medical Expenses immediately following).

The following charts will help you determine whether an individual qualifies as a dependent.

WHO MAY QUALIFY AS YOUR DEPENDENT?

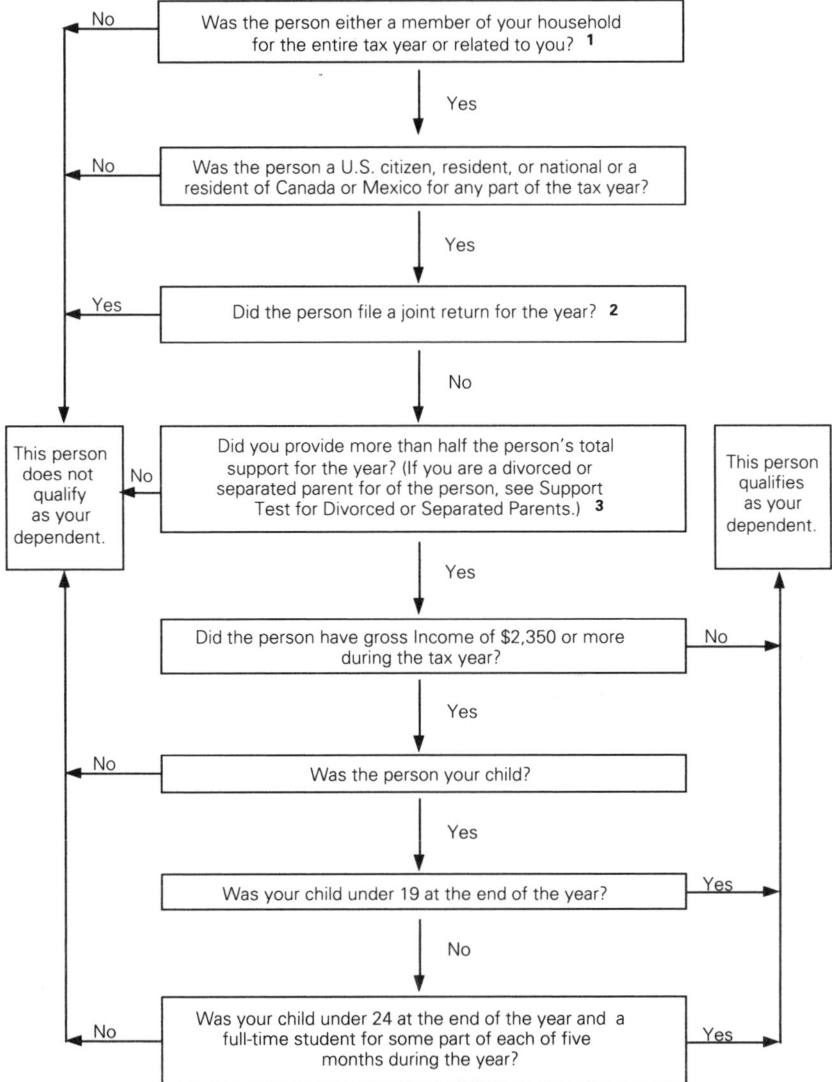

Start Here
Was the person either a member of your household for the entire tax year or related to you? 1
No
Yes
Was the person a U.S. citizen, resident, or national or a resident of Canada or Mexico for any part of the tax year?
No
Yes
Did the person file a joint return for the year? 2
Yes
No
Did you provide more than half the person's total support for the year? (If you are a divorced or separated parent for of the person, see Support Test for Divorced or Separated Parents.) 3
No
This person does not qualify as your dependent.
This person qualifies as your dependent.
Yes
Did the person have gross Income of $2,350 or more during the tax year?
No
Yes
Was the person your child?
No
Yes
Was your child under 19 at the end of the year?
Yes
No
Was your child under 24 at the end of the year and a full-time student for some part of each of five months during the year?
No
Yes

1 If the person was your legally adopted child and lived in your home as a member of your household for the entire tax year, answer "yes" to the question.
2 If neither the person nor the person's spouse is required to file a return but they file a joint return to claim a refund of tax withheld, you may answer "no" to this question.
3 Answer "yes" to this question if you meet the multiple support requirements under Multiple Support Agreement.

WORKSHEET FOR DETERMINING SUPPORT

Income

1) Did the person you support receive any income, such as wages, interest, dividends, pensions, rents, social security, or welfare? (If yes, complete lines 2, 3, 4, and 5) YES NO

2) Total income received $________

3) Amount of income used for support $________

4) Amount of income used for other purposes $________

5) Amount of income saved $________

(The total of lines 3,4, and 5 should equal line 2)

Expenses for Entire Household (where the person you support lived)

6) Lodging (complete item a or b)

a) Rent paid $________

b) If not rented, show fair rental value of home. If the person you support owns the home, include this amount in line 20. $________

7) Food $________

8) Utilities (heat, light, water, etc., not included in line 6a or 6b) $________

9) Repairs (not included in line 6a or 6b) $________

10) Other. Do not include expenses of maintaining home, such as mortgage interest, real estate taxes, and insurance. $________

11) Total household expenses (Add lines 6 through 10) $________

12) Total number of persons living in household. ________

Expenses for the Person you Support

13) Each person's part of household expenses (line 11 divided by line 12) $________

14) Clothing $________

15) Education $________

16) Medical, dental $________

17) Travel, recreation $________

18) Other (specify) $________

19) Total cost of support for the year (Add lines 13 through 18) $________

20) Amount the person provided for own support (line 3, plus line 6b if the person you support owns the home) $________

21) Amount others provided for the person's support. Include amounts provided by state, local, and other welfare societies or agencies. $________

22) Amount you provided for the person's support (line 19 minus lines 20 and 21) $________

23) 50% of line 19 $________

If line 22 is more than line 23, you meet the support test for the person. If the person meets the other dependency tests, you may claim an exemption for that person. If line 23 is more than line 22, you may still be able to claim an exemption for that person under a multiple support agreement.

Medical Expense Deduction

An individual is entitled to an income tax deduction for medical expenses for the individual and for his or her dependents. For these purposes, dependent is defined as above, except that the *Gross Income Test* and the *Joint Return Test* do not have to be satisfied. The person must have qualified as a dependent when the medical services were provided or when the bill was actually paid.

A number of hurdles must be passed before medical expenses may be deducted. First, medical expenses are deductible *only* to the extent they exceed 7.5 percent of your adjusted gross income. For example, if your adjusted gross income for a given year is $30,000, only expenses in excess of $2,250 (7.5%) may be deducted.

One potential strategy is to try to time your expenses so a deduction will be possible. For example, if you receive a bill in December, have had little in the way of medical expenses during the year and anticipate large expenses during the next year, you should consider waiting until January to pay your bill since you might then exceed the limitation.

Second, medical expenses may be deducted only if you itemize your deductions. Taxpayers who do not have significant itemized deductions are entitled to take the standard deduction instead. For 1996, the standard deduction is equal to $6,700 for married taxpayers filing joint returns, $5,900 for heads of household and $4,000 for singles. Similarly, you cannot take the medical expense deduction if you use Form 1040A or Form 1040EZ because you must figure the deduction on Schedule A, Form 1040, commonly called the "long form."

Third, you cannot deduct expenses that are paid by insurance. Only expenses that you pay, that are not reimbursed by your insurance company, may be deducted.

Fourth, medical expense deductions, along with many other itemized deductions, are reduced for taxpayers whose incomes are above certain threshold amounts. For 1996, the reduction generally applies to taxpayers with adjusted gross income in excess of $117,950.

Most parents with children who have disabilities deduct larger amounts of medical expenses than other families. As a result, they may draw special notice from the Internal Revenue Service. The IRS computer may single out for review those taxpayers who deduct proportionately higher medical expenses in relation to their income level. To reduce the IRS's suspicions, you can describe your child's disability in a letter written by yourself or your child's doctor and attach it to your tax return. Store your receipts and cancelled checks carefully. One key to good tax planning is good record keeping.

According to the IRS a medical expense includes *any amount paid for the diagnosis, cure, mitigation, treatment, or prevention of disease, or for the purpose of affecting any structure or function of the body, and transportation cost on a trip primarily for and essential to medical care.* Following is a list of items that you should consider in figuring your medical expense deduction. The items are listed in alphabetical order.

Alcoholism

You may include in medical expenses payments to a treatment center for alcohol or drug addiction. This includes meals and lodging provided by the center during medical treatment.

Ambulance

You may include in medical expenses amounts you pay for ambulance service.

Analysis

You may include payments for psychoanalysis. You may not include payments for psychoanalysis that you must get as a part of your training to be a psychoanalyst.

Artificial limb

You can include the amount you pay for an artificial limb.

Birth control pills

You can include the amount you pay for birth control pills prescribed by your doctor.

Braille books and magazines

You may include the difference in cost of braille books and magazines over regular books and magazines.

Capital expenses

Amounts you pay for special equipment installed in your home or other special improvements that increase the value of the property may be partly deductible as medical expenses, if their main purpose is medical. The amount paid for the improvement is reduced by the increase in the value of the property. The rest is a deductible medical expense.

Example: Your daughter has a heart ailment. On her doctor's advice, you install an elevator in your home so that she will not have to climb stairs. The elevator costs $2,000. An appraisal shows that the elevator increases the value of your home by $1,400.

You figure your medical deduction as follows: The amount you paid for the improvement ($2,000) minus the increase in the value of your home ($1,400) equals your medical expense deduction ($600).

If a capital expense qualifies as a medical expense, amounts you pay for operation and upkeep also qualify as medical expenses, so long as the medical reason for the capital expense exists. This is so even if you are not allowed to deduct any part of the capital expense because the increase in the value of your home is equal to, or more than, the capital expense.

Example: If, in the previous example, the elevator increased the value of your home by $2,000, you would have no medical deduction for the cost of the elevator. However, the cost of electricity to operate the elevator and repairs to maintain it are deductible so long as the medical reason for the elevator exists.

Amounts paid by a person with a disability to buy and install special plumbing fixtures in a rented house, mainly for medical purposes, are medical expenses.

Example: John Smith has cerebral palsy and a heart condition. He cannot climb stairs or get into a bathtub. On his doctor's advice, he installs a bathroom with a shower stall on the first floor of his two-story rented house. The landlord did not pay any of the cost and did not lower the rent. John may include in medical expenses the whole amount paid.

Car

You may include in medical expenses the cost of special hand controls and other special equipment installed in a car for the use of a person with disabilities. If you have a car designed to hold a wheelchair you may include its costs beyond the cost of a regular car. You may not deduct the cost of operating a specially equipped car, except as noted under **Transportation**.

Crutches

Cost of bought or rented crutches is allowable.

Chiropractors

You can include fees you pay to a chiropractor for medical care.

Christian Science practitioners

You can include amounts you pay to Christian Science practitioners.

Cosmetic surgery

Generally, you cannot include in medical expenses the amount you pay for unnecessary cosmetic surgery. This applies to any procedure that is directed at improving the patient's appearance and does not meaningfully promote the proper function of the body or treat illness or disease. Procedures such as face lifts, hair transplants, hair removal (electrolysis), and liposuction generally are not deductible.

You can include in medical expenses the amount you pay for cosmetic surgery if it is necessary to improve a deformity arising from, or directly related to, a congenital abnormality, a personal injury resulting from an accident or trauma, or a disfiguring disease.

Dancing lessons, swimming lessons, etc.

You may not deduct the cost of dancing lessons, swimming lessons, etc., even if they are recommended by your doctor for the general improvement of one's health.

Dental fees

You may include in medical expenses the amounts you pay for dental treatment. This includes fees paid to dentists, X-rays, fillings, braces, extractions, and false teeth.

Diaper service

Diaper service is usually not deductible. However, if your child will always wear diapers because of a disability, diaper service is probably deductible.

Eyeglasses

You may include amounts you pay for eyeglasses and contact lenses you need for medical reasons. You may also include fees paid for eye examinations.

Foods, special

You may include in your medicine and drug expenses the cost of special foods or drinks your doctor prescribed to relieve or treat an illness. They must be in addition to your normal diet and not a part of your normal nutritional needs. Do not include the cost of special foods or drinks that replace what you normally eat or drink. You should attach to your return a statement from your doctor showing that you need the special foods or drinks.

Example 1: Your doctor prescribes 2 ounces of whiskey twice a day for relief of angina pain. The cost of the prescribed amount of whiskey is a deductible medical expense.

Example 2: You have an ulcer and your doctor puts you on a special diet. You may not deduct the cost of your foods or drinks because the special diet replaces what you normally eat or drink. However, the difference in cost between a normal diet and a specially, medically prescribed diet is deductible. The special food must be intended to cure a specific ailment rather than merely to improve general health.

Funeral expenses

Not deductible.

Guide dog or other animal

You may include in medical expenses the cost of a guide dog or other animal for those with visual or hearing impairments. You can also include the cost of a dog or other animal trained to assist persons with other disabilities. Amounts you pay for the care of the dog or other animal are also medical expenses.

Health club dues

You cannot include health club dues, YMCA dues, or amounts paid for steam baths for your general health or to relieve physical or mental discomfort not related to a particular medical condition.

Health Maintenance Organization (HMO)

You may include in medical expenses amounts you pay to entitle you to receive medical care from a health maintenance organization. These amounts are treated as medical insurance premiums.

Hearing aids

You may include in medical expenses the cost of a hearing aid and the batteries you buy to operate it.

Health insurance credit

If your adjusted gross income is less than $21,250, you may be entitled to claim the health insurance credit. If you claim the credit, you must subtract the amount of the credit from your total medical expenses.

Hospital services

You may include in medical expenses amounts you pay for hospital services. See **Meals**.

Household help

You may not deduct the cost of household help, even if your doctor recommends it because you are physically unable to do housework. See **Nursing services**.

Insurance-premiums, policies, and plans

Your medical insurance premiums are amounts paid for medical care, whether the payments under the policy are made directly to the provider of the care (hospital, doctors, dentists, etc.), to the patient, or to you.

You can include in medical expenses premiums you pay for policies that provide payment for: physician fees, hospitalization, surgical fees, X-rays, etc.; prescription drugs; replacement of lost or damaged contact lenses; or membership in an association that gives cooperative or so-called "free-choice" medical service, or group hospitalization and clinical care.

If you have a policy that provides more than one kind of payment, you can include the premiums for the medical care part of the policy if the charge for the medical part is reasonable. The cost of the medical portion must be separately stated in the insurance contract or given to you in a separate statement.

If you are covered under Social Security (or if you are a government employee who paid Medicare tax), you are enrolled in Medicare A. The tax paid for Medicare A is not a medical expense. If you are not covered under Social Security (or were not a government employee who paid Medicare tax), you may voluntarily enroll in Medicare A. In this situation the premiums paid for Medicare A can be included as a medical expense on your tax return. Medicare B is a supplemental medical insurance. Premiums you pay for Medicare B are a medical expense.

Premiums you pay before you are 65 for insurance for medical care for yourself, your spouse, and your dependents after you reach 65 are medical care expenses. These premiums are included in your medical expenses in the year paid if they are:

1) Payable in equal yearly installments, or more often, and
2) Paid for at least 10 years, or until you reach age 65 (but not for less than 5 years).

You cannot include premiums you pay for: life insurance policies; policies providing payment for loss of earnings; policies for loss of life, limb, sight, etc.; policies that pay you a guaranteed amount each week for a stated number of weeks if you are hospitalized for sickness or injury; or the part of your care insurance premiums that provides medical insurance coverage for all persons injured in or by your care since the portion of the premium for you and your dependents is not stated separately.

Insurance reimbursement

You must reduce your total medical expenses for the year by all reimbursements for medical expenses that you receive from insurance or other sources during the year. This includes payments from Medicare.

If you pay the entire premium for your medical insurance or all the costs of a similar plan and you receive a reimbursement equal to your total medical expenses for the year, you do not have a medical deduction. If insurance payments or other reimbursements are more than your total medical expenses for the year (excess reimbursement), you do not have a medical deduction. Do not include the excess reimbursement in your gross income.

If both you and your employer contribute to your medical insurance plan and your employer's contributions are not included in your gross income, you must include in your gross income the part of your excess reimbursement that is from your employer's contribution.

Example. You are covered by your employer's medical insurance policy. The annual premium is $2,000. Your employer pays $600 of that amount and the balance of $1,400 is taken out of your wages. The part of any excess reimbursement you receive under the policy that is from your employer's contributions is figured like this:

Total annual cost of policy	$2,000
Amount paid by employer	600
Employer's contribution in relation to the total annual cost of the policy ($600/$2,000	30%

You must include in your gross income 30% of the excess reimbursement you received for medical expenses under the policy.

If your employer or your former employer pays the total cost of your medical insurance plan and your employer's contributions are not included in your income, you must report all of your excess reimbursement as income.

Laboratory fees

You can include the amount you pay for laboratory fees that are part of your medical care.

Lead-based paint removal

You may include in medical expenses the cost of removing lead-based paints from surfaces in your home to prevent a child who has or had lead poisoning from eating the paint. These surfaces must be in poor repair (peeling or cracking) or within the child's reach. The cost of repainting the scraped area is not a medical expense.

If, instead of removing the paint, you cover the area with wallboard or paneling, you would treat these items as capital expenses. See **Capital Expenses**. Do not include the cost of painting the wallboard as a medical expense.

Learning disability

Tuition or tutoring fees you pay on your doctor's advice for a child who has severe learning disabilities caused by mental or physical impairments may be included in medical expenses. Your doctor must recommend that the child attend the school.

You can also include tutoring fees you pay on your doctor's recommendation for the child's tutoring by a teacher who is specially trained and qualified to work with children who have severe learning disabilities.

Legal fees

You may include legal fees paid to allow treatment for mental illness. If part of the legal fees is not for medical care, you may not include that part in medical expenses.

Lifetime care

You may include in medical expenses a life-care fee or "founder's fee" you pay monthly or as a lump sum under an agreement with a retirement home. The part of the payment you include is the amount properly allocable to medical care. The agreement must require a lump-sum payment or advance payment as a condition for the home's promise to provide lifetime care that includes medical care.

You may include advance payments to a private institution to provide for the lifetime care, treatment, and training of a dependent with physical or mental disabilities when you die or become unable to provide care. The payments must be a condition for the institution's future acceptance of your dependent and must not be refundable.

Lodging

You can include in medical expenses the cost of meals and lodging at a hospital or similar institution if your main reason for being there is to receive medical care. See **Nursing home**, later.

You can include in medical expenses the cost of lodging (not provided in a hospital or similar institution) while away from home if you meet all of the following requirements.

- The lodging is primarily for and essential to medical care.
- Medical care is provided by a doctor in a licensed hospital or in a medical care facility related to, or the equivalent of, a licensed hospital.
- The lodging is not lavish or extravagant under the circumstances.
- There is no significant element of personal pleasure, recreation, or vacation in the travel away from home.

The amount you include in medical expenses cannot exceed $50 for each night for each person. Lodging is included for a person for whom transportation expenses are a medical expense because that person is traveling with the person receiving the medical care.

For example, if a parent is traveling with a sick child, up to $100 per night is included as a medical expense for lodging (meals are not deductible).

Do not include the cost of your meals and lodging while you are away from home for medical treatment that you do not receive at a medical facility, or for the relief of a specific condition, even if the trip is made on the advice of your doctor.

Example. You have a heart condition. You live in an area that has cold winters, which makes your condition worse. Your doctor advises you to spend the winter in a warmer place. You and your family spend the winter in a rented house in Florida. The trip was made for a specific medical reason. You cannot include any of the expenses for food and lodging between your home and Florida or while you are in Florida as a medical expense. However, your share of transportation expenses between your home and Florida is included as a medical expense. Your family's transportation is not deductible. See **Transportation** later.

Medical information plan

You may include in medical expenses amounts paid to a plan that keeps your medical information by computer and that can give you the information when you need it. For example, some organizations can store medical information on your child. This information is accumulated while the parents are alive, and is especially helpful for the guardian of the child after the parents die.

Medical services

You can include amounts you pay for medical services provided by physicians, surgeons, specialists, or other medical practitioners. You cannot include amounts you pay for illegal operations or treatments.

Medicines

You can include in medical expenses amounts you pay for prescribed medicines and drugs. A prescribed drug is one which requires a prescription by a doctor for its use by an individual. You can also include amounts you pay for insulin.

Mental retardation, special homes

You may include in medical expenses the cost of keeping a person with mental retardation in a special home, not the home of a relative, on the recommendation of a psychiatrist to help the person adjust from life in a mental hospital to community living.

Nursing home

You may include the cost of medical care, including meals and lodging, for yourself, your spouse, or your dependents in a nursing home or home for the aged, if the main reason for being there is to get medical care.

Do not include the cost of meals and lodging if the reason for being in the home is personal. You can, however, include in medical expenses the part of the cost that is for medical or nursing care.

Nursing services

You can include wages and other amounts you pay for nursing services. Services need not be performed by a nurse as long as the services are of a kind generally performed by a nurse. This includes services connected with caring for the patient's condition such as giving medication or changing dressings, as well as bathing and grooming the patient.

Only the amount spent for nursing services is a medical expense. If the attendant also provides personal and household services, these amounts must be divided between the time spent performing household services and the time spent for nursing services.

You can also include part of the amounts you pay for the attendant's meals. Divide the food expenses among the household members to find the cost of the attendant's food, to the extent allocable to nursing services (calculated as described above). If you had to pay additional amounts for household upkeep because of the attendant, you may deduct the extra amounts. This includes extra rent or utilities you pay because you moved to a larger apartment to provide space for the attendant, or the extra cost of utilities for the attendant.

You may deduct any Social Security taxes you pay for a nurse, attendant, or other person who provides medical care.

Operations

You may include in medical expenses amounts you pay for legal operations.

Oxygen

The costs you pay for oxygen or oxygen equipment to relieve breathing problems caused by a medical condition may be included.

Personal use items

You cannot include an item ordinarily used for personal, living, and family purposes unless it is used primarily to prevent or alleviate a physical or mental disability or illness. For example, the full cost of a wig purchased upon the advice of a physician for the mental health of a patient who has lost all of his or her hair from disease can be included with medical expenses.

When an item purchased in a special form primarily to alleviate a physical disability is one that in normal form is ordinarily used for personal purposes, the excess of the cost of the special form over the cost of the normal form is a medical expense (for example, Braille books and magazines).

Psychiatric care

You may include amounts you pay for psychiatric care. This includes the cost of supporting a dependent with mental illness at a specially equipped medical center where the dependent receives medical care.

Psychologist

You may include in medical expenses amounts you pay to a psychologist for medical care.

Schools, special

You can include in medical expenses payments to a special school for a person with mental or physical disabilities if the main reason for using the school is its resources for relieving the disability. You can include, for example, the cost of a school that:

- Teaches braille to a visually impaired child,
- Teaches lip reading to a hearing impaired child, or
- Gives remedial language training to correct a condition caused by a birth defect
- Certifies that it provides training to a child with mental retardation.

The cost of meals, lodging, and ordinary education supplied by a special school can be included in medical expenses only if the main reason for the child's being there is the resources the school has for relieving the mental or physical disability. You cannot include the cost of sending a child to a special school for benefits the child may get from the course of study and the disciplinary methods.

Smoking program

You cannot include the cost of a program to stop smoking that you join for the improvement of your general health, even if your doctor suggests the program.

Sterilization

You may include in medical expenses the cost of a legally performed operation to make a person unable to have children.

Telephone

You may include the cost and repair of special telephone equipment that lets a person with a hearing impairment use a regular telephone.

Television

You may include the cost of equipment that displays the audio part of television programs as subtitles for the hearing impaired. This may be the cost of an adapter that attaches to a regular set, or the cost of a specially equipped set to the extent it exceeds the cost of the same model regular television set.

Therapy

You may include in medical expenses amounts you pay for therapy received as medical treatment. For example, payments you make to someone for giving "patterning" exercises are deductible. (These exercises consist mainly of coordinated physical manipulations of the child's arms and legs to imitate crawling and other normal movements.)

Transplants

You may include in medical expenses payments for surgical, hospital, laboratory, and transportation expenses for a donor or a possible donor of a kidney or other transplant.

Transportation

Amounts paid for transportation primarily for, and essential to, medical care qualify as medical expenses.

You can include:

- Bus, taxi, train, or plane fare, or ambulance service,
- Actual car expenses, such as gas and oil (do not include expenses for general repair, maintenance, depreciation, and insurance),
- Parking fees and tolls,
- Transportation expenses of a parent who must go with a child who needs medical care,
- Transportation expenses of a nurse or other person who can give injections, medications, or other treatment required by a patient who is traveling to get medical care and is unable to travel alone, or

- Transportation expenses for regular visits to see a dependent with mental illness, if these visits are recommended as part of treatment.

Instead of deducting actual car expenses, you can take 9 cents a mile for each mile you use your care for medical reasons. Add the cost of tolls and parking to this amount.

Do not include:

- Transportation expenses to and from work, even if your condition requires an unusual means of transportation, or
- Transportation expenses if, for nonmedical reasons only, you choose to travel to another city, such as a resort area, for an operation or other medical care prescribed by your doctor.

Trips

You can include in medical expenses amounts you pay for transportation to another city if the trip is primarily for and essential to receiving medical services. You may be able to include up to $50 per night for lodging. See **Lodging**.

You cannot include in medical expenses a trip or vacation taken for a change in environment, improvement of morale, or general improvement of health, even if you make the trip on the advice of a doctor.

Tuition fees

You may include charges for medical care that are included in the tuition fee of a college or private school if the charges are separately stated in the bill, or given to you by the school.

Weight loss program

You may not deduct the cost of a weight loss program even if a doctor advises the program for general health.

Wheelchair

You may include in medical expenses amounts you pay for an autoette or a manual or motorized wheelchair used mainly for the relief of sickness or disability, and not just to provide transportation to and from work. The cost of operating and keeping up the autoette or wheelchair is also a deductible medical expense.

X-ray fees

You may include in medical expenses amounts you pay for X-rays.

The following list may help you keep track of your medical expenses.

1. Transportation for taking your child to Special Schools, Institutions, Hospitals, Doctors Office, Special Therapy, Pharmacies, etc.

   a. Mileage (Standard rate .9 cents per mile) or actual expenses (gas/oil) ________

   b. Parking ________

   c. Toll ________

   d. Cost of an attendant to go with child ________

   e. Cost of attendant to ride bus to school ________

2. Medical Expenses-Standard ________

3. Hospital Expenses-Standard ________

4. Medicine, Drugs, Vitamins - prescribed by a doctor only ________

5. Special Education Expenses

   a. Tests and Evaluations at special school ________

   b. Special instruction in braille, lip-reading speech ________

   c. Tutoring by a qualified teacher if recommended by a doctor ________

   d. Room, board and tuition at residential facility if main reason for attending is to alleviate medical condition ________

6. Sheltered Workshop Expenses
   a. If you have to pay the sheltered workshop for their services __________
7. Special Equipment
   a. Any special equipment prescribed by a doctor, i.e. air-conditioning, ramp, elevators, etc. __________
   b. Repair of equipment including TTD __________
   c. Closed Caption TV/Adaptor __________
8. Attendant Care
   a. Nursing Services __________
   b. Meals for Attendants __________
9. Aids for Persons with Visually Impaired
   a. Audio tapes __________
   b. Special typewriters __________
   c. Special lenses, etc. __________
   d. Cost and care of guide dogs __________
10. Lifetime Care Payments
    a. If you have to pay non-refundable advance payments to a private institution for the privilege of having them care for your child in the future, those payments are deductible. __________
11. Transitioning Expenses
    a. The costs involved in helping a person with mental retardation adjust to life in a community setting __________
12. Miscellaneous
    a. Expenses involved in providing "patterning exercises." ________
    b. Disposable diapers for incontinent child or adult if prescribed by a doctor __________
    c. Special food and beverage costs are weighed against costs of "normal" food. __________
    d. Dental care __________
    e. Eyeglasses, contacts, eye examinations __________

f. Hearing aid, batteries, hearing evaluations ________

g. Wheelchair, braces, other adaptive equipment ________

h. Birth control pills ________

i. Legal operation to prevent having children ________

j. Oxygen equipment and oxygen ________

k. Medical and Hospital insurance premiums (see Formula) ________

l. Social Security tax for worker providing medical services ________

m. Cost and care of dog or other animals aiding blind, deaf and other persons with disabilities ________

n. Legal abortion ________

Impairment-Related Work Expenses

The law permits you to deduct, as a business expense, amounts which you incur to enable you to work (impairment-related work expenses). These expenses are not subject to the 2 percent of adjusted gross income limit that applies to other employee business expenses or the 7.5 percent of adjusted gross income limitation that applies to medical expenses. Therefore, it is often better to characterize an expense as an impairment-related work expense, as opposed to a medical expense.

Impairment-related work expenses are deductible only when they are incurred by the person with a disability. Impairment-related work expenses which you incur on behalf of a child with a disability are not deductible by you, though they would be deductible by your child if incurred by your child.

The following examples illustrate whether expenses are medical or business expenses. The expenses in each example are unreimbursed.

Example 1

You are blind. You must use a reader to do your work. You use the reader both during your regular working hours at your place of work and outside your regular working hours away from your place of work. The reader's services are only for your work. You can deduct your expenses for the reader as a business expense.

Example 2

You use a wheelchair. Sometimes you must go out of town on business. Your friend or spouse goes with you to help with such things as carrying your luggage or getting up steps. You do not pay your helper a salary, but you do pay for your helper's travel, meals, and lodging while on such trips. In your home town, you do your job without a helper. Because the expenses for travel, meals, and lodging of your helper are directly related to doing your job you can deduct them as business expenses.

Example 3

You use a wheelchair. You must go on overnight out-of-town business trips as a part of your job. Your friend goes with you on these trips to help with your wheelchair, your luggage, and your daily medication. You do not pay a salary to your friend. You do pay for all of your friend's travel, meals, and lodging while on these trips. However, you also need your friend's help regularly during the hours you are not working, while at home and out of town. The expenses for the travel, meals, and lodging of your friend are nursing services. You include them as medical expenses.

If, instead of your friend, your spouse goes with you on the out-of-town business trips, you can include as medical expenses only the out-of-pocket expenses for your spouse's travel. Expenses for your spouse's meals and lodging are not deductible.

Child and Dependent Care Credit

If you pay someone to care for a dependent under age 13, or for a dependent or spouse with a disability, you may be able to take a tax credit for up to 30% of your expenses. Unlike the tax deductions described above, tax credits are subtracted directly from taxes due and are therefore more valuable. To illustrate, if you are in a 30 percent tax bracket a $2,000 deduction will be worth $600 to you. A $2,000 credit, on the other hand, will be worth $2,000.

You can use Form 2441, Credit for Child and Dependent Care Expenses, to figure your credit. To be able to claim the credit, you must meet *all* the following tests.

1.The care must be for one or more qualifying persons.

A qualifying person is (i) a dependent under 13 for whom you can claim a personal exemption deduction, (ii) a dependent who is over age 13 if he or she is not able to care for himself or herself, (iii) a person you could claim as a dependent except that he or she has gross income in excess of the applicable limitation ($2,550 for 1996) who is not able to care for himself or herself, or (iv) your spouse if he or she is physically or mentally not able to care for himself or herself.

Persons who are not able to dress, clean, or feed themselves because of physical or mental disabilities are not able to care for themselves. Also, persons who require constant attention to prevent them from injuring themselves or others are considered not capable of self care.

If you are divorced, legally separated under a decree of divorce or separate maintenance, or separated under a written separation agreement, your child qualifies if you had custody for a longer time during the calendar year than the other parent. The child does not have to be your dependent, but your child must (i) be under 13, or not able to care for himself or herself, (ii) be in the custody of one or both parents for more than half of the year, and (iii) receive more than half support from one or both parents.

2. You (and your spouse if you are married) must keep up a home that you live in with the qualifying person or persons.

You are keeping up a home if you (and your spouse if you are married) pay more than half the cost of running it. Upkeep expenses normally include property taxes, mortgage interest, rent, utility charges, home repairs, insurance on the home, and food eaten at home.

Do not include as upkeep any payments for clothing, education, medical treatment, vacations, life insurance, transportation, mortgage principal, or for the purchase, improvement, or replacement of property. For example, the cost of replacing a water heater is not considered upkeep, but the cost of repairing a water heater can be included.

Payments such as Aid to Families with Dependent Children (AFDC) received from the state that you use to keep up your home are considered to be provided by the state, not by you. If you do not provide more than half the cost of keeping up your home from your own funds, you cannot claim the child and dependent care credit.

3. You (and your spouse if you are married) must have income from work during the year.

Earned income includes wages, salaries, tips, other employee compensation, and net earnings form self employment. Earned income also includes strike benefits and any disability pay you report as wages.

Earned income does not include pensions or annuities, Social Security payments, workers' compensation, interest, dividends, or unemployment compensation.

Your spouse is treated as having earned income for any year that he or she is a full time student or physically or mentally not capable of self care. You are a full time student if you are enrolled at or attend a school for the number of hours or classes that the school considers full time. You must have been a student for at least some part of 5 calendar months (not necessarily consecutive) during the year.

The term "school" includes elementary schools, junior and senior high schools, colleges, universities, and technical, trade, and mechanical schools. It does not include on-the-job training courses, correspondence schools, or night schools.

4. You must pay child and dependent care expenses so you (and your spouse if you are married) can work or look for work.

Child and dependent care expenses must be work related to qualify for the credit. Expenses are considered work related only if they allow you (and your spouse if you are married) to work or look for work and they are for a qualifying person's care.

Qualifying expenses include expenses paid for household services (for example, baby-sitters). Expenses incurred for services provided by a day care center qualify only if the center complies with applicable state and local regulations. The cost of overnight camp is not a qualifying expenditure.

5. If you are married at the end of your tax year, you must file a joint return with your spouse to qualify for the credit.

If you are legally separated from your spouse under a decree of divorce or of separate maintenance, you are not considered married. You may claim the credit on a separate return. If you are married and file a separate return, you will not be considered married and will be permitted to take the credit if (i) your home was the home of a qualifying person for more than half the tax year, (ii) you paid more than half the cost of keeping up your home for the tax year, and (iii) your spouse did not live in your home for the last 6 months of the tax year.

6. You must identify the care provider on your tax return.

To identify the care provider, you must give the provider's name, address, and taxpayer identification number. If the care provider is an individual, the taxpayer identification number is often the Social Security number. If the care provider is an organization, then it is the employer identification number (EIN).

The taxpayer identification number is not required if the care provider is one of certain tax-exempt organizations (such as a church or school). In this case, write "Tax-Exempt" in the space where the tax form calls for the number.

If the provider refuses to give you the required information, you should report whatever information you have (such as the name and address) on the form you use to claim the credit. Write "See Page 2" in the columns calling for the information you do not have. On the bottom of page 2, explain that you requested the information from the care provider, but the provider did not give you the information. This statement will show that you used due diligence in trying to furnish the required information.

7. You must pay someone other than a child of yours who is under 19 or a person you can claim as your dependent.

When figuring your credit, you may not use payments you made to your dependent or your child if he or she was under 19 at the end of the year. You may use payments you made to relatives who are not your dependents, even if they lived in your home.

Figuring the Credit

If your adjusted gross income is $10,000 or less, your credit is generally equal to 30% of work-related expenses. The 30% figure is reduced by one percent for each $2,000 or part of $2,000 of adjusted gross income above $10,000 until the percentage is reduced to 20% for income above $28,000. The limit on work-related expenses is $2,400 for one qualifying person and $4,800 for two or more persons.

Example

A widower pays a housekeeper $5,000 a year to take care of his home and his daughter while he is working. He earns $20,000 during the year. Since there is only one qualifying person, the daughter, the maximum work-related expenses he can claim are $2,400, even though he spent at least $5,000. Therefore, the largest credit he can claim is 25% of $2,400 or $600. The 25% credit is calculated by reducing the 30% credit by one percent for every $2,000 of income above $10,000. Since the widower had income of $20,000, the 30% credit is reduced by 5%.

Earned Income Limit

During any tax year, the amount of work-related expenses that you may use to figure your credit may not be more than

1. Your earned income for the year, if you are single at the end of your tax year, or

2. Your earned income or the earned income of your spouse, whichever is less, for the year, if you are married at the end of your tax year.

If you are married and for any month your spouse is either a full-time student or not able to care for himself or herself, your spouse will be considered to have earned income of $200 a month if there is one qualifying person in your home, or $400 a month if there are two or more qualifying persons in your home. A spouse who cannot care for himself or herself is a qualifying person.

Employer Provided Plans

The amount of any benefit you receive under an employer-provided dependent care assistance plan may be excluded from your income. This means that you do not have to include the amount of the benefit in your income for tax purposes. The plan must meet certain requirements. Your employer can tell you whether the plan qualifies. If it does, you must subtract this excludable amount from the dollar limit ($2,400 or $4,800, whichever applies) to get the reduced limit on the amount of work-related expenses you can use to figure the credit.

Example

You are widower with one child and earn $20,000 a year at work. You pay work-related expenses of $1,600 for your 4-year old child and qualify to claim the credit for child and dependent care expenses. Your employer pays an additional $1,000 under a qualified employer-provided dependent care assistance plan. This $1,000 is excluded from your income. The dollar limit for your work-related expenses is $2,400 (one qualifying person). However, your credit is figured on only $1,400 of the $1,600 work-related expenses you paid because the dollar limit is reduced to $1,400 as a result of the subtraction of the $1,000 excludable benefit from $2,400.

How to Claim Credit

To claim the credit, you must file your return on Form 1040 or Form 1040A. If you file Form 1040, you must complete Form 2441, Credit for Chid and Dependent Care Expenses, and send it in with your Form 1040. If you file Form 1040A, you must complete Schedule 2, Child and Dependent Care Expenses for Form 1040A, and attach it to your Form 1040A. You cannot claim the credit on Form 1040EZ.

Tax Preparers

Now you should realize there are many medical deductions and credits available to families with children who have disabilities. If you are uncertain about whether an expense qualifies as a deduction or about your taxes in general, there are many sources of assistance available. You should look for tax help early in the tax year. Select a tax professional by reference from friends and professionals. Once you find someone to help you with your taxes, agree to a general fee before hiring. Although your tax preparer should sign your tax return, make sure you understand everything that is written on it because you are responsible for any errors.

In addition to tax services, three useful tax guides exist: *Your Federal Income Tax*, available from IRS offices or the Superintendent of Documents, Washington, D.C.; *The Master Tax Guide* published by Commerce Clearance House and available at most libraries; and J.K. Lasser's *Your Income Tax*, available at many book stores.

The following list describes different types of services available that will either prepare your return for you or help you fill it out.

The Internal Revenue Service

The IRS provides many services at no charge. First, you can call the IRS on a toll-free number, available from your local IRS office, to get answers to specific questions. You can also use the TeleTax system, which offers recorded messages of basic tax information. To use the recorded-message system you dial the TeleTax number and then follow instructions. Each tape has a different 3 digit tape number: For example: Dependent: who can be claimed? Tape 155. Medical and Dental Expenses: Tape 302. Child and Dependent Care Credit: Tape 401. For information on how to use TeleTax ask the IRS for publication 910.

Second, you can walk into any IRS office for free tax help. The problem with this free help is that the IRS staff is usually very busy and can spend little time in computing, let alone planning, your taxes. Normally, you will be one of a group being helped by an IRS employee. Only people with disabilities receive one-on-one assistance. In general, seek help at a local IRS office only if your financial situation is not complex. If you seek IRS help, by the way, the IRS cannot ask you to substantiate your deductions. For these visits, they are there to help, not to audit.

Third, the IRS has a program called Outreach in which the Agency will go into communities to offer help, sometimes in cooperation with local organizations.

Telephone help for hearing impaired taxpayers is available for those who have access to TDD equipment. Residents of all states call 1-800-829-4059. Braille materials are made available through the IRS for distribution through the Library of Congress.

Other Free Assistance

Several organizations offer free help in preparing tax returns. One such program is called Tax Counseling for the Elderly, which is run by the American Association of Retired Persons (AARP) and provides help to anyone age 60 or older. Volunteers, many of whom are retired accountants or businessmen, are trained by the IRS and the Association to give one-on-one help to the elderly. For more information, call the IRS after February 1 in any year.

Another free service is called the Volunteer Income Tax Assistance Program, or VITA. Groups from colleges, community associations, and other organizations are trained by the IRS to provide help in their own communities for those with relatively uncomplicated tax returns. For further information, watch for publicity in your area or call the IRS and ask for the Taxpayer Education Coordinator.

Commercial Preparers

These services, such as H&R Block, are convenient, relatively inexpensive, and competent to handle the not-too-complicated tax return. Commercial preparers fill out tax returns, but they do not plan your taxes on an on-going basis.

Enrolled Agents

These tax preparers are not attorneys or certified public accountants, but they have passed an IRS examination and received what is known as a "Treasury Card," which means their background has been checked. Enrolled agents will represent you before the IRS but cannot represent you in court.

Accountants

As your income becomes greater and your tax return more complicated, you should consider hiring an accountant. An accountant deals with taxes regularly and can help you plan your taxes throughout the year. Usually, it is better to hire a certified public accountant (CPA) than a regular accountant, because CPA's have passed a comprehensive accounting exam. CPA's will represent their clients before the IRS but cannot represent clients in court.

Inquire about the type of client the CPA most often handles. From this information, you can determine whether his or her specialty meets your needs—individual tax planning, small business accounting, professional corporations, or whatever.

Tax Attorneys

Generally, tax attorneys deal with the most complicated tax questions. Tax attorneys will often handle tax issues for wealthy individuals, corporate returns, tax forms concerning estates and trusts, or business deals that have tax ramifications. The tax attorney is the only tax preparer who can represent you in court.

(Note: Much of the information in this chapter and the charts and diagrams are based on IRS Publication 501, 502, 503 and 907. You can obtain these publications and others from your local IRS office.)

CHAPTER 12

PERSONAL INJURY AWARDS

OFTEN A DISABILITY RESULTS FROM AN INJURY THAT GIVES RISE to a cause of action under the law. For example, your child may have received a head or spinal chord injury in a car accident and the driver of another car may have been at fault, or your child may have been the victim of medical malpractice which resulted in a brain injury.

In such cases, the law gives your child the right to sue the party responsible for his or her injuries. This is accomplished by having an attorney file a lawsuit against the responsible party. The lawsuit will then either be settled by the parties, which will generally result in your child receiving a cash payment or the right to a series of payments over a period of time, or the lawsuit will proceed to trial where the court will determine whether your child is entitled to anything and, if so, how much. In most cases, this determination will be made by a jury.

Personal injury cases are often very complex. The party who is sued (the defendant) often asserts a variety of defenses relating to whether he or she was really at fault and whether the injuries of the party bringing the lawsuit (the plaintiff) are as severe as claimed. Therefore it is very important that you hire an attorney who is expert in handling personal injury cases similar to yours. Such an attorney will likely be able to respond to the defenses raised by the defendant and to present your case in the most favorable light. The attorney will also be able to advise you as to your chances of success and the type of damage award that you can expect, and to represent you in any settlement negotiations. It is not advisable to seek to settle a personal injury claim on your own.

Moreover, most personal injury attorneys work on contingency fee arrangements. This means that you pay nothing unless the attorney successfully collects from the party who is sued. The typical arrangement is for the attorney to receive one-third of whatever is collected, in addition to reimbursement for whatever expenses are incurred in bringing the case.

Calculating the Personal Injury Award

The general theory behind the personal injury award is that the award is supposed to *compensate* the injured party for his or her injury. Of course in actual practice this theory is a fiction. No amount of money could ever compensate a quadriplegic for the loss of the use of his or her limbs.

Nevertheless, the theory is compensatory. The injured party receives an amount that the court views as adequate compensation for his or her injury. The greater the extent of the injury, the larger the award.

This is not to say that damage awards are susceptible to precise calculation. They are not, because the award is supposed to compensate the injured party for items such as pain and suffering, or reduced quality of life, which are not objectively determinable.

Moreover, if the defendant's conduct is considered particularly egregious, the jury may award *punitive* damages in addition to *compensatory* damages. Punitive damages are damages awarded to the injured party in excess of the amount a jury determines to be sufficient compensation for the injury. They are awarded to punish the defendant for conduct considered sufficiently bad.

Example One

Fred purchases an automobile from a large manufacturer. The manufacturer becomes aware that, due to negligence on the part of an inspector, a possibility exists that a small number of cars that were shipped from a particular plant may have contained a defective bolt which is critical to the braking system. The plant foreman has found three defective bolts out of the thousand that remain on the shop floor and is unsure whether any cars containing defective bolts were actually shipped.

Although the manufacturer is aware of the potential danger, the manufacturer decides not to order a recall of cars shipped from the plant or to take any other remedial action. The manufacturer is unsure whether any defective cars were shipped and, even if some defective cars were shipped, the number is likely to be relatively small— because nine hundred and ninety seven out of the thousand bolts that were inspected had no defect. The manufacturer is also unsure whether any harm will result even if defective cars were shipped because the bolt may never give way. Finally, the manufacturer is concerned about the potential cost and adverse publicity resulting from a recall.

Unfortunately, the automobile that Fred purchases is defective. The bolt gives way while Fred is driving on the highway. The brakes fail, and Fred is severely injured.

The jury determines that Fred is entitled to $1 million as compensation for items such as medical expenses, pain and suffering, and lost wages resulting from a prolonged absence from work. The jury also may decide to award punitive damages, and the amount may be quite substantial, to punish the manufacturer for failing to order a recall when it had evidence of the possibility that defective automobiles were shipped.

As is apparent, the amount that Fred should receive is not susceptible to precise calculation. It is not possible to determine how to adequately compensate Fred for his pain and suffering, or how to punish the manufacturer for its decision to ignore a known risk. Even medical expenses remain an unknown; Fred may have future medical expenses as a result of his injury.

How much should Fred receive? How much should a person with a brain injury be paid as *compensation* for the reduced quality of life resulting from his or her injury? What is the proper amount to pay someone who has mental retardation as a result of medical malpractice?

In practice, the answer depends on the extent of the injury and the sense of outrage that the jury feels over the defendant's conduct. In cases of severe injury, it is now common for attorneys to have a day in the life of the injured party videotaped to enable the jury to experience firsthand the devastating consequences of the injury.

Another factor that is often relevant is the financial wherewithal of the defendant. While a punitive damage award of one hundred thousand dollars might be sufficient to "send a message" to an individual whose conduct is considered particularly venal, such an award might not be adequate to punish a large company. A woman who suffered severe burns when coffee she was drinking spilled was awarded $2.7 million because the jury felt that the restaurant had knowingly served coffee that was too hot (the judge in the case later reduced the award to $480,000). Similarly, a bowling alley was ordered to pay $5.8 million in punitive damages for serving too many beers to a customer who later killed a young woman in a car accident. The largest punitive damage award that the authors are aware of involved the company responsible for a large oil spill in Alaska. The company was ordered to pay punitive damages of $5 billion.

The following are some of the elements to be considered in determining the adequacy of a settlement offer.

Liability: Is it clear that the defendant was at fault, or is it possible an injury resulted from an accident which was no one's fault? If a jury finds that there was no fault, the injured party will receive nothing.

Bad faith: Was the defendant's conduct merely negligent, or was it something more? Was there an element of intentionality or recklessness that could cause a jury to award punitive damages? The presence of intentionality or recklessness will likely cause a jury to award higher compensatory damages as well, particularly in regard to items such as pain and suffering and diminished life-style which are not objectively determinable.

Pain and suffering: Obviously, the more severe the injury, the higher the award.

Diminished life-style: What was the injured person's life like before the injury? What will it be like afterwards? This is where videotaping can be helpful.

Lost wages: How much work was missed as a result of the injury? What was the injured person's salary and what was the salary likely to be in the future? Is work still possible after the injury and at what salary? Is retraining possible? Has there been a loss of fringe benefits such as medical insurance or pension coverage? Note that reduced earnings will generally cause a reduction in pension benefits as well.

Medical expenses: How much was spent on doctors and hospitals? Is the injury likely to result in future medical expenses? If so, what is the expected cost? (Note that the opinion of experts is helpful here.)

Future needs: If the injury is sufficiently severe that substantial lifetime care will be required, what is the projected cost?

The chart in Chapter 5 relating to the calculation of supplementary care costs, which is repeated here for your convenience, is helpful to this calculation. You should note, however, that the projected future needs should not serve as a cap on the damages ycu request because the calculation does not take account of items such as pain and suffering or reduced quality of life. However, information as to the future needs of a person who is injured severely is relevant in determining the adequacy of a settlement offer.

PROJECTED CARE COSTS PER MONTH (Current Dollars)

$ ______ Housing

______ Rent/Month

______ Utilities

______ Maintenance

______ Cleaning Items

______ Laundry Costs

______ Other

$ ______ Care Assistance

______ Live-in

______ Respite

______ Custodial

______ Guardianship/Advocacy (approx. $50-$75 per hr.)

______ Other

$ ______ Food

______ Meals, snacks-home

______ Outside of home

______ Special foods/ gastric tube

______ Other

$ ______ Clothing

$ ______ Furniture

$ ______ Medical/Dental Care

______ General medical/ dental visits

______ Therapy

______ Nursing Services

______ Meals of attendants

______ Evaluations

______ Transportation

______ Medications

______ Other

$ ______ Insurance

______ Medical/Dental

______ Burial

______ Car

______ Housing/Rental

______ Other

$ ______ Automobile

______ Payments

______ Gas, Oil, Maintenance

______ Other

$ ______ **Recreation**

______ Sports

______ Special Olympics

______ Spectator Sports

______ Vacations

______ TV/VCR

______ Summer Camp

______ Transportation costs

______ Other

$ ______ **Education, Training, Etc.**

______ Transportation

______ Fees

______ Books

______ Other

$ ______ **Employment**

______ Transportation

______ Workshop fees

______ Attendant

______ Training

______ Other

$ ______ **Personal Needs**

______ Haircuts, Beauty Shop

______ Telephone

______ Cigarettes

______ Church/Temple Expenses

______ Hobbies

______ Books, Magazines, Etc.

______ Allowance

______ Other

$ ______ **Special Equipment**

______ Environmental control

______ Elevator

______ Repair of equipment

______ Computer

______ Audio books

______ Ramp

______ Guide dog/other special animals

______ Technical instruction

______ Wheelchair

______ Other

$ ______ **Emergency Reserve**

TOTAL PROJECTED EXPENSES $__________

After calculating the total required expenses, you are ready to calculate the minimum settlement required to fund those expenses. The calculations are complex, and you may need an accountant, a financial planner, or a specialist in settlement planning to assist you. In general, you will need to build in an inflation factor to account for cost increases over time, and a return rate to account for the investment income that the settlement funds will generate. You will then need to account for taxes attributable to the investment income and possibly a fee to compensate a financial planner for investment services. It may also be advisable to build in a reserve for unanticipated emergency expenses.

For example, suppose that after filling out the worksheets provided above you decide that your injured child will need $3,000 in funds each month. If we assume an inflation factor of 4 percent, an anticipated after-tax rate of return of 5 percent, and a life expectancy for your child of another 40 years, a settlement of $1,144,944 will be required.

Structured Settlements

The *structured settlement* has become an increasingly popular method of settling personal injury claims in the case of severe injuries where the injured party is expected to require substantial care throughout his or her life.

Talk to any personal injury attorney, and you will be told horror stories of clients who dissipated substantial settlements on luxury items, and were later unable to pay for the basic necessities of life. A structured settlement is designed to deal with this problem by matching damage awards to the injured party's needs. Instead of receiving a single lump sum settlement, the injured party receives a series of payments over his or her lifetime that is carefully structured to meet his or her financial needs.

Example Two

Linda suffers severe injuries when the car she is driving collides with a train. Apparently the gate at the crossing was defective, and Linda's car was struck by an oncoming train. Although Linda has a loving family, her parents are not experienced in dealing with substantial sums of money and they fear that they could make mistakes if they receive a large settlement amount. This is particularly troubling because it is anticipated that Linda will need to live on her settlement for the rest of her life.

Linda's attorney hires a structured settlement specialist who determines that Linda will need $50,000 per year in today's dollars to satisfy ongoing medical and personal needs. Instead of accepting a single lump sum payment, Linda, through her parents and attorney, agrees to release her claim against the driver in exchange for an initial payment of $500,000 to pay Linda's medical expenses and attorney fees, and a series of payments that begin at $50,000 in the year of the settlement and increase by 3 percent each year (to account for inflation) for the rest of Linda's life.

If it is possible to determine that Linda will have extraordinary needs at some point in the future, the settlement can be structured so that Linda receives larger payments in those years. For example, Linda may have a young child who is expected to begin college in five years. In such a case it would be possible to structure the settlement so that Linda receives a larger cash payment at that time. Similarly, Linda may need a special wheelchair or a customized van, and it is possible to structure the settlement so that larger payments can be made when it is anticipated that a new wheelchair or van will be needed, or she may need vocational rehabilitation, and larger payments can be made in those years.

Careful attention to any rehabilitation report that may have been prepared on Linda's behalf can be helpful in anticipating Linda's needs. It can also be helpful to consult medical experts as well as structured settlement specialists to project future medical needs. For example, it may be possible to predict that a young child who is injured will require reconstructive surgery at a definite point in the future.

Structuring the Settlement

A structured settlement is an agreement between the defendant and an injured party, whereby the injured party agrees to accept a series of payments over a period of time, often for life, in lieu of a single settlement amount. In most cases the injured party will not want to rely on the promise of the defendant to make the payments. The payments may continue for a long period of time, and the defendant may have financial difficulties and become unable to make the payments in the future.

As a result, several methods have been developed to reduce the risk of default. In the typical case, the defendant will pay a structured settlement company to assume the obligation to pay the injured person. The *structured settlement company* then purchases an *annuity* (see Chapter 5) from a life insurance company to fund the obligation. In many cases the insurance company will own the structured settlement company. In some cases the defendant will purchase the annuity directly and a structured settlement company will not be involved.

Example Three

Linda suffers severe brain trauma as a result of an automobile accident. A structured settlement is agreed to, the terms of which provide that Linda is to receive an initial payment of $500,000 to fund her medical expenses and attorney fees, and a series of payments that begin at $50,000 in the year of the settlement and increase by 3 percent each year (to account for inflation) for the rest of Linda's life.

Under the terms of the settlement, the defendant pays a structured settlement company to assume its obligation to make future payments to Linda. The structured settlement company purchases an annuity that pays Linda $50,000 in the year of the settlement, with payments increasing by 3 percent each year during Linda's life. The initial $500,000 is paid by the defendant to Linda directly. If it is possible to determine that Linda will have extraordinary needs at some point in the future, the annuity can be structured so that Linda receives larger payments in those years.

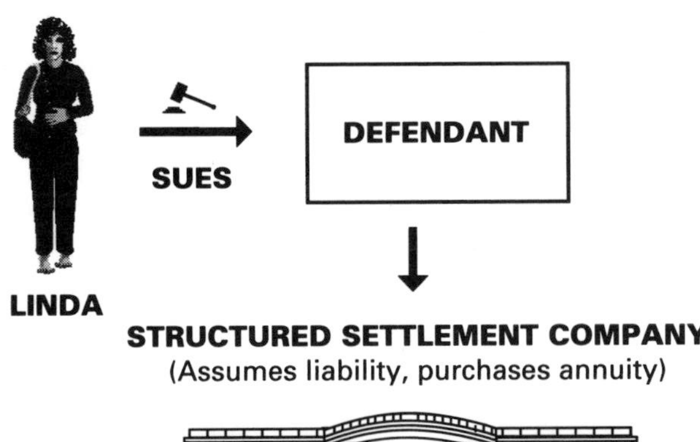

STRUCTURED SETTLEMENT COMPANY
(Assumes liability, purchases annuity)

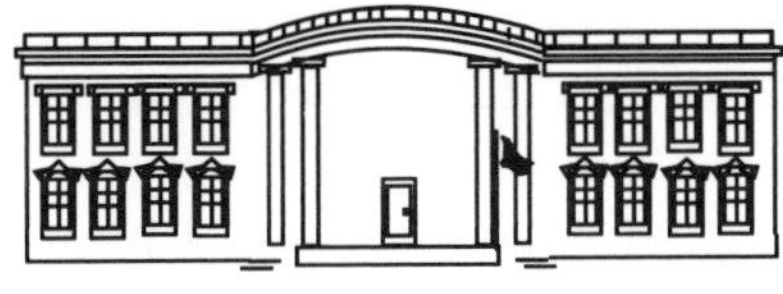

Sometimes United States Treasury Obligations, as opposed to annuities, are used to reduce the default risk. Under such an approach the defendant purchases United States Treasury Obligations which are held by a bank in a custodial account, and the injured party is given a security interest. This means that the injured party gets the right to take possession of the Treasury Obligations if the defendant misses a payment. Alternatively, the Treasury Obligations can be held in trust.

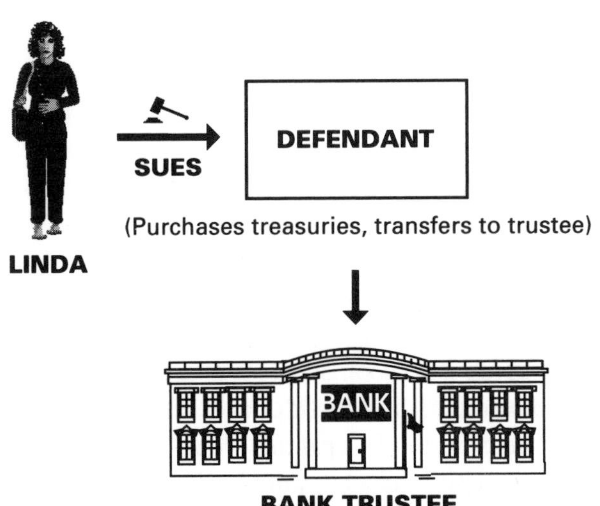

BANK TRUSTEE

Treasury Obligations offer greater security than annuities because it is possible that the insurance company selling the annuity will go bankrupt and will be unable to make the required payments. The United States government is less likely to go bankrupt.

However, Treasury Obligations are less flexible. While it is possible to structure an annuity so that payments are made for the life of the injured party, Treasury Obligations have maximum terms of 30 years.

What are the advantages of a structured settlement approach?

The primary advantage has already been discussed. The structured settlement gives the injured party the right to receive a guaranteed income stream for his or her entire life that cannot be outlived or dissipated prematurely. This is to be contrasted with a single lump sum payment which can be spent unwisely or invested poorly. Obviously, the value of this benefit depends at least partly on the financial sophistication of the injured person and his or her family.

Example Four

Linda suffers from mental retardation as a result of oxygen deprivation during delivery. The hospital and doctors are sued, and settlement discussions commence. Linda's parents are not experienced in financial matters and her attorney suggests a structured settlement, so Linda will have a guaranteed income stream for her life. While it would be possible for Linda's parents to get advice from qualified experts to make up for their lack of expertise, there is a chance that they could hire the wrong person and get poor advice, or they could make unwise expenditures. In addition, substantial management fees could be incurred.

If Linda's parents were sophisticated investors with a great deal of financial discipline, the benefit of a structured settlement would be reduced because Linda's parents would be less likely to dissipate her settlement by purchasing unnecessary luxury items or investing unwisely. However, even in such a case, Linda's parents may not wish to risk her future on their expertise, and they may instead prefer the security of a structured settlement approach.

Another option is for the court to appoint a guardian of Linda's estate. See Chapter 3. In such a case the court supervises expenditures and investments to protect against premature dissipation. While this supervision is useful in many cases, the constant need for court approval can be cumbersome and fees charged by attorneys and guardians can be high. In addition, even where a guardian of the estate is appointed, it is possible that the injured person will outlive the damage award.

Structured settlements offer income tax benefits as well. The tax law generally provides that damages received in a personal injury case are not subject to income tax. The same is true of personal injury settlements. However, earnings from investment of personal injury awards are subject to tax, unless the award is invested in tax-exempt vehicles such as municipal bonds.

Example Five

John suffers brain trauma as a result of a motorcycle accident in which the other driver is clearly at fault. He accepts a cash settlement of $500,000 which is invested in an annuity that pays John $40,000 per year for 20 years plus $500,000 at the end of 20 years. The $500,000 that John receives in settlement of his injury is not subject to tax. However, John's earnings as a result of investing in the annuity are subject to tax. If we assume that John is in the 15 percent tax bracket, the $800,000 in earnings ($40,000 per year for 20 years) yield a total tax of $120,000. If John is in the 28 percent bracket, the $800,000 in earnings give rise to a tax of $224,000. (For ease of explanation, we ignore the effect of graduated rates and other deductions.)

Suppose that instead of settling for $500,000 and investing the proceeds in an annuity, John agrees to a structured settlement that is identical from an economic perspective. That is, the defendant agrees to pay John $40,000 per year for 20 years and $500,000 at the end of 20 years. The defendant would presumably secure its obligation to John by purchasing the same annuity that John was going to buy.

Although John's situation is unchanged economically, his tax position improves substantially. Instead of receiving $500,000 tax free as a result of his injury and $800,000 in taxable investment earnings, John receives the entire $1,300,000 in compromise of his personal injury claim. As a result, no tax is owing. This results in a savings of $120,000 if John is in the 15 percent tax bracket and $224,000 if John is in the 28 percent tax bracket. In effect, the government pays part of the settlement.

Of course, John could take the $500,000 and receive tax free treatment on the earnings by investing in a municipal bond. However, the return on tax-exempt bonds is generally two to four percent less than the return on an annuity. John could perhaps take the $500,000 and invest in a taxable instrument that would have a higher return than an annuity, maybe even be enough to offset the tax advantage of the structured settlement. However, this tends not to occur very often.

One point to keep in mind. The tax benefit of the structured settlement approach depends upon John's tax bracket. If John has substantial medical expenses each year, the benefit of a structured settlement will be reduced because John's medical expenses will be deductible. In addition, as discussed in Chapter 11, the definition of medical expense is quite expansive, and includes items such as nursing care.

Example Six

John suffers brain trauma as a result of a motorcycle accident in which the other driver is clearly at fault. He accepts a cash settlement of $500,000 which is invested in an annuity that pays John $40,000 per year for 20 years plus $500,000 at the end of 20 years. John's medical expenses are $20,000 per year.

The $500,000 that John receives in settlement of his injury is not subject to tax. However, John's earnings as a result of investing in the annuity are subject to tax. If we assume that John is in the 15 percent tax bracket, the $400,000 in earnings ($40,000 in investment income less $20,000 in medical expenses times 20 years) yield a total tax of $60,000. If John is in the 28 percent bracket, the $400,000 in earnings give rise to a tax of $112,000.

Thus, the tax benefit of a structured settlement is reduced to $60,000 if John is in the 15 percent bracket and $112,000 if John is in the 28 percent bracket. This is because earnings on a lump sum settlement over 20 years result in tax of those amounts while, as discussed in Example 5, the proceeds from a structured settlement are entirely tax free.

If John's annual medical expenses are $40,000 or more, a structured settlement has no tax advantage because the lump sum approach results in no tax. John has $40,000 of gross earnings per year, but no tax is owing after medical expenses and personal exemptions are deducted.

Are there any disadvantages to a structured settlement?

The most obvious is the risk of nonpayment. As stated previously, a structured settlement is an agreement between the defendant and an injured party, whereby the injured party agrees to accept a series of payments over a period of time, often for life, in lieu of a single settlement amount. As such, there is a possibility that the defendant will be unable to pay.

There are, however, a number of methods of reducing the nonpayment risk and several of these methods have already been discussed. In the typical case, the defendant will pay a structured settlement company to assume its payment obligation. The structured settlement company is often owned by an insurance company and has typically been established specifically to act as payer on personal injury claims. The structured settlement company will then purchase an annuity from the insurance company with money provided by the defendant in order to fund its payment obligation. The insurance company will also typically guarantee payment. This means that the insurance company will pay the injured party directly if the structured settlement company does not.

Obviously, it is very important that the injured party and his or her attorney be confident of the insurance company's financial wherewithal. A.M. Best Company publishes periodic reports which rate the financial strength of various insurance companies. Some structured settlement specialists attempt to reduce the risk by using more than one insurance company. In addition, many states have guarantee funds organized by resident insurance companies to guarantee payment of annuity contracts in the event that a member insurance company becomes insolvent. The funds typically limit their liability to $100,000 in cash value or $300,000 per claim. Finally, as discussed previously, the nonpayment risk can be reduced even further by funding the structured settlement with treasury bills.

A second disadvantage to a structured settlement is inflexibility. Once a structured settlement is agreed to, it is set in stone, and there is little flexibility to respond to changed circumstances. For example, if you agree to a structured settlement of $30,000 per year for life, you cannot later change your mind if you decide you need more money shortly after the injury and less later. As discussed in Example 2, it is possible to try and anticipate future needs and structure the settlement so payments match needs. However, it may not be possible to accurately forecast future needs and, once agreed to, a structured settlement cannot be changed.

Example Seven

Linda suffers severe brain trauma as a result of an automobile accident. A structured settlement is agreed to, the terms of which provide that Linda is to receive an initial payment of $500,000 to fund her medical expenses and attorney fees, and a series of payments that begin at $50,000 in the year of the settlement and increase by 3 percent each year (to account for inflation) for the rest of Linda's life.

Unfortunately, Linda develops additional medical problems and the $50,000 proves insufficient. Had Linda accepted a cash settlement, she might have had sufficient resources to fund the emergency.

Finally, if you accept a structured settlement you bear the risk that inflation will increase and the settlement will no longer be sufficient to satisfy your needs. As discussed in Example 2, it is possible to structure the settlement so that payments increase over time. There is no guarantee, however, that inflation will not occur at a higher rate than the payments increase.

Example Eight

Linda suffers severe brain trauma as a result of an automobile accident. Careful analysis determines that Linda will require $500,000 initially to pay immediate expenses, and $50,000 per year in today's dollars to meet ongoing needs. A structured settlement is agreed to, the terms of which provide that Linda is to receive an initial payment of $500,000, and a series of payments that begin at $50,000 in the year of the settlement and increase by 3 percent each year (to account for inflation) for the rest of Linda's life. Unfortunately, inflation rises to 5 percent and the settlement proves to be inadequate.

Obviously, the decision as to whether you should accept a structured settlement is complicated, and what is right for one person is not necessarily right for another. If you do decide to accept a structured settlement, you will want to be sure that a certain number of minimum payments is guaranteed. This is very important to protect against premature death.

Example Nine

Linda suffers severe brain trauma as a result of an automobile accident. In lieu of a $1 million cash settlement, her representatives accept an initial payment of $400,000 to fund medical expenses and attorney fees, and a series of payments that begin at $40,000 in the year of the settlement and increase by 3 percent each year (to account for inflation) for the rest of Linda's life.

While this might be a good idea if Linda lives for a long time, it would not be advisable if she lives for only a short time after the accident. Linda's representatives can protect against this risk by insisting that payment be made for a specified period, say ten years, even if Linda dies prematurely. Depending on Linda's age, a ten year guarantee will likely add little to the cost of the annuity used to fund the structured settlement.

It is also advisable that you be aware of the cost of a structured settlement to the defendant before you accept the offer. This is because an offer may sound attractive, but its cost may be significantly less than the amount you would be likely to receive if your case actually went to trial.

Example Ten

Linda is injured severely when a drunk driver crashes into her car while pulling out of the parking lot at the local tavern. Although the driver is uninsured and lacks substantial assets of his own, it turns out that the tavern owner continued to serve the man drinks despite the fact that the man was obviously drunk. Under the dram shop laws in the state where the accident occurred, the tavern owner is potentially liable for Linda's injuries. Linda is 35 years old when the injury occurs.

After consultations with her attorney, Linda decides she is willing to accept $500,000 in settlement, but not less. The tavern owner offers Linda a structured settlement of $2,000 per month for the rest of Linda's life, with a ten year guarantee period.

Linda would be ill advised to accept the settlement. This is because, under prevailing interest rates, the cost to the tavern owner of purchasing an annuity for a 35 year old will be approximately $350,000, which is considerably less than Linda was willing to accept.

In general, the cost of an annuity is based on three factors: the size of the payments to be made, the life expectancy of the injured party and the prevailing interest rate. The importance of interest rates is easily understood if you think about how insurance companies make money from annuity sales— by investing the proceeds. If an annuity costs $100,000 and the insurance company can invest the $100,000 at 8 percent, it can pay a higher monthly annuity than if it earned just 6 percent.

Similarly, if the injured party has a lower life expectancy, an annuity will cost less because the insurance company can expect to be making the payment for a shorter period. For example, if in Example Ten Linda was 60 years old, the annuity paying $2,000 per month with a ten year guarantee period would have a cost of $280,000. This dependency on life expectancy can be used by both the injured party and the defendant to lower the annuity cost or increase benefits.

Example Eleven

Linda is injured severely when a drunk driver crashes into her car while pulling out of the parking lot at the local tavern. Although the driver is uninsured and lacks substantial assets of his own, it turns out that the tavern owner continued to serve the man drinks despite the fact that the man was obviously drunk. Under the dram shop laws in the state where the accident occurred, the tavern owner is potentially liable for Linda's injuries. Linda is 35 years old when the injury occurs.

After consultations with her attorney, Linda decides she is willing to accept $350,000 in settlement, but not less. The tavern owner offers a Linda a structured settlement of $2,000 per month for the rest of Linda's life, with a ten year guarantee period. Given that Linda is 35-years old, the annuity should have a cost of $350,000.

However, it may be possible for the tavern owner to convince the insurance company issuing the annuity that Linda has a reduced life expectancy as a result of her injuries. If the insurance company decided that Linda had the life expectancy of a 60 year old, this is known as having a rated age of 60, the cost would be $280,000. Similarly, if the tavern owner was willing to spend $350,000, Linda would receive a much better settlement if she could find a financially sound insurance company that gave her a rated age of 60.

Obviously, knowing her rated age is very important for Linda in determining whether a settlement offer is acceptable.

Settlements And Government Benefits

The cost of lifetime care for a person with a severe injury can be staggering, and often settlements and personal injury awards that initially appear very large can prove insufficient. This is because costs can increase over time, and it is not always possible to predict the full range of expenses that will be incurred with absolute certainty. Moreover, the defendant in the personal injury case will present a variety of arguments and defenses, and it will not always be possible to obtain a settlement that will be sufficient to fund the victim's lifetime needs. The resulting shortfall can cause great hardship.

Example Twelve

Linda suffers severe physical injuries from an automobile accident which result in complete paralysis. Because liability is unclear, there are arguments which suggest that Linda may have been partly at fault, she accepts a settlement of $1 million. After attorney fees and five years of medical expenses, she runs out of money. Linda may now qualify for government benefit programs such as Medicaid and SSI (see Chapter 4). However, Medicaid and SSI will pay for the basic necessities of life alone— room, board and medical care, and Linda will miss out on many of the "extras" that make life worth living, such as vacations, meals out, and occasional outings with friends. There may even be opportunities for experimental treatments that may not be available through the Medicaid program.

Fortunately, as a result of legislation contained in the Omnibus Budget Reconciliation Act of 1993 (enacted at the end of 1993), Linda can direct that the settlement be paid into a trust for her benefit. Linda can use Medicaid to pay her medical expenses, and the trust can be available to meet other needs.

Two types of trusts are potentially available. The first, which has already been discussed (see Chapter 6), is a special needs trust which satisfies the requirements for "Trusts Created With A Beneficiary's Own Assets" discussed at the end of Chapter 6. Three requirements must be satisfied.

First, the beneficiary of the trust must be under the age of sixty-five at the time the trust is created, and must be considered disabled within the meaning of the social security regulations (see Chapter 4). It is irrelevant whether the beneficiary turns 65 after the trust has been created; the trust continues to qualify.

Second, the trust must be created by a parent, grandparent, or guardian of the person with a disability, or by a court. Note that the trust cannot be created by the beneficiary of the trust.

Third, the trust must provide that amounts remaining in the trust after the death of the beneficiary must be used to reimburse the state to the extent that the state has paid the beneficiary's medical expenses under its Medicaid program.

It is also possible for the personal injury victim to retain eligibility for government benefits by directing that the settlement be transferred to a pooled income trust set up by a nonprofit association. The nonprofit association sets up a separate account for the beneficiary, and funds remaining at the death of the beneficiary must be used to repay the state for amounts expended under its Medicaid program on the beneficiary's behalf, except to the extent the funds are retained by the nonprofit association for charitable purposes.

Example Thirteen

Linda suffers severe physical injuries from an automobile accident which result in complete paralysis. Linda accepts a settlement of $1 million and directs that the settlement be paid into a special needs trust that meets the requirements specified above. Linda remains eligible for government benefits, and the funds are available to satisfy needs beyond those that the government provides.

It may even be possible to use special needs trusts in cases that settled many years ago. For example, if Linda accepted a $1 million settlement some time ago, it may be possible to transfer any remaining money into a special needs trust to avoid further depletion of trust assets. A 1993 case in New York permitted such a result.

The case involved a man by the name of Michael Moretti who has been in a coma since he was struck by an automobile on September 8, 1984 at the age of 15. A personal injury action was brought on Mr. Moretti's behalf, and he received a settlement in the amount of $1 million. In 1992, Mr. Moretti's mother brought an action requesting that the $200,000 remaining from Mr. Moretti's settlement be placed in a special needs trust so as to avoid further depletion of Mr. Moretti's assets. After initially denying Mrs. Moretti's request on September 24, 1992, the court later granted the request, citing the 1993 legislation discussed previously as authorization for the creation of the trust.

Government Benefits And Structured Settlements

As stated previously, it is sometimes advisable for an injured person to accept a settlement structured as a series of payments over years, as opposed to a lump sum settlement. Such payments can be structured to avoid loss of government benefits as well.

Example Fourteen

Linda suffers severe physical injuries from an automobile accident which result in complete paralysis. Linda accepts a settlement of $50,000 per year for the rest of her life, with a guaranteed term of twenty years, and directs that the settlement be paid into a special needs trust that meets the requirements specified above. Linda remains eligible for government benefits, and the funds are available to satisfy needs beyond those that the government provides.

An interesting issue arises relating to the choice of beneficiary in a structured settlement designed to maintain eligibility for government benefits. As stated previously, it is generally advisable to have a guaranteed term to protect against premature death. For example, in Example 14 Linda accepted a structured settlement with a guaranteed term of twenty years. If Linda died within the twenty year period, her beneficiary would have the right to receive the payments until the end of the period. The issue in the case of a structured settlement designed to maintain eligibility for government benefits is whether guaranteed payments have to be made available for government reimbursement.

Example Fifteen

Linda suffers severe physical injuries from an automobile accident which result in complete paralysis. She accepts a settlement of $500,000 and directs that the settlement be paid into a special needs trust that meets the requirements specified above so as to maintain eligibility for government benefits. Linda incurs medical expenses in excess of $500,000 which are paid by Medicaid, and dies within ten years of the accident. Because the trust has been created to maintain eligibility for government benefits, the remaining funds must be used to reimburse the government for costs incurred under the Medicaid program on Linda's behalf.

Suppose instead that Linda accepts a structured settlement, naming a special needs trust as primary beneficiary and a loved one as contingent beneficiary in the event Linda dies within the guarantee period. If we assume that Linda is thirty-five years old, the $500,000 will buy a structured settlement of $36,000 per year with a twenty year guarantee period. If Linda dies five years after the settlement, her beneficiary will be entitled to $36,000 per year for a fifteen year period (the remaining term of the guarantee period). In effect, by naming someone other than the special needs trust as contingent beneficiary, the requirement that the government be repaid from trust moneys has been avoided.

Does the approach work? The answer is unclear. It is possible the government could argue that the 1993 legislation requires that the special needs trust be named as contingent beneficiary during the guarantee period. However, our reading of the statute suggests no such requirement.

Conclusion

Handling personal injury claims is complicated, and it is vital that you get attorneys and other advisors who are expert in the area to represent you. In addition to actually bringing the lawsuit, it is important that your advisor be knowledgeable about the benefits and detriments of structured settlements as well as the intricacies of government benefit programs.

If you decide to create a special needs trust in connection with a personal injury, it is generally advisable that you contact the Medicaid department in the state where you reside and inform them of your plans so as to avoid unexpected problems. If the state Medicaid agency has provided services prior to the settlement, the agency may seek reimbursement. Though the matter is not free from doubt, the 1993 legislation appears to indicate that a special needs trust can be used to defer reimbursement for such services until the death of the beneficiary, even if the services were provided before the settlement.

If medical payments relating to the injury were paid for by Medicare, Medicare will also have a right to reimbursement. Medicare's rights apparently cannot be deferred through use of a special needs trust.

It is vitally important that the injury victim's attorney be aware of all reimbursement claims before funding the trust. This is because the attorney can potentially be liable if reimbursement claims are not satisfied before the trust is funded.

Chapter 13

The Final Step:
Putting Your Estate In Order

Now that you have completed our book, you should be aware of the importance of estate planning and have likely developed some general ideas about what your estate plan will look like. You have thought about what your child's life will be like after you are gone: where your child will live, how he or she will continue to enjoy favorite activities, and who will serve as your child's advocate and look out for his or her interests after you are no longer able to do so. Perhaps you have even been made aware of some government programs that might be of benefit to you.

You have probably had some general thoughts about how you want to divide your property, whether you want to establish a trust for your child, and, if so, who you will want to act as trustee. You have thought about whether you want a living trust and what type of estate-tax planning, if any, will be required.

All that is left is to begin the process— to take the first steps toward preparation of your estate plan. As we have repeatedly stressed throughout this book, you should not attempt to prepare an estate plan yourself. It is too important, and it is too easy to make mistakes.

In many states there are experts in estate planning for families with children who have disabilities. You can probably get referrals from many of the agencies listed in the Directory of Organizations found in Appendix III of this book. Referrals can also be obtained from social workers or agencies you may have worked with in the past, as well as from other parents of children with disabilities who may have been through the estate-planning process themselves. Shop carefully, and make sure you select advisors who are trustworthy, well informed, and good-hearted.

As you work through the planning process, you will want to involve those you intend to rely on to carry out your wishes. Seek out their ideas and make sure you feel confident in their willingness and ability to help.

As a general rule we advise our clients to keep their original documents in a fireproof safe, a safe deposit box, or with their attorney. We also supply our clients with a binder that contains all the information that others will need to carry on after the clients are gone.

The binder should be kept in a place that is readily accessible, so you can update it periodically, and so the people who will act as your child's advocate after you are gone will be able to find it. Many of our clients purchase small fireproof safes for this purpose.

The binder generally contains separate folders in which we place the following:

1. An overview of the estate plan in plain English— that is, without any "legalese"— which we prepare.

2. Important legal papers for any children with disabilities (for example, birth certificates, Social Security cards, and health-insurance cards).

3. A description of the goals and purposes of the Special Needs Trust, which we prepare.

4. A copy of the Letter of Intent, which you should update at least once per year.

5. Unsigned copies of any wills.

6. A letter spelling out any wishes regarding final arrangements (burial, cremation, or religious services or other ceremonies that may be desired).

7. Living wills and/or Power of Attorney for health care that may have been prepared.

8. Extra signed copies of any trusts— special needs trusts, living trusts, or insurance trusts— that may have been prepared. Remember, signed copies will be needed to complete property transfers, and extra signed copies will prove to be useful.

9. A list of major assets and information about where they are kept (for example, a list of insurance policies, stocks, mutual funds, bank accounts, with policy and account numbers and storage locations, and the names of any brokers, insurance agents, and investment advisors).

10. Guardianship papers, if any, and a list of advocacy organizations that may be helpful.

11. The names of government agencies or case workers that the client may have dealt with and the client's thoughts about them.

12. A list of government benefits that the client's child may receive, as well as copies of any filled-out application form. (These application forms will help you the next time you apply for benefits and will be especially helpful to future caregivers who may not understand the complexity of these applications.)

13. Other miscellaneous papers, such as tax returns filed by the child, information about housing options, schooling, photographs of the family, parent's Social Security numbers, parent's birth and marriage certificates, certificates and awards for the person with a disability.

14. Information about where the original documents are kept.

The estate-planning process is long and can often be heart wrenching. But when you are through, you can feel confident that you have done all that you can to assure your child's happiness after you are gone. We wish you the best of luck.

APPENDIX I

GLOSSARY

A

Account: To account for financial transactions is to provide a written statement of money earned, accrued, spent, and invested, and to explain how and why these transactions have taken place.

Adminstrator\Administratrix: Person appointed by probate court to administer a decedent's estate if an executor or personal representative is not properly appointed by will.

Advocate: An advocate is a friend, family member, or institution that looks out for the interests of a person with a disability. Advocates lack the legal standing of guardians.

Age of Majority: At the age of majority a person is entitled by law to manage his or her own affairs. The age of majority in most states is 18.

Annual Exclusion Gift: A gift of property worth $10,000 or less, often intended to reduce the estate tax owing at the donor's death.

Annuity, Annuitant: An annuity is the regular payment of money for life or for a specified period of time. The receiver or beneficiary of such payments is the annuitant.

Annuities are available in many forms but usually involve the payment of money to an organization for the promised return of one or more payments at a future time. An annuity that begins payments as soon as it is funded is sometimes referred to as an immediate annuity. An annuity that begins payments on a specified future date is sometimes called a deferred annuity.

Below are the most common methods of annuity payments:

1.A fixed annuity guarantees the annuitant an unchanging amount of money regularly for a specified period of time (most commonly, for life).

2. A variable annuity pays the annuitant an amount that depends on the investment performance of the company offering the annuity.

Attestation Clause: A clause often found in wills and other legal documents wherein witnesses attest to the signature of the person preparing the document.

B

Beneficiary: In general, a beneficiary is a person or institution named to receive property. For example, the beneficiary named in a life insurance policy will receive the insurance proceeds at the death of the insured. The beneficiary of a trust receives income and/or principal from the trust. The beneficiary under a will receives property from the decedent's estate.

Bond, Bond Fee: In court a bond is an amount of money that is pledged to secure performance. The bond will be forfeited if the person does not follow through properly on his or her obligation. Such bonds are sometimes called "performance" or "surety" bonds, and certain companies or individuals (bondsmen) specialize in guaranteeing payment of these bonds. The charge for such a service is called a bond fee.

As an investment, "bond" refers to a certificate of creditorship by which a borrower promises to repay borrowed money, plus interest, to a lender.

C

Codicil: A codicil is a formally executed addition to or change in the terms of a will, not requiring the complete rewriting of the will.

Conservator: In some states, a conservator is the same as a full guardian of the person and the estate. In other states, a conservator is a guardian of an adult as distinguished from a guardian of a child. The conservator of an estate or of any property is appointed by the court to care for that estate or property.

Credit-Shelter Trust: Trust used to increase the amount a married couple is able to pass on to others without estate tax from $600,000 to $1.2 million. Also known as marital bypass trust.

D

Decedent: A decedent is a person who has died. The term is used frequently in the course of estate settlement.

Developmental Disability: Any severe chronic disability that:

1. Is attributable to a mental or physical impairment or impairments,
2. Manifests itself prior to age 22,
3. Will likely continue indefinitely,
4. Results in substantial functional limitations in three or more of the seven major life activities: (a) self-care, (b) receptive and expressive language, (c) learning, (d) mobility, (e) self-direction, (f) capacity for independent living, and (g) economic sufficiency, and
5. Reflects the individual's need for a combination and sequence of special services that are either of extended or life-long duration and that are individually planned and coordinated.

Discretionary Trust: A trust in which the trustee has the discretion to determine whether or not to make distributions to the beneficiary.

Distribute, Distributee: To distribute property is to pass it on to those entitled to it. For example, a probate court distributes or passes estate property on to whoever is legally entitled to it. The trustee of a trust fund distributes or passes income or principal from the trust fund to the trust beneficiary, sometimes called the distributee.

Diversity, Diversification: If investments are diversified, they are spread into several different types of properties in order to minimize the risk of loss should one investment fail. Diversification is the process of spreading investments.

Dividend: A dividend is the money or other property that the owners of a corporation's stock receive out of the corporation's profits.

Donor/Donee: A donor is a person who gifts property to another. A donee is the person who receives the gift.

E

Earned Income: Earned income is wages, salaries, or fees derived from labor as opposed to income derived from invested capital such as rents, dividends, and interest.

Endowment Insurance: Endowment insurance is a type of protection that combines life insurance and investment. If the insured outlives the policy, the face value is paid to the insured. If he or she does not, the face value is paid to the beneficiary.

Estate, Probate Estate, Taxable Estate: A person's estate is all the money and all the real and personal property owned by that person or treated as owned by the person under the Internal Revenue Code.

A decedent's probate estate is that part of an estate that passes through the probate system.

A decedent's gross estate is the total property for estate-tax purposes, and his or her adjusted gross estate or taxable estate is the gross estate less certain deductions. The estate pays an estate tax based on the taxable estate. Thus, a decedent's estate is itself a taxpayer, managed as such by an administrator or executor.

Estate Planning: Estate planning is the process of creating and preserving one's property during one's lifetime and arranging for its transfer at one's death. Most frequently, the term is associated with advantageous investment and tax planning that does not sacrifice personal and family security and welfare.

Estate Tax: Tax due on death of decedent whose taxable estate exceeds $600,000.

Executor/Executrix: An executor is a person or institution named in a will to carry out the terms of the will. Executrix is the female version of executor.

F

Fiduciary: A fiduciary is a person or institution that takes the responsibility of acting on behalf of another person. In reference to wills, estates, and trusts, the following act in a fiduciary capacity for the maker of the will, for the estate, and for the beneficiaries: the attorney(s), executor(s), trustee(s), and guardian(s). All are bound by good faith and trust.

Funded Trust: A funded trust is a trust to which assets have been transferred.

G

Generation-Skipping Trust: Trust used to bypass children and pass money to grandchildren or more remote generations. Often used by the wealthy to save on estate taxes.

Gift, Gift Tax: A gift is a voluntary transfer of money and/or property from one person to another who accepts it without giving something of equal value in return. If the gift is to an individual or an organization not qualifying as nonprofit, it may be subject to a gift tax. If such a tax is due, it is computed on the amount of money given or on the fair market value of the property given.

Grantor: The grantor of a trust, also known as the settlor, is the person who creates a trust.

Group Home: A residential facility designed for several people with disabilities.

Guardian: A guardian is a person appointed by the court to control and manage another person's affairs and/or property. Most typically, a guardian is appointed to manage the affairs of a minor or of an adult who is considered incapable of looking after his or her own affairs.

A guardian is limited in power by the court making the appointment. The guardian must submit regular accountings to the court and must follow the direction of the court at all times. Guardians can also be appointed by will to look after the affairs of minor children.

Guardian Ad Litem: A guardian ad litem is a guardian appointed by the court for the purpose and duration of a law suit or similar action. Typically guardians ad litem are appointed for people determined by a court to need assistance in protecting their interests in the law suit.

Guardian-Discharge or Modification: Procedures for removing a guardian or a request for change in duties and powers of the guardian.

Guardian-Limited: A guardian appointed to exercise care and custody of the ward and/or management of the ward's estate in a restricted sense. This restriction takes the form of a determination by the court that the person is unable to act only in specific areas.

Guardian-Natural: The parent who is lawfully in control of a minor child; natural guardianship ceases when the child attains the age of majority.

Guardian of the Estate: A person appointed by the court to handle the care, management, and investment of the estate (real and personal property) of another person, with the duty to protect and preserve such property.

Guardian of the Person: An individual appointed by the court to see that the person with a disability has proper care and protective supervision in keeping with personal needs.

Guardian-Plenary: A person appointed by the court to exercise total legal control and management of the person, estate, or both.

Guardian-Public: A public official empowered to accept court appointment as a legal guardian.

Guardian-Successor: A legal guardian appointed by a court when an already functioning guardian dies, is removed by the court, or resigns.

Guardian-Temporary: A legal guardian appointed by a court for a temporary period of time when the court is given notice that a person is in immediate need of guardianship, generally for an emergency situation. A temporary guardian may be of the person, of the estate, or both.

Guardian-Testamentary: A testamentary guardian is a person designated by the last will and testament of a natural guardian.

I

Independent Living: A residential situation in which people with disabilities live by themselves with limited assistance from others.

Inherit: To inherit property is to receive it by will or by applicable state statutes (laws of descent or distribution) at the death of the owner of that property.

Insured: The person who obtained or who is otherwise covered by insurance on his or her health, life, or property.

Intermediate Care Facilities (ICFs): Group residential facilities, often funded by Medicaid and other government benefit programs.

Integrated Employment: A type of employment whereby people who have disabilities work alongside those who do not.

Integrated Living: A type of living arrangement in which people who have disabilities live alongside those who do not.

Inter Vivos: Made during one's lifetime (literally, between living persons). An inter vivos trust becomes effective during the creator's lifetime.

Intestate: To die intestate is to die without having a will. Intestacy is the state of being without a will. If a person dies intestate, the person's property passes to the heirs as required by the applicable state statute (the laws of descent and distribution), regardless of how the person who died may have intended the property to pass.

Invest, Investment Company: To invest is to use money to make more money. An investment company (commonly referred to as a mutual fund) will arrange to put an individual's money to work by adding it to sums from other people and investing it on a larger and/or more diverse scale than the individual would be capable of achieving alone. The money is managed by the investment company or another company retained as its investment advisor. The company sells shares of ownership in its own company, which represent ownership of its group of investments.

A "closed end" investment company or mutual fund sells only a fixed number of shares, and these are bought and sold (after the original purchase) in the open market like shares of common stock. An "open fund" investment company sells a continuous offering of shares, and the price of a share is determined by the current market value of the company's investments plus, in some cases, a sales charge (or load). Shares of an open end mutual fund may be redeemed (sold back to the company) at any time. The profits from both types of investment company come from the money they make in dividends, interest, and capital gains from their investments.

Irrevocable: Unchangeable. An irrevocable trust is a trust that cannot be changed.

Irrevocable Insurance Trust: Trust used to enable the grantor to pass insurance payable as a result of his or her death to loved ones without imposition of estate tax.

Itemized Deductions: Certain personal expenditures that are allowed by the Internal Revenue Code as deductions from adjusted gross income.

J

Job Coach: A person who assists people with disabilities in integrated employment situations.

Joint Return: Tax return filed for federal or state income taxes by a husband and wife together, each being individually liable. It includes the income of both spouses. Usually it is more beneficial for a couple to file a joint return than a separate return.

Joint Tenancy With Right Of Survivorship: Two or more persons owning property with each having the legal right of survivorship, by which the ownership on the death of any joint tenant remains with the survivors. See Tenancy In Common.

L

Least-Restrictive Alternative: A policy based on the belief that persons should be free to live as they please and that when government must interfere with a person's liberty, the services should be designed to maximize the developmental potential of the person and should be provided in the setting that is least restrictive of personal liberty.

Legacy, Legatee: A legacy (also known as a bequest) is a gift of personal property by will. The recipient of such a gift is the legatee.

Letters of Office: A document issued by the court indicating the appointment of a guardian of the person, a guardian of the estate, or both.

Life Estate: A person with a life estate (or life interest) in property has a right to use the property during his or her own or another designated person's lifetime.

Life Tenant: A life tenant is the person who has the use of property during his or her lifetime.

Limited Payment Insurance: Limited payment insurance is a type of life insurance for which premiums are payable for a definite period of time, after which the policy is fully paid. Also known as vanishing premium insurance.

Liquid, Liquid Assets, Liquidate: If property is liquid, it is easily sold or convertible to cash. Cash in hand is considered property in its most liquid form. To liquidate property generally means to convert it to cash or other easily marketable assets and then distribute the proceeds to the person or persons entitled to them.

Living Trust: A living trust is a trust created and funded during the life of the person who creates it.

Living Will: A living will is a document prepared for health care providers expressing the creator's desire not to be kept alive by artificial means.

M

Marital Bypass Trust: See Credit-Shelter Trust.

Marital Deduction: Mechanism by which transfers of property to spouse, whether during life or after, is exempted from gift and estate tax. Each person has an unlimited marital deduction, which means that any amount of property can be transferred to a spouse without imposition of gift or estate tax.

Minor: A person who has not reached the age of majority (18 years old in most states).

Municipal Bond: A municipal bond is a certificate of debt issued (sold) by a state or local government or government agency. Generally, the interest paid to the purchaser on such bonds is exempt from federal income tax, and, in some cases, state and local taxes as well.

Mutual Fund: See Investment Company.

N

Nonprobate Estate: Property of a deceased person which passes to beneficiaries or persons sharing ownership in the property without being subject to the probate process.

Nursing Home: A home designed to provide medical or custodial care to its residents. Typically the residents are aged or ill.

P

Per Capita: Used in wills and trusts to refer to distributions without representation. For example, leaving property to your descendants, per capita, means that each of your descendants receives an equal share.

Personal Property: All property owned by a person or institution except real estate.

Personal Representative: Same as executor. Some states use the term "personal representative" instead.

Per Stirpes: Used in wills and trusts to refer to distributions with representation. For example, leaving property to your descendants, per stirpes, means that your property is divided equally among your children, with grandchildren dividing the shares of children who have died.

Petitioner: A person who asks the court (a) for action or relief, or (b) to exercise its authority in some way. In guardianship proceedings, the petitioner is generally the person asking that a guardian be appointed for a person with a disability.

Portfolio: As a financial term, a person's or institution's portfolio is the total of all investments or the collection of investment assets.

Pour-Over Will: A will that directs that all, or a portion of, a testator's estate to flow into an already-existing or independently established trust.

Power of Attorney/Health Care: A power of attorney for health care is a legal document used to appoint someone to make health care decisions for you if you are not able to do so.

Power of Attorney/Property: A power of attorney for property is a legal document used to appoint someone to make property decisions for you, such as selling your property or making investment decisions.

Principal: In a trust, the principal amount is all the capital, the property that produces income.

Probate, Probate Court: The court process of probate specifically involves the validation of a will as the genuine and legally acceptable last directions of the maker of the will (the testator) and the carrying out of those directions. Most commonly, a state will have a special court that handles estates and probate proceedings. This court is called probate court in most states and by other names in other states (for example, surrogate or orphan's court).

Prudent Person Rule: Trustees (as fiduciaries) must manage trust property in accordance with the prudent person rule. This requires the trustee to handle the trust property with the same care that a prudent, honest, intelligent, and diligent person would use to handle the property under the same circumstances. If a trustee is accused of mismanaging the assets, the court will often judge the trustee's conduct by applying the prudent person rule as the standard against which to measure the trustee's actions.

Q

QTIP: Stands for Qualified Terminal Interest Property. Property left in a QTIP trust for a person's spouse is considered the spouse's for estate-tax purposes, and therefore qualifies for the marital deduction, even though the spouse's ability to use property can be restricted.

R

Real Property: Real property (also known as real estate or realty) is land and the buildings or other fixed improvements on that land.

Remainderman: The remainderman of a trust receives the remaining principal of the trust when the income beneficiary or life tenant dies.

Representative Payee: A person or organization that is authorized to cash and manage public assistance checks (Social Security, Supplemental Security Income) for a person deemed incapable of doing so.

Residue, Residual (or Residuary) Clause, Residual Estate: The residue is what remains, what is left over. A residual estate is what remains of an estate after all claims and taxes have been paid and all specific distributions have been made. A residual (residuary) clause in a will arranges for the distribution of this residual property of the estate.

Respondent: The person who makes an answer to a bill or other proceeding in court. In guardianship proceedings, the respondent is the person for whom a guardian has been requested.

Revocable: A revocable trust is a trust that can be revised or revoked at any time during the grantor's life.

S

Sheltered Workshop: A sheltered workshop is a workshop for people with disabilities where work is brought in from the community at large. It tends to be segregated from the community.

Special Needs Trust: A discretionary trust prepared for a person who has a disability. Also known as a supplemental needs trust. The trust is intended to supplement, not replace, government benefits.

Spendthrift Clause: Also known as "Protection from Claims by Strangers," a spendthrift clause in a trust agreement provides that the named beneficiary has a right to trust distributions only and thus cannot voluntarily dispose of the capital assets (principal) of the trust or the income before it is earned and paid. As a result the trust principal and unpaid income are protected from creditors of the beneficiary.

Sprinkling, Sprinkle and Spray Trust: A provision for "sprinkling" in a trust agreement allows the trustee to use personal judgment in distributing income from the trust fund. He or she controls the timing and the amount of the distributions and decides which beneficiaries will receive those distributions. A trust with such a provision is sometimes referred to as a "sprinkle and spray" trust.

Statute: A law.

Stocks: Certificates representing ownership in a corporation; they may yield dividends and can increase or decrease in value.

Supported Employment: An employment option for people with disabilities that is integrated into the community at large. The person with a disability generally receives assistance from a job coach, who may be a fellow employee or an employee of an adult service agency.

Surety: Surety is a financial guarantee that an act will be carried out or that a debt will be paid by another person. To post bond is to provide such surety.

Successor: A successor is one who follows another in a particular office. For example, a successor guardian is a person named to follow the originally named guardian if the originally named individual or institution can no longer hold office. A successor trustee is a person who takes over management of a trust after the initial trustee ceases to act.

T

Tax-Exempted Securities: Obligations issued by a state or municipality whose interest payments (but not profits via redemption or sale) are exempted from federal income taxation. The interest payment may be exempted from local taxation, too, if purchased by a state resident.

Tenancy In Common: Form of joint ownership in which tenants do not have right of survivorship. For example, if two individuals each own a one-half interest in a house as tenants in common, each of them can dispose of his or her interest by will. See Joint Tenancy With Right Of Survivorship.

Term Insurance: Term insurance is a form of pure life insurance having no cash surrender value and generally furnishing insurance protection for only a specified or limited period of time, though term insurance is usually renewable from term to term.

Testament, Testamentary Capacity: A person's testament is the final disposition of his or her personal property. Anything that is testamentary relates to a will. Testamentary capacity is the legal competence to make a will.

Testamentary Trust: A trust set up by will.

Testator/Testatrix: A testator is a person who is making a will. Testatrix is the female version of testator.

Trust: Property in trust is held and managed by a person or institution (the trustee) for the benefit of those persons or institutions for whom the trust was created (the beneficiaries). The creator of a trust is commonly referred to as the settlor, grantor, or trustor.

Trust Property: Trust property is the principal amount (the corpus or body) of a trust. It is the income-producing property of a trust.

U

Unearned Income: Unearned income is income from investments, rental property, etc., as distinguished from income derived from labor.

Universal Life Insurance: Like whole life insurance except the growth of the policy's cash value depends on investment performance. See Whole Life Insurance.

V

Vanishing Payment Insurance: See Limited Payment Insurance.

Vocational Rehabilitation: Vocational rehabilitation is a federally funded state-operated program designed to increase or develop employment skills.

W

Ward: A person, either a minor or an individual with a disability, under the care of a guardian.

Whole Life Insurance: With whole life insurance, the insured can fix a premium which remains constant for the insured's life. It is also possible to arrange premiums so the policy is paid off after a specified period. Because premiums exceed the insurance cost, the policy builds a cash value that the insured can borrow. The cash value grows at a rate specified in the insurance contract.

Will: A will is a legal document by which an individual can direct to whom his or her property will pass at death.

Workstation/Enclave: A type of employment wherein a group of people with disabilities work in a group in an integrated employment environment, typically for a particular job.

Y

Yield: The yield of an investment is the amount of money it pays to the owner annually, usually expressed as a percentage of the principal value of the investment.

APPENDIX II

DIRECTORY OF ORGANIZATIONS

THE FOLLOWING IS A LIST OF ORGANIZATIONS THAT MAY BE HELPFUL to you. Occasionally organizations will change addresses or phone numbers. You can obtain current information from the September issue of *Exceptional Parent* each year or by contacting the National Information Center for Children and Youth with Disabilities.

L. Mark Russell
Attorney at Law
820 Davis Street
Suite 215
Evanston, IL 60201
(847) 869-8868

Advocacy and Information Centers

Alexander Graham Bell Association for the Deaf
3417 Volta Place, NW
Washington, DC 20007
202-337-5220
(VOICE/TDD)

Alliance of Genetic Support Groups
35 Wisconsin Circle #440
Bethesda MD, 20815-7015
(800) 336-GENE

Alzheimer's Disease and Related Disorders Association
919 North Michigan Avenue
Suite 1000
Chicago, IL 60611
(800) 621-0379

American Association on Mental Retardation (AAMR)
444 N. Capital St. NW
Suite 846
Washington, DC 20001-1512
(800)424-3688

American Association of University Affiliated Programs
30 Fenton
Silver Springs, MD 20910
(301) 588-8252

American Council of the Blind
1155 15th Street, NW
Suite 720
Washington, DC 20005
(800) 424-8666

American Deafness and Rehabilitation Association
P.O. Box 251554
Little Rock, AR 72225
(501) 868-8850 (Voice/TDD)

American Foundation of the Blind
11 Penn Plaza
New York, NY 10001
(800) 232-5463
(212) 502-7600

American Heart Association
7272 Greenville Avenue
Dallas, TX 75231-4596
(800) 242-8721

American Paralysis Association/Spinal Injury Hotline
(800) 526-3456

American Society for Deaf Children
2848 Arden Way
Suite 210
Sacramento, CA 95825-1373
(800) 942-2732

Apple Computer's Office of Special Education and Rehabilitation
(408) 974-7910

Association of American Inc. Sickle Cell Disease, Inc.
200 Corporate Pointe
Suite 495
Culver City, CA 90230-7633
(800) 421-8453

Association of Birth Defect Children (ABDC)
827 Irma Avenue
Orlando, FLA. 32803
(800) 313-2232

Association for Children with Down Syndrome
2616 Martin Avenue
Bellmore, NY 11710
(516) 221-4700

The Association of Persons with Severe Handicaps (TASH)
29 W. Susquehanna Avenue
Suite 210
Baltimore, MD 21204
(800) 828-8274

Association for Retarded Citizens of the United States
500 East Border Street
Suite 300
Arlington, TX 76101
(817) 261-6003

AT&T National Special Needs Center
(800) 223-1222

Autism Society of America
7910 Woodmont Avenue
Suite 650
Bethesda, MD 20814
(800) 328-8476
(301) 657-0881

Batten Disease Support and Research Association
2600 Parsons Avenue
Columbus, OH 43207
(800) 448-4570

The Beach Center on Families and Disability
The University of Kansas
Inst. for Life Span Studies
3111 Halworth Hall
Lawrence, KS 66045
(800) 854-4938
(913) 864-7600

Caring, Inc.
P.O. Box 400
Milton, WA 98354
(206) 922-8607

Center for Special Education Technology Council for Exceptional Children (CEC)
920 Association Drive
Reston, VA 22091-1589
(800) 873-8255

Children With Attention Deficit Disorder (CADD)
499 NW 70th Avenue
Suite 101
Plantation, FL. 33317
(800) 233-4050
(305) 587-3700

Chromosome 18 Registry and Research Society
6302 Fox Head
San Antonio, TX 78247
(210) 657-4968

Clearinghouse on Handicap and Gifted Children Council for Exceptional Children
1920 Association Drive
Reston, VA 22091
(703) 620-3660

Cooley's Anemia Foundation
12909 26th Avenue
Flushing, NY 11354
(800) 552-7222

Cornelia De Lange Syndrome Foundation
60 Dryer Avenue
Collinsville, CT 06022
(800) 223-8355

Council for Exceptional Children
1920 Association Drive
Reston, VA 22091
(703) 620-3660

Creative Management Associates
P.O. Box 5488
Portsmouth, NH 03801

Cystic Fibrosis Foundation
6931 Arlington Road
Bethesda, MD 20892
(800) FIGHT-CF

Department of Health and Human Services National Institute of Health
Bethesda, MD 20892
(800) 638-6833

Directory for Exceptional Children
Porter Sargent Publishers
11 Beacon Street
Boston, MA 02108

The Disability Bookshop
P.O. Box 129
Vancouver, WA 98666

Epilepsy Foundation of America
4351 Garden City Drive
Landover, MD 20785
(800) 332-1000

Federation for Children with Special Needs
312 Stuart Street
2nd Floor
Boston, MA 02116
(617) 482-2915

Fetal Alcohol Syndrome
7802 S.E. Taylor Street
Portland, OR 97215
(503) 246-2635

The 5p-Society
11609 Oakmont
Overland Park, KS 66210
(913) 469-8900

Heredity Disease Foundation
606 Wilshire Blvd.
Suite 504
Santa Monica, CA 90401

Higher Education and Adult Training for People with Handicaps (HEATH)
One Dupont Circle NW
Suite 800
Washington, DC 20036-1193
(800) 544-3284

Human Growth Foundation
P.O. Box 3090
Falls Church, VA 22043
(800) 451-6434

Human Services Research Institute
2336 Massachusetts Avenue
Cambridge, MA 02140
(617) 876-0426

Huntington Disease Society of America, Inc.
140 West 22nd Street
New York, NY 10011-2420
(212) 242-1968
(800) 345-HDSA

Hydrocephalus Association
870 Market Street
Suite 955
San Francisco, CA 94102
(415) 776-4713

Immune Deficiency Foundation
25 W Cheasapke Avenue
Suite 206
Townson, MD 21204
(800) 296-4433
(410) 321-6647

International Rett Syndrome Assoc.
9121 Piscataway Road
Suite 2B
Clinton, MD 20735
(800) 818-7388
(301) 856-7388

Klinefelter Syndrome Associates
P.O. Box 119
Roseville, CA 95661-0119

Learning Disabilities Association of America
4156 Liberty Road
Pittsburgh, PA 15234
(412) 341-1515
(412) 341-8077

Listen, Inc.
P.O. Box 27213
Tempe, AZ 85285
(602) 921-3886

March of Dimes Birth Defects Foundation
1275 Mamaroneck Avenue
White Plains, NY 10605
(914) 428-7100

Mental Health Law Project
1101 Fifteenth Street, NW
Suite 1212
Washington, DC 20005

Monosomy 9p Support
43304 Kipton Nickel Plate Road
LaGrange, Ohio 44050
(216) 775-4255

Muscular Dystrophy Association
3300 E. Sunrise
Tucson, AZ 85718
(800) 572-1717
(520) 529-2000

National Alliance for the Mental Ill
200 N. Glebo Rd.
Suite 1015
Arlington, VA 22203-3745
(703) 684-7722

National Association for the Deaf (NAD)
814 Thayer Avenue
Silver Springs, MD 20910-4500
(301) 587-1788
(301) 587-1789
(VOICE/TDD)

National Association of Development Disabilities Councils
1234 Massachusetts Avenue NW
Suite 103
Washington, DC 20005
(202) 347-1234

National Association for Down Syndrome Congress
P.O. Box 4542
Oak Brook, IL 60521
(708) 325-9112

National Down Syndrome Society
666 Broadway
Suite 810
New York, NY 10012
(800) 221-4602

National Association for Parents of the Visually Impaired
PO Box 317
Watertown, MA 022272-0317
(800) 562-6265
(617) 972-7441

National Association of Private Residential Facilities for the Mentally Retarded
4200 Evergreen Lane
Suite 315
Annandale, VA 22003
(703) 642-6614

National Association of Private Schools for Exceptional Children (NAPSEC)
1625 I Street
Suite 506
Washington, DC 20006
(202) 223-2192

National Association of Protection and Advocacy Systems
900 2nd Street NE
Suite 211
Washington, DC 20002
(202) 408-9514

National Association of Social Workers
(202) 408-8600

National Association for the Visually Handicapped
22 West 21st Street, 6th Fl.
New York, NY 10010
(212) 889-3141

National Ataxia Foundation
750 Twelve Oaks Center
15500 Wayzata Blvd.
Wayzata, MN 55391
(612) 473-7666

National Autism Hotline/ Autism Services Center
Prichard Building
605 Ninth Street
P.O. Box 507
Huntington, W. VA. 25701
(304) 524-8014

National Birth Defects Center
30 Warren Street
Brighton, MA 02135

National Catholic Office for Persons with Disabilities
P.O. Box 29113
Washington, DC 20017

National Maternal and Child Clearing House (NCEMCH)
2070 Chain Bridge Road
Suite 450
Vienna, VA 22182
(703) 821-8955 ext. 317

National Clearinghouse for Professions in Special Education
1800 Diagonal Road
Suite 320
Alexandria, VA 22314
(703) 519-3800

National Council on the Handicap
800 Independence Avenue SW
Suite 184
Washington, DC 20591

National Council on Independent Living
2539 Telegraph Avenue
Berkeley, CA 94704

National Down Syndrome Congress
1605 Chantilly Drive
Suite 250
Atlanta, GA 30324
(800) 232-6372

National Easter Seal Society
230 W. Monroe
Suite 1800
Chicago, IL 60606
(312) 726-6200

National Federation of the Blind
1800 Johnson Street
Baltimore, MD 21230

National Foundation for Jewish Genetic Diseases, Inc.
250 Park Avenue
Suite 1000
New York, NY 10177
(212) 371-1030

National Fragile X Foundation
1441 York Street Suite 215
Denver, CO 80206
(800) 688-8765

National Head Injury Foundation
1776 Massachusetts Ave. NW
Suite 100
Washington, DC 20063
(800) 444-6443

National Health Information Center
P.O. Box 1133
Washington, DC 20013-1133
(800) 336-4797

National Hemophilia Foundation (NHF)
110 Greene Street. Room 303
New York, NY 10012
(212) 219-8180
(800) 424-2639

National Hydrocephalus Foundation
1670 Green Oak Circle
Lawrenceville, GA 30243
(800) 431-8093

National Information System and Clearinghouse

provides information on services for children in every state (800) 922-9234

National Information Center for Children and Youth with Disabilities
P.O. Box 1492
Washington, DC 20013
(800) 695-0285
(202) 884-8200

National Information Center on Deafness
Gallaudet University
800 Florida Avenue, NE
Washington, DC 20002

National Information Center for Orphan Drugs and Rare Diseases
P.O. Box 1133
Washington DC 20013-1133

National Marfan Foundation
382 Main Street
Port Washington, NY 11050

National Center for Education Maternal and Child Health Clearinghouse
2000 15th Street North
Suite 701
Arlington, VA 22201-2617
(703) 524-7802

National Mental Health Association
1021 Prince Street
Alexandria, VA 22314
(800) 969-6642

National Multiple Sclerosis
733 Third Avenue
6th Floor
New York, NY 10017
(800) 227-4867

National Network of Parent Centers TAPP Project
312 Stuart Street
2nd Floor
Boston, MA 02116

National Neurofiberomatosis Foundation
95 Pine Street, 16th floor
New York, NY 10005
(800) 323-7938

National Organization on Disability
910 16th Street NW
Suite 600
Washington DC 20006
(202) 293-5960

National Organization for Rare Disorders (NORD)
P.O. Box 8923
100 Route 37
New Fairfield, CT 06812-8923
(800) 999-NORD

National Parent Network on Disabilities
1727 King Street
Suite 305
Alexandria, VA 22314
(703) 684-6763

National Parent Resource
95 Berkeley Street
Suite 104
Boston, MA 02116
(617) 482-2915

National Parkinson Foundation
1501 NW 9th Avenue
Miami, FL 33136
(800) 327-4545
(800) 433-7022 (If calling from Florida)

National Rehabilitation Information Center (NARIC)
8455 Colesvill Road
Suite 935
Silver Springs, MD 20910-3319
(800) 346-2742

National Sickle Cell Research
P.O. Box 8095
Houston, TX 77004

National Spinal Cord Injury Association
545 Concord Avenue
Suite 29
Cambridge, MA 02138
(800) 962-9629
(617) 441-8500

National Spinal Cord Injury Hotline
2201 Argonne Drive
Baltimore, MD 21218
(800) 526-3456

National Tay-Sachs and Allied Disease Association
2001 Beacon Street
Suite 304
Brookline, MA 02146
(617) 277-4463

National Tuberous Sclerosis Association
8000 Corporate Drive
Suite 120
Landover, MD 20785
(800) 225-NTSA

Neurofibromatosis, Inc.
8855 Annapolis
Suite 110
Lanham, MD 20706-2924

Office of Special Education and Rehabilitation Services US Department of Education
Switzer Building
330 C Street, SW
Washington, DC 20202
(202) 205-8723
(202) 205-8241

Osteogensis Imperfecta Foundation, Inc.
5005 W. Laurel Street
Suite 210
Tampa, FL 33607
(813) 282-1161

Parent /Family Information and Support
(800) 922-9234 Ext. 301

Parenting Preemies
P.O. Box 530
Stevens Point, WI 54481
(715) 824-2596

Parents of Chronically Ill Children
1527 Maryland Street
Springfield, IL 62702
(217) 522-6810

Prader-Willie Syndrome Association
2510 S. Brentwood Blvd.
Suite 220
St. Louis, MO 63144
(800) 926-4797

Progeria International Registry
New York State Institute for Basic Research Department of Human Genetics
1050 Forest Hill Road
Staten Island, NY 10314
(718) 494-5230

Retintis Pigmentosa
International Society for Degenerative Eye Diseases
P.O. Box 900
Woodland Hills, CA 91365
(800) 344-4877
(800) FIGHT-RP

Rett Syndrome Association
8511 Rose Marie Drive
Fort Washington, MD 20744
(301) 248-7031

Rubinstein-Taybi Syndrome
414 East Kansas
Smith Center, KS 66967
(913) 282-6237

Sibling Information Network
249 Glenbrook Road
PO Box U64
Storrs, CT 06269-2064
(860) 486-4985

Soto Syndrome USA Support Association
Three Danada Square East # 325
Wheaton, IL 6018˙
(847) 682-8815

Special Needs Parent Information Network (APIN)
P.O. Box 2067
Augusta, ME 04330

Spina Bifida Association of America
4590 McArthur Blvd. NW #250
Washington, DC 20007-4226
(800) 621-3141

Specialized Information Services
National Library of Medicine
8600 Rockville Pike
Bethesda, MD 20894

Sturge-Weber Foundation
PO Box 418
Mount Freedom, NJ 07970
(800) 627-5482
(201) 895-4445

Struge-Weber Foundation
P.O. Box 460931
Aurora. CO 80015
(800) 621-3141

Support Organization for TrisomyY 18,13 and Related Disorders
2982 S. Union Street
Rochester, NY 14624
(800) 716-7638
(716) 594-4621

Technical Assistance to Parent Programs (TAPP) Network Federation for Children with Special Needs
95 Berkeley Street
Suite 104
Boston, MA 02116

Tourette Syndrome Association
Park 50 TechneCenter
100 TechneCenter Drive
Suite 116
Milford, OH 45150-2713
(513) 831-2976 or
(513) 543-2675

Tourett Syndrome Association
42-40 Bell Blvd.
Bayside NY 11361-2861
(718) 224-2999

Turner's Syndrome Society
768-214 Twelve Oaks Center
15500 Wayzata Blvd.
Wayzata, MN 55391
(612) 475-9944

Turner's Syndrome Society
7777 Keele Street
Concord, Ontario
Canada, L4K 147
(905) 660-7766
(800) 465-6744

UCPA, Inc. National Office
1660 L Street NW
Suite 700
Washington, DC 20036
(800) USA-5UCP

United Cerebral Palsy Assoc. Inc.
1660 L Street NW
Suite 700
Washington DC 20036-5602
(800) 872-5827
(202) 776-0406

United Leukodystrophy Foundation, Inc.
2304 Highland Drive
Sycamore, IL 60178
(800) 728-5483

The USA Sotos Syndrome Parent Support Group
Research and Education
Scott and White Clinic
2401 South 31st Street
Temple, TX 76508
(817) 774-2350

Williams Syndrome Association
P.O. Box 3297
Ballwin, MO 63020
(314) 227-4411

Williams Syndrome Association
PO Box 297
Clawson, MI 48107-0297
(810) 541-3630

Wilson Disease Association
P.O. Box 75324
Washington, DC 20013
(800) 399-0266

Xerderma Pigmentosum Registry
UMD-NJ Medical School
Dept. of Pathology, Rm. C-520
185 S. Orange Avenue
Newark, NJ 07103-2714
(201) 982-6255

Xerderma Pigmentosum Support Group
P.O. Box 431
Yuba, CA 95991
(919) 696-0328

Corporate, Guardianship, Trust, and Lifecare Programs

Arizona

Arizona Proxy Plan Foundation
2241 E Filmore St.
Phoenix, AZ 85008
(602) 244-8166

Green Valley
210 W. Continental Rd.
Suite 116
Green Valley, AZ 85614
(602) 625-4338

Arkansas

Guardianship, Inc.
519 _. 5th St.
Little Rock, AR 72202
(501) 376-2420

California

ndland Counties Master Trust
P.O. Box 2664
San Bernadino, CA 92406
(909) 370-0902 ext. 215

National Continuity Program California Institute on Human Services Sonoma State University
1801 E. Cotati Avenue
Rohnert Park, CA 94928
(707) 664-2416

Proxy Parent Services Foundation
1336 Wilshire Blvd., 2nd Floor
Los Angeles, CA 90017
(213) 413-1130

The Good Shepherd Fund
P.O. Box 629
Santa Cruz, CA 95061
(408) 458-1199

Connecticut

Plan of Connecticut
P.O. Box 370312
W. Hartford, CT 06137-0312
(203) 523-4951

Florida

Guardianship Association of Pinellas County
P.O. Box 1826
Pinellas, FL 34664
(813) 938-0929
(813) 391-1216
(800) 382-9100

West Central Florida Guardianship Services, Inc.
P.O. Box 6
Wauchula, FL
(813) 773-6511

Georgia

Plan of Georgia
1256 Brair Cliff Road NE
Room 421S
Atlanta, GA 30306
(770) 853-0494

Illinois

Pact, Inc.
555 E. Butterfield Rd.
Suite 201
Lombard, IL 60148
(847) 960-9700
(847) 960-9849

Self-Sufficiency Trust
340 W. Butterfield Road
Suite 3C
Elmhurst, IL 60126
(708) 832-9700

Indiana

Arc of Indiana Master Trust
22 East Washington St.
Suite 210
Indianapolis, IN 46204
(317) 632-4387

Kansas

ARCare, Inc.
Mark 1 Building, Suite 205
10100 W. 87th St.
Overland Park, KS 66212
(916) 648-2319

TARC Beneficiary Trust
TARC Guardianship Program
Topeka Association for Retarded Citizens
2701 Randolph
Topeka, KS 66611
(913)232-0597

Kentucky

Citizen Advocacy Council for Retarded Citizens
1146 South Third St.
Louisville, KY 40203
(502) 584-1239

New Jersey

Plan of New Jersey
1275 Bound Brook Rd.
Suite 1
Middlesex, NJ 08846-1486
(908) 563-0300

New Mexico

ARC Guardianship Program
3500 G. Commanche NE
Albuquerque, NM 87107
(505) 883-4630

New York

Foundation for the Benefit of Disabled Persons
United Cerebral Palsy of New York City, Inc.
105 Madison Avenue
New York, NY 10016
(212) 683-6700 ext. 203/204

Life Services for the Handicap, Inc.
352 Park Avenue, South
Suite 703
New York, NY 10010
(212) 532-6740

Plan of New York
432 Park Avenue, South
Suite 1201
New York, NY 10016
(212) 545-7063

North Carolina

Life Trust Plan, Inc.
P.O. Box 50545
Raleigh, NC 27619
(919) 782-4632

Ohio

Plan of Northeast Ohio
3130 Mayfield Rd.
Suite GW112
Cleveland Hts., OH 44118
(212) 321-3611

Oregon

GAPS - Guardianship,
Advocacy and Planning Services
1745 State St.
Salem, OR 97301
(503) 581-2726

Pennsylvania

Plan of Pennsylvania
110 West Lancaster Avenue
Wayne, PA 19087
(610) 687-4036

Tennessee

Comcare, Inc.
P.O. Box 1385
Greenville, TN 37744
(615) 638-3926

Guardianship and Trusts Corporation
P.O. Box 121685
Nashville, TN 37212
(615) 638-3926

Texas

Plan of North Texas
Executive Tower, Suite 723
3300 W. Mockingbird Lane
Lockbox #2
Dallas, TX 75235
(214) 956-9933

Virginia

Army and Air Force Mutual Aid Association
102 Sheridan
Ft. Myer, VA 22211-1110
(800) 336-4538

Personal Support Network
100 N. Washington St. #234
Falls Church, VA 22046
(703) 532-3303

Washington

Guardianship Services of Seattle
200 First Avenue, W
Suite 308
Seattle, WA 98119
(206) 284-6225

Lifetime Advocacy Plus
424 North 130th St.
Seattle, WA 98133
(206) 367-8055

Wisconsin

The ARC of Eau
513 S. Barstow St.
Eau Claire, WI 54701
(715) 834-7204

Recreation Organizations

Access America: An Atlas and Guide to the National Parks for Visitors with Disabilities
Northern Cartographic, Inc.
Department AA-91
P.O. Box 133
Burlington, VT 05401
(802) 860-2886

AHRC Camping Services
200 Park Avenue South
New York, NY 10003
(212) 254-8203 ext. 250

American Camping Association
5000 State Road 67 North
Martinsville, IN 46151
(317) 342-8456

Annual Special Camp Guide Resources for Children with Special Needs
200 Park Avenue South
Suite 816
New York, NY 10003
(212) 677-4650

Boy Scouts of America Scouting for the Handicapped
1325 Walnut Hill Lane
P.O. Box 152079
Irving, TX 75015
(214) 580-2000

Directory of Summer Camps for Children with Learning Disabilities (ACALD)
4156 Library Road
Pittsburgh, PA 15234
(412) 341-1515/9077

National Lekotek Center
2100 Ridge Avenue
Evanston, IL 60201
(847) 328-0001

Camps for Kids Muncy Manuscripts
P.O. Box 1561
Grapeville, TX 76051
(817) 329-0060

National Park Camping Guide
Superintendent of Documents
US Government Printing Office
Washington, DC 20402
(202) 783-3238

Camping for the Handicapped
2056 South Buffalo Road
Traverse City, MI 49684

National Park Service
Division of Special Programs
P.O. Box 37127
Washington, DC 20013
(202) 343-4747

North American Riding for the Handicapped Association
1-800-369-RIDE

Girl Scouts
830 3rd Avenue & 51st Street
New York, NY 10022
(212) 940-7500

Guide to Summer Residential Programs for Individuals with Disabilities
20 Park Plaza
Room 330
Boston, MA 02108
(617) 272-5540

Guide to Summer Camps and Summer Schools
Porter Sargent
11 Beacon Street
Boston, MA 02108
(617) 523-1670

The Parent Information Center
P.O. Box 1422
Concord, NH 03302
(603) 224-7005

Residential Camping Program List
National Easter Seal Society
2023 West Ogden Avenue
Chicago, IL 60612
(312) 243-8400

Toys for Special Children
385 Warburton Avenue
Hastings, NY 10706
(914) 478-0960

Special Olympics
1350 New York Avenue NW
Suite 500
Washington, DC 20005-4709
(202) 628-3630

"There are many times when a parent of one of our residents asks what they can do now to insure not only the financial future of their child, but also their future emotional well-being. This book meets the needs of families who are faced with these challenges."

—Robert C. Wissinger, President,
Martha Lloyd Community Services, Troy, Pennsylvania

"*Planning For The Future* is a valuable reference book for both parents who have children with handicaps and for professionals who offer consultation to parents and their children with handicaps...I enthusiastically endorse the text.

—Bernard R. Wagner, Ph.D., President,
Evergreen Presbyterian Ministries, Inc.

"The book *Planning For The Future* came to us at exactly the right time. We are holding an estate planning seminar in the near future. This book will give parents something concrete to use...It is easy to read and covers the topics so vital to the future for people who are disabled. Congratulations on a book well done!"

—Marian Mullet, Executive Director, Pathfinder Village

"Provides compelling and powerful instructions for implementing the important things a parent needs to include in their disabled child's life and financial plan ... It will be used as a primary planning tool for parents who come to the Pathfinder Village International Information and Conference Center on Down Syndrome in Edmeston."

—Paul A. Donnelly, Special Project Consultant,
International Information and Conference Center on Down Syndrome

"*Planning For The Future* is the perfect book for families who have a loved one with a disability. One must consider how to provide for long-term care therefore making this book a must read for all."

—Patricia M. Johnson, Executive Director, Publisher,
A Positive Approach Magazine

"Our work has been positively and significantly enhanced by this resource that removes the mystery from an extremely complex, too often avoided, legal and personal dilemma for families confronted with the many issues of disability. Going beyond my expectations, these authors have created a resource readable and practical for families experiencing disability and the professionals who support family efforts."

—Ronnie Barclay, Parent Education Coordinator,
Illinois Next Step Network, Illinois Dept. of Rehabilitation Services

"*Planning For The Future* provides families with a manageable way of organizing their knowledge, hopes and fears for the future. Reading it increases parents' chances of getting to sleep at night."

—Carolyn Beckett, Program Specialist,
Parent Educational Advocacy Training Center

"As the mother of a son who suffered from paranoid schizophrenia, I have worked for several years with a dedicated group of people who were concerned about the future of family members with severe disabilities. This book has the answers to all the questions that have haunted me. I congratulate the authors for their expertise, and their obvious compassion for people with disabilities."

—Gwill Newman, President Emeritus,
National Association For Research On Schizophrenia And Depression;
Vice Chairman, Chicago Brain Research Foundation

"*Planning For The Future* is an extremely comprehensive and step by step approach—from education and social activities to legal and financial elements—to enable parents to ensure the future quality of life for their child with a disability."

—Jeffrey A. Ditty, Ph.D., President, Neuro Education Center

"Using this book is probably the single most important planning step that you can take for your child."

—Professor Kenneth Friedman, from a review in *The Association for Persons with Severe Handicaps (TASH) Newsletter*